THE
NEW SCIENCE
JOURNALISTS

THE
NEW SCIENCE
JOURNALISTS

Edited by

TED ANTON
and
RICK McCOURT

BALLANTINE BOOKS

New York

Introduction and compilation copyright © 1995 by Ted Anton and Rick McCourt

All rights reserved under International and Pan-American Copyright Conventions. Published in the United States by Ballantine Books, a division of Random House, Inc., New York, and simultaneously in Canada by Random House of Canada Limited, Toronto.

Permission acknowledgments appear on page 338, which is an extension of the copyright page.

Library of Congress Catalog Card Number: 94-94557

ISBN: 0-345-38365-6

Cover design by Kathleen Lynch
Book design by Ruth Kolbert

Cover photo of bumblebee © Charles Fitch/FPG Int'l. Photo of calliope hummingbird © Stan Osolinski/FPG Int'l. Photo of Earth over land © Charly Franklin/FPG Int'l. Photo of astronaut Bruce McCandles, space walk © Telegraph Colour Library/FPG Int'l. Photo of beaker boiling over © Jook Leung/FPG Int'l. Photo of autumn leaves © Telegraph Colour Library/FPG Int'l.

Manufactured in the United States of America

First Edition: April 1995

10 9 8 7 6 5 4 3 2 1

FOR
Maja, Cam, and Marja

FOR
Becky and Cole

CONTENTS

ACKNOWLEDGMENTS

So many people shared their ideas in the making of this book that it is impossible to name them all. Our thanks go, in particular, to Sharon Friedman, Sharon Dunwoody, Chris Anderson, Janet Hopson, Carol Rogers, James Trefil, David Quammen, Anne Gudenkauf, Blake Edgar, Terri Randall, John Wilkes, Ann Finkbein, Stuart Zola-Morgan, Joanne Rodgers, Janet Basu, Patricia Gadsby, Leon Lederman, Paul Grannis, Dianne Dumanoski, Tom Levenson, Dava Sobel, and to our students.

We owe a special thanks to our student assistant Joana Frasor, who worked so diligently and contributed so thoughtfully during the months of article selection. DePaul University provided crucial support in the form of Quality of Instruction and Competitive Research grants.

Our editor, Sherri Rifkin, steered us through and offered insightful suggestions along the way.

Our deepest acknowledgment goes to Sam Vaughn, who believed in this project, made suggestions, offered encouragement, and brought his wealth of experience to every stage in the making of this anthology.

We are especially grateful to the writers who took time away from their work to talk with us.

THE
NEW SCIENCE
JOURNALISTS

INTRODUCTION

*"Science is the foremost intellectual adventure
of our time. It is what painting and sculpture were
to the Renaissance; it's what philosophy was in
the age of Kant; it's the game in town."*
                                        —*Timothy Ferris*

For years something extraordinary has been happening in science writing. Once mostly the province of "gee whiz" reporting that extolled the latest breakthrough, science writing in the past ten years has exploded in volume, style, controversy, and impact. Today science books become best-sellers and Hollywood movies, science articles make or break careers, and science reporting affects billions of dollars of government and private investment and the decisions of researchers and institutions. Sparked by the hubris of research and the crucial role of technology in our lives, this new science writing is revealing dramatic conflicts, brilliant investigation, and deep repercussions inside and outside of labs.

The best of the new science writers work on the frontier of knowledge, examining the future of our universe and psyches with innovations of journalistic style and reporting technique. Whether writing with the art of the novelist or taking the art of investigation to new heights, they are exposing both the successes and failures of science by exploring its culture, conflicts of interest, and even the construction of its languages. From the *New York Times* to

Discover magazine, this generation of journalists is changing the way we think about science by reporting and writing in articles so intricate they ultimately confront the question: What is truth?

There's nothing fundamentally new about the appeal and impact of good science writing. Darwin's *Origin of Species*, written for the general public as well as his peers, sold out its first day of publication in 1859 and transformed our sense of place in the cosmos. A century later Rachel Carson's *Silent Spring* sparked an environmental revolution, while James Watson's *The Double Helix* gave an uncensored view of the race to discover the most basic genetic structure of life.

The difference today lies in the larger scale, faster pace, and more varied uses for science writing. More science books are being published more quickly today for a mass audience that ranges from business investors to newly discriminating medical patients. The selections in this volume come from a wide variety of national and local publications and were written by a range of authors—from senior scientists and veteran reporters to a young internist and a writer who flunked chemistry. Their work has dominated Pulitzer Prizes in feature journalism over the last three years. As the public's grasp of advanced science falters, the problems facing us—those of energy, environment, and global cooperation—are growing more and more crucial. The work of those who explain science to the public, dubbed by Pulitzer Prize winner Jon Franklin as "a borderline world, part science, part art, part smoke, part mirrors," is now more important than ever.

Each of these pieces offers an innovation in science reporting or writing. These writers fall roughly into three categories—those who write in original style, those who investigate with new zeal, and those who pull together the data of specialized studies to identify important new trends.

The first group of writers in this collection captures the childlike wonder of the universe with the passion of the lyric poet. They include Diane Ackerman, Charles Bowden, Elisabeth Rosenthal, Elissa Ely, Jim Kelly, Dennis Overbye, and John Seabrook. In their work the world shines anew in encounters that challenge our most basic assumptions about everything from solar systems to baboons.

The second group comprises the investigators who detail the inside story of science research—from AIDS to energy to animal research and cancer. The Chicago *Tribune*'s John Crewdson, for instance, upset medicine's largest breast cancer study with revelations that one of its doctors lied on data for ten years. The Sacramento *Bee*'s Deborah Blum takes a sympathetic look at the opposing passions of animal researchers and animal activists. Gary Taubes and the Hartford *Courant*'s Robert S. Capers and Eric Lipton dissect human foibles as old as vanity and greed that led to billion-dollar American science tragedies.

The third group of writers include those who dig through the new data to uncover revelations that researchers themselves may tend to miss. James Gleick's early work on chaos theory, for instance, aided scholars in fields as diverse as religion and rhetoric to rethink their approach to their subjects. The Atlanta *Constitution*'s Mike Toner changed the view of doctors and pesticide manufacturers about their most common cures (his newspaper's fax hot line rang nonstop for three days after his Pulitzer Prize–winning series ended). In *U.S. News & World Report*, Shannon Brownlee chronicled a new course for cancer research, while Timothy Ferris charted the recent redefinition of the self in cognitive science. In his profile of Hungarian mathematician Paul Erdös, Paul Hoffman confronts the twentieth century's legacy of fascism and the cold war. The *New York Times*'s Natalie Angier refined our conception of the purposes of work in the animal kingdom, and in the closing piece, Pulitzer Prize–winning entomologist Edward O. Wilson addresses the most direct question of our future.

The work of writers like these is critical now because the traditional mode of science communication with the public is changing so rapidly. In the past professionally reviewed journals presented science findings in dryly written papers and conference presentations—occasionally filtered for the public by an insider crew of science journalists. That still happens. But the speed of information technology, the prospect of lucrative patent or business deals, the combat for grant funds, and the flaws of peer review itself are breaking down that system. When University of Utah chemists Stanley Pons and Martin Fleischmann announced cold fusion by press conference in 1989, for instance, their spectacular fraud was not revealed by professional journals or mainstream journalists—the two scientists had written numerous flawed peer-review papers on other subjects—but by a new underground press of E-mail and contentious and often informal science meetings.

The new science writing shares some traits with what Tom Wolfe thirty years ago called the new journalism; some of its writers *are* the new, or literary, journalists— Wolfe in *The Right Stuff* (1979), Tracy Kidder in *The Soul of a New Machine* (1981), and John McPhee in books on subjects like atomic energy, ecology, and geology. Many of the new generation of science writers cite these works as inspiration; some employ the same narrative techniques. Both styles of writing are popular and yet still admired by insiders. Like literary journalists, many of these new science writers offer a personal view. Both reflect a historical moment: The literary journalism originated in the social ferment of the 1960s, while the new science writing springs from a new fin de siècle when our biggest global problems and minutest questions of the self and matter are, in essence, science questions.

The new science writing, however, comes with its own innovations and flaws. It is deeply contentious. Its writers critique each other and their field—for being too soft, too esoteric, too melodramatic, too personal, or too objective. The boosterism of traditional science journalism continues today to inflate successes or crises in the interest of the news or literary market. At the same time media coverage of science is profoundly altering science careers and research in a way the literary journalism never did. As these selections attest, the field is rich with drama. In short, science writing is in a state of radical transformation.

Today more science writers have advanced science degrees or have been trained in graduate-level science writing programs; many more of them are women focusing on women. Some writers work for news services and data banks or for the rapidly expanding press offices of universities, companies, and research institutions. While still marred by flaws, the best science reporting demonstrates struggle to get at the sometimes ugly truth at a time when the increasingly and incredibly complex stories include issues of funding, ethics, and rabid personalities as well as the search "to see a world in a grain of sand," as William Blake wrote.

This anthology highlights some of the best examples of science communication at a time when the issues have grown pressingly urgent. What has been the impact of new science coverage on the way we think and the way scientists work? Have new science-trained writers and graduate programs created better journalism, or is the new science writing "all breathlessness and black net stockings," as a recent *New York Times Book Review* article by Ann Finkbeiner claimed? In the end, communicating the work of the mind is almost as daunting as doing the work itself. "Science is an intensely human enterprise," says the Sacramento *Bee*'s Deborah Blum. "We fail as reporters if we fail to convey that."

A HISTORY OF SCIENCE WRITING

For most of history, save for the odd church upheaval, science communication was a relatively small field. Science as a method of discovery took hold only as recently as the Renaissance, when Galileo first suspected the stars were physical, not metaphysical. At the time his art was as obscure as magic and often just as hidden. Even today, when it has transformed our world, we forget that science is not a body of knowledge at all—not the fields of astronomy, physics, chemistry, biology, and botany covered in this collection—but a method of observation. Most of us learned it in high school, even invented it on our own: testing theories by experiment, with objective observation, controls, and repeatable results. As such it continually calls into question our most basic beliefs. Its search for truth is, or should be, relentless.

For years the reporting of science remained a specialized activity of scientists. Interestingly the best researchers seemed in many cases to be the best communicators. Centuries later, building the world's most powerful energy accelerator in the cornfields of Illinois, physicist Robert Wilson asserted that great science, like aesthetics, had to *communicate*. But science communication could, in the eighteenth century, take its time. Newton took twenty years to publish his findings. Unlike Wilson, Newton never had to testify before Parliament about the economic benefits to be gleaned from gravity because he didn't need a billion dollars to do his research.

At the start of this century, however, World War I showed that science meant power—whether in the killing power of laboratory-developed mustard gas or the transport potential of the monoplane. Academia and journalism responded. The American Chemical Society set up the first science news service in 1919. E. W. Scripps followed with a science news service in 1921 that flourishes among a dozen others today. By 1934 science journalists had formed their own national association; like the first Christian disciples, they numbered all of twelve members.

World War II and *Sputnik* catapulted scientists to glamour status. As the cold war's space and weapons races fueled big-ticket research, writers helped to make the men and women of vision into stars. In her 1988 book *Selling Science*, sociologist Dorothy Nelkin quotes many examples of the time, including *Family Health* magazine's 1977 headline on Nobel Prize–winning medical researcher Rosalyn Yalow: SHE COOKS. SHE CLEANS. SHE WINS THE NOBEL PRIZE. Scientists put up with the adulation because it seemed clipping a *New York Times* article to a grant request "somehow, some way made fate smile," says Jon Franklin.

Though few scientists admit it, the media helped advance knowledge, too, by transmitting news to researchers. A *New England Journal of Medicine* study proved this relationship by looking at research journals in the period when the *New York Times* went on strike in 1978. Normally, after a *Times* profile, citations of a scientist vastly increase in professional journal reports of new experiments. But those who published research during the strike months barely were noticed—not by the milkman or by their professional peers.

By the late 1970s that adulation flip-flopped as Vietnam and Watergate unleashed reporters' mistrust of divine authority. At the wrong moment science faltered, at Three Mile Island and Chernobyl, and when the *Challenger* blew up on national TV. In stories on the environment, radiation, and medical research, reporters unveiled the sometimes unbelievable flaws in science methods, personalities, and culture. The candid accounts of James Watson or *The New Yorker*'s medical writer Berton Roueché paved the way for William Broad and Nicholas Wade's more critical *Betrayers of the Truth* (1983). Other books, like Gary Taubes's *Nobel Dreams* (1986), Stephen Hall's *Invisible Frontiers* (1987), and Natalie Angier's *Natural Obsessions* (1988) had writers spending months with the scientists, revealing their betrayals as well as the beauty of ideas. New science newspaper sections and magazines sprouted— *Omni* in 1979, and *Science '80*, and *Discover* in 1980, —offering work to a new generation of writers.

The new science writing found its most explosive subject in AIDS. Randy Shilts's *And the Band Played On* attacked the arrogance and indolence of the medical and government establishment in 1984. John Crewdson followed with an Odyssean investigation of AIDS researcher Robert Gallo that challenged science reporting to do better. "He showed us the heights to which science investigation should be taken," says *Science* magazine's Chris Anderson, one of a new generation of writers. In a 52,000-word supplement to the Chicago *Tribune* on Sunday, November 19, 1989, Crewdson proved that Gallo had not isolated a new AIDS virus as he claimed but had found the same virus as French researchers. In the end Gallo's oft-changed side of the story—that he never willfully stole the virus—ended with no medical censure or criminal charges. But Crewdson unveiled a science chicanery that included forged documents and a hubris that endangered lives and the truth. If Crewdson signaled a "new breed of science writer," according to Dorothy Nelkin, Gallo signaled a new kind of scientist and science story. Or, at least, a new way of covering research hubris.

Still many scientists and reporters, including some in this collection, derided Crewdson's avalanche of Freedom of Information Act requests as a vendetta that slowed vital research. "I wouldn't go after a guy's raw data," responds Dennis Overbye. "I wouldn't know what to do with it."

The worst science news of the last years would seem to bear out the need for investigative zeal. Cold fusion, the $2 billion loss in the unfinished superconducting super-collider, and more medical fraud cases—four at the University of Pittsburgh alone—hint that "science reporters are fatter and lazier than they should be," complains Timothy Ferris, who noted his discomfort at the slick handling of an American Astronomical Conference in Washington where papers were all packaged and summarized by the press office. In a world increasingly media savvy, the battle is for spin control.

Like the oracle at Delphi, scientists have long held the role as translators of the gods (and generally their pronouncements have been just as ambiguous). They lost that role and now are trying to regain it through press offices. Some science reporters feel only scientists can critique their colleagues' work. "When scientists ask me to get involved in their own competition," says award-winning *Economist* writer Alexandra Wyke, "it makes me very uncomfortable." Others disagree. "We should interpret science as an art critic interprets art, and judge it for ourselves," says Shannon Brownlee. "We then have to communicate it to a public that has to make key decisions."

LEVELS OF THE GAME

Today science is covered in a number of venues—from the sound bites of daily newspapers and TV news to the Discovery channel, to the best newspaper science section and science magazines, to books and speeches and Op Ed pages. Giant institutions that fund research—drug companies, trade associations, and even the government—feature their own publications, which in turn pour out material. The field is much broader than the scope of its mainstays, including *Science, Science News, Audubon, Smithsonian, Natural History,* and *The Sciences.*

Despite its many levels, science writing is often a flawed product. At big-city or national newspapers like the *Wall Street Journal,* Los Angeles *Times,* Boston *Globe, Newsday,* Dallas *Morning Herald,* and Chicago *Tribune,* the number of sections devoted exclusively to science has dropped in recent years, although science and technology *are* covered in the news and business sections and, more and more often, on the front page in Pulitzer-chasing series of articles on specific topics. Some smaller newspapers like the Sacramento *Bee,* Tucson *Citizen,* and Hartford *Courant,* all represented here, publish outstanding science journalism. When they're not being too awestruck, magazines like *Discover* and *The Sciences* do a good job.

The general fare in journalism, however, even in the most august science section of all, Tuesday's *New York Times,* is often uneven, overhyped, and occasionally downright wrong. Some of the errors are caused by the rigors of daily deadline. "You're like a hockey goalie trying to field pucks flying at you," says Phil Hilts, former *New York Times* science reporter, of the regimen of newspaper work. "Some of them are bound to get through." They can include the sensationalism of taking the latest article from the *New England Journal of Medicine* and dressing it up the day it's published—sometimes prepackaged by a scientist or institutional press office. EXPERTS ASSERT, such articles might proclaim. "Imagine," says Gary Taubes, "a political reporter resorting to 'politicians assert.' "

The most common error in science writing is to overblow the "breakthrough" of a new discovery. To see how often that word is overused, consult the word in an InfoTrac search of magazines three years ago, then examine those stories to see how many, three years later, stand up as real breakthroughs. Few will. But bad science writing, like bad science, can sell to an ignorant public.

The writers in this collection are doing things right despite the enormous complications they face. Among the best writers and scientists, a savvier, if edgy, new relationship has recently been evolving. "The best scientists return your calls," says Ricki Lewis, a science author with a Ph.D. in genetics. The improvements in these relationships, in science writing, and in the critical nature of science issues have all contributed to the dominance of the field in recent Pulitzer Prizes. Included in this volume are the 1992 Pulitzer winner in beat reporting, Deborah Blum on monkey research; the 1992 winner in explanatory journalism, Robert S. Capers and Eric Lipton on the Hubble telescope fiasco; and the 1993 winner in explanatory journalism, Mike Toner's Atlanta *Constitution* series on microbes' resistance to antibiotics. In 1994, for the third year in a row, the Pulitzer Prize in explanatory journalism went to a science series, this time by the Chicago *Tribune*'s Ron Kotulak, whose chronicle of the latest research on the mind showed, for instance, that inner-city violence causes a psychological and genetic transformation due to the high stress of dangerous neighborhoods. Another 1994 Pulitzer winner for science came in national reporting for the Albuquerque *Tribune*'s series on secret government radiation experiments forty years ago. The field of science is so rich that competing writers following the same story from distant locations can win simultaneous awards, as Deborah Blum and Richard Preston did with reports that began with the same story of a deadly monkey virus.

You can see the growing interest to better science writing in a number of other ways. Today some eighteen graduate science writing programs are training science journalists, and many more undergraduate programs and courses are being offered, though some disagree as to whether the new graduates have either the requisite "controlled outrage" or sense of story of the best reporters. Membership has doubled in the last five years in the National Association of Science Writers, where truly contentious debates on the role and training of science writers fly on E-mail and at annual meetings. How you join the debate depends on who you are. More than half of the new NASW members are information officers of universities or laboratories who want the best possible publicity for their institutions. Many of their scientists would like journalism to inspire young people with the truly difficult advance of research, as *they* had been inspired by science writing as children. Critics say writers must catch bad science before it wins billion-dollar federal grants.

For their part scientists are realizing that if they want to succeed in the new climate, they have to mix it up with the public. "It's like communicating what you do to your father-in-law or other hostile audience," says physicist Leon Lederman, coauthor of a new book, *The God Particle*. "We should be able to do it. We have to."

FACING THE MONSTER: THE CHALLENGE OF SCIENCE WRITING

At the end of a two-week-long roller-coaster ride of interviews with chemist Rick Smalley, the twenty-three-year-old Houston *Press* writer Jim Kelly asked the star researcher why he insisted on jogging five miles, daily, in Houston in midsummer at noon. Smalley shrugged and said, "Gotta go face the monster."

Talk to scientists and science writers about communicating with the public and they speak, in some way, of facing the monster. The move from the lab, with its control and elegance, to the madding crowd is a formidable exercise in translation. Science loves complexity and, often, consensus. Journalism loves simplicity and, preferably, a fight. The writer's challenge is first to understand the subject, then to tell it accurately while handling a close relationship with brilliant people in which the capacity to betray is tempting, and finally to convince the reader, long after his or her initial enthusiasm may have waned, of the significance of the quest. Overcoming the challenge is in many ways as difficult as doing good science. It requires many of the same skills—a discipline bordering on obsession, imagination, competitiveness, and street smarts.

First, like Rick Smalley on his first mile, a writer must relish the trial. "I love walking the line," says *The New Yorker*'s John Seabrook. "I love bringing all this stuff together," says Gary Taubes. John Crewdson speaks of his delight in poring over reams of lab data, and Diane Ackerman talks of the excitement of seeing her world in a new way. "For weeks or months I'll think of nothing else," she says.

Like many of the new science writers, Deborah Blum lifted her reporting on primate research into something approaching a religious quest: "The question was, who are we?" she says of her work. "How do we treat our fellow species?"

Clash of Cultures

Such obsession is crucial because the first thing that happens in science writing is a kind of culture shock. At some point in every science story the initial bravado will fade. Editors pressure you to punch it up, scientists push you to be fair and accurate if not fawning, and your innermost self begs you to do at least part of that great job it envisioned all along. A deadline waits. That's when the clash of cultures between science and reporting can overwhelm.

The writer's allegiance is to an audience the scientist rarely encounters: the general public. Writers compete with MTV and the latest tabloid story. They must put findings in context, explain what is new in a field and what has changed, and entertain while they educate. To writers the grand outline of a theory's architecture is as important as its bricks and mortar, the scientists' data. And so they ask the same questions over and over, trying to get catchier quotes, sharper angles, more dramatic anecdotes from their subjects.

Every instinct of good scientists, on the other hand, is to qualify and hedge. They have spent a lifetime among the bricks and mortar; any tinkering with the architecture is saved for late-night talks with close colleagues or tentative proposals in conference presentations—certainly not with a writer or the public. Scientists have to be good communicators, yes, to get ideas across to each other. And the best are excellent persuaders. But the wonder, the downright awestruck oh-my-god surprise of their work, seems out of place in an interview. Scientists often put on poker faces to tell their most wonderful secrets.

Still writers must deliver readers, and science researchers, who are responsible for the careers of lab colleagues and postdoctoral and graduate students working on their projects, must sell administrators, grant suppliers, and their peers. At this moment writer and scientist, for all their differences, experience the same terrors, and needs, and this can lead to abuses of the truth. This is when the rubrics of science writing come into play. "Like a great researcher you need a sixth sense," says Taubes, "something that tells you what sounds right and what doesn't."

For science writers, that sense derives from the tools of their art—the elements of simplification, story, immersion, and heart.

Simplification

The great thrust of science is to uncover general principles in the chaos of life. The challenge of science writing is to simplify those science principles without distorting them. When trying to put it all together, then, the biggest key is knowing what to leave out. "You're always adjusting the dials to be accurate without being too precise," says nature essayist David Quammen. "If you leave all the qualifications in, you can kill the writing."

The problem is sometimes you can leave out or simplify so much you get the whole thing wrong—or make it completely senseless, as *Time* magazine did in its story following Crewdson's revelation of breast cancer fraud. To find a balance writers resort to a few common rules. "I use plain language," says Jim Kelly. "I make sure I understand it first before I talk to someone else," suggests John Seabrook. Make the scientists explain it over and over, they say. Get them to the point where they're furious and blurt something out in the sharpest possible terms. Avoid jargon.

In the end, though, you have to accommodate the complexity of science. Some of these writers, like James Gleick and Paul Hoffman, selectively use esoteric terms like spices in cooking. "There's no way to simplify a term like staphylococcus," says Mike Toner. If the ancient Greeks liked to make simple subjects complex, science writers must make complex subjects clear. To address the problem, Diane Ackerman resorts to a science ploy. "I pick out contingency samples," she says. "Like a NASA space probe that detects the history of a planet in a single soil sample. I'll pick a few of those samples to focus on in depth when I simplify."

Story

"Science writing differs from every other kind of writing in that its fans, avid though they may be, don't usually have a good sense of science," says Natalie Angier. "You must teach without being didactic. That's where story comes in."

As every fiction writer knows, the elements of story are character and plot. If the scientist is a good character, as mathematician Paul Erdös was for Paul Hoffman or astronomer Beatrice Tinsley was for Dennis Overbye, the writer is in luck. If the plot is delicious—as with the story of cold fusion or the tangled emotions surrounding Deborah Blum's series on primate research—the writing will follow (Blum includes, for instance, the dreams and memories of researcher Allen Merritt as he dissects a monkey). If the setting is spectacular, as with Charles Bowden's bat cave, the piece will come together. But often scientists are boring people with really interesting ideas, says physicist and science popularizer James Trefil. Turning *ideas* into a story is the untold art of science writing.

Some writers dramatize ideas to the point where they are plain wrong. Terms like "crisis," "miracle cure," "all-out competition," and "all the built-in cosmic clichés," according to Timothy Ferris, will appear in article proposals as in grant proposals. "No verb goes unadverbed," notes Ann Finkbeiner, a science writer teaching at Johns Hopkins. "Chapters begin and end with one-sentence stunners." Since Archimedes the biggest cliché of any science story is the Eureka! moment of discovery, usually in some intimate moment following a gripping crisis of self-doubt. "My favorite is the line 'Either I'm totally wrong or this is the greatest discovery since . . . ,'" says Gary Taubes. "That means there's a 99 percent chance they're totally wrong."

The funny thing is, sometimes science does happen that way. Nobel Prize winner Kary Mullis dreamed up a crucial method of reproducing genes in a test tube while driving down a lonely California highway. Even everyday medicine can be brilliantly dramatic, as Jon Franklin has shown.

"Take the readers into the labs and let them hear the screams," he once wrote of the new science journalism.

When it doesn't happen, authors will use some of the tricks of lyric or epic poetry. Most every science article traces some form of the same plot: the quest for knowledge. It can be told as a detective story, a race against time, or simply a discursive rumination on a particular topic, like laziness or the weather. Natalie Angier and Diane Ackerman move almost in a stream-of-consciousness technique from topic to topic in their quests to understand. Dennis Overbye uses the hook of group relations—a "Big Chill" of cosmology (which is perhaps why Tom Hanks optioned the film rights to his book). Timothy Ferris draws on the rhythm and refrain structure of the mind. Elisabeth Rosenthal starts off with a photograph—a common technique of the contemporary short story. Stylish writing, simile, puns, a distinctive voice—all help a science writer.

The glue that holds a science story together, though, is often an apt metaphor. Overbye's chapter "The Endless Good-bye," from *Lonely Hearts of the Cosmos*, subtly counterpoints the evidence of an ever-expanding universe that might, eventually, die, with the poignant story of rebel Beatrice Tinsley's losing battle with cancer. Metaphor means, literally, to "bring across," and almost every piece of really good science writing will connect its subject to an unexpected object or larger meaning. The device can be literal—Elissa Ely reading a newspaper article in an intensive care unit at two in the morning. It can be figurative—as in Natalie Angier's comparison of animal inactivity to human laziness. It can be both, as when Capers and Lipton describe the accuracy of the Hubble space telescope mirror: "If its surface were the size of the Atlantic Ocean, no wave could be higher than three inches." But to work, a metaphor must be accurate.

Accuracy

Gary Taubes lived with scientists at the Geneva-based particle accelerator called CERN (Centre Européenne pour la Recherche Nucléaire) for six months before writing his first book, *Nobel Dreams*. Paul Hoffman spent weeks with mathematician Paul Erdös. Natalie Angier learned the topic of animal inactivity better than most researchers. Many of these authors will speak of making four or five phone calls to verify one sentence. Even under the stress of deadline, good science reporters will consult Rolodexes chock-full of independent experts with whom they check figures and interpretations.

Because editors and fact checkers usually are not well versed in science, a science writer's accuracy ultimately derives from internal motivation. Making three extra phone calls, awakening in the night to jot down a contradiction, learning a wholly new subject—as Edward O. Wilson did in learning statistical research in midcareer—all are common practices cited by these writers. Most tape-record their interviews and then listen to them carefully afterward. Even ignorance, or fear, or deadline pressure can be useful. "I'd leave my tape recorder on," says Jim Kelly, of interviewing Rick Smalley. "Along about the time I was panicking in confusion, I would look around the office while he talked, gathering sense details." Afterward Kelly listened to the tapes carefully and called other chemists to explain the concepts—because he was afraid to bother Smalley. Some of these writers will show their work to their subjects—a taboo with most journalists. Some snip out only the critical numbers to run these past the scientists, negotiating a version that fits the editor's need for drama, the reader's need for clarity, and the scientist's need for accuracy.

But at some point the writer and subject will be at odds. You cannot write a "scientist-approved" piece or you've sold your soul, yet it's particularly tough to be independent when the scientist knows so much more than the writer. One way to get around this problem is to spend more time with the crowd. "Living with the scientists," says Taubes, "I came to see just how flawed some of their work was." Scientists themselves forget their rules, as in Crewdson's breast cancer story, and the writer has to remain skeptical even when immersed in a story. Too often even *New York Times* science writers will accept a specialist's opinion about the meaning of a finding without getting a second opinion or looking at the study themselves. "If your mother tells you she loves you, your attitude should be, 'Check it out,' " suggests Crewdson.

While it's extremely difficult for outsiders to critique the work of specialists, accuracy demands at least a look at opposing evidence and a good book on statistics like Victor Cohn's *News and Numbers.*

Heart

There's one key that brings together these writers: They love the pursuit of their subject. John Seabrook once penciled in his most memorable passage—a childhood memory—on a galley page as his article went to press. Diane Ackerman thought about nothing other than the world of the senses for months. Mike Toner talked to parents of the children who received no relief from expensive antibiotics.

In the middle of a long night in an intensive care ward Elissa Ely imagined the family past of an elderly patient who would never awaken. "As an intern you erect a barrier between yourself and the patient," she says, "but staying up all night, you let your guard down. Then, for a moment you become whole."

THE SCIENTISTS' VIEW

The barrier between the public and the scientist, even if it is occasionally only a facade, still presents a real challenge. One might think it due to conceit of the intellect. But the root emotion is even more human than that. Scientists truly believe they are on a quest for truth, an ideal that is never achieved but still worth going for. Fresh from a round of inside jokes in the lab, a scientist will sit down, get serious, and write a dispassionate account of one of the more exciting events in her or his life. The scientist has found out something *new* but is too bashful to write with emotion. It is simply not done.

Here another emotion takes hold: fear. Somewhere someone will find he or she has made a mistake. It is inevitable. No theory is ever left alone. Ideas change. And how would it look to get euphoric about something that isn't really quite perfect and after all only applies to a very restricted set of cases and conditions? Better to be quietly in error and footnoted politely in history than to stroke out with a pompous grin on one's face.

Scientists are also busy. So for the most part science writing has been left to nonscientists. A science writer can afford to be amazed, offended, cynical, and everything else that would be so out of place in a scientist's presentation. Science writers are not afraid, and are perhaps over-eager, to humanize the players. That's why there became, and still is, an expanded niche for science writers.

Now more scientists are writing or working with authors to help explain the purpose of their research, compete for grants in a post-cold-war era of shrinking funds, and get their word out amidst an antiscience backlash that has unmasked some of science's pretensions. "Researchers are in trouble right now," says Joann Rodgers, Director of Public Information at Johns Hopkins Medical Institutions. Some are picking up the pen, taking seminars in media and press relations, or hiring literary agents to try to emulate the success of Stephen Hawking's *A Brief History of Time*. Commenting on the recent rise of coauthored science books like *Wrinkles in Time* by astronomer George Smoot and Keay Davidson and *The God Particle* by Leon Lederman and Dick Teresi, Timothy Ferris notes: "They look suspiciously front-loaded. I'm not saying that's bad, but I wouldn't confuse them with Lucretius either."

Science is responding in a number of other ways, some benign and some corrupt. Laboratory requests for the *National Association of Science Writers' Manual* for communicating with the press have remained high. The booklet explains how to hold a press conference and write a press release and conveys such sound advice as "Never give anything off the record." It tells the story of a noted cancer researcher whose conference paper on a promising new treatment neglected to mention that one patient had died from the treatment. The follow-up articles destroyed an otherwise important finding.

"If you don't play the game," writes University of California atmospheric researcher Stephen Schneider of the battle for grants and good coverage, "you're not above the game, you've abdicated."

Other reactions of scientists have even, paradoxically, included opening themselves to more public scrutiny. Alexandra Wyke notes that scientists are more available to speak with her than ever before. Some of this openness may be driven by a newfound respect for the power of the press or by congressional hearings. In America "federal lab administrators know we're making Freedom of Information Act requests. That has to affect how they budget and describe their research," says *Science*'s Chris Anderson. Writers, if they want to, can sit in on endless, monotonous planning meetings at the Fermilab high-energy accelerator in Illinois.

"I find the attitude has changed," says Sharon Friedman, chair of the Journalism Department at Lehigh University and a founder of the field of science journalism education. "One on one, scientists are more willing to discuss the problems they're having." As evidence Friedman recalls the reception Nicholas Wade received during a meeting of the American Association for the Advancement of Science many years ago. "One scientist almost shouted him down. Today that would never happen."

When openness exists, it can be carefully controlled. In federal laboratories access to scientists is slowed down by, or filtered through, public information officers. Science public relations provides perhaps the best job market for aspiring writers and career journalists today. At Rutgers University the public relations office regularly faxes research announcements in an operation so smooth it has been dubbed the "quote-a-matic." So many other institutions do the same that newspaper science reporters often turn off their fax machines.

Science journalists may also be the target of professional flattery. Industry and science groups—from General Motors to Westinghouse—annually give thirty-two annual awards to science writing. Early in her career Shannon Brownlee won a $10,000 General Motors grant for her work on cancer research. Now she asks, "I wonder, if I had written a story that car exhaust is a significant cause of cancer, whether my story would have been considered."

More insidiously, drug companies have occasionally offered freelance science writers fat fees to plug their products without revealing their connection to the companies. Industries often offer to cosponsor symposia, free lunch and all, with science writers. Even pure science can fall into the P.R. trap. "Science has become far too capable of jumping onto political or social fads, like AIDS, or the Greenhouse effect, or the ozone hole. If the public can be panicked, it will spend money," comments Jon Franklin.

Among science publicists, keeping a low profile is high art.

SCIENCE WRITING PROGRAMS

While many graduate journalism programs have long offered a science writing course or a sequence of courses, the field of graduate writing programs specializing solely in science has lately blossomed—up to eighteen at last count. Of these the four best are at Boston University, Johns Hopkins, New York University, and the University of California at Santa Cruz. Of the top four Santa Cruz is the most unusual. It's the only program that requires all entrants to have a science degree and full-time research experience, and it's also the only program that does not offer a degree, only a certificate. "I couldn't get into my own program," says Santa Cruz's program founder and only regular faculty member, John Wilkes. An English Ph.D., Wilkes doesn't offer a master's degree "because I would have to hire academics. I wanted science writers." His students follow a one-year sequence that includes illustration as well as reporting, editing, and essay writing and ends with a professional summer internship.

While Santa Cruz focuses on reporting, other programs favor writing. For those "more interested in sentences and paragraphs," as well as the literature of science, Johns Hopkins admits about twenty undergraduates and up to eight master's students a year in its Program in Writing About Science, says faculty member Ann Finkbeiner. The editor-in-chief of *Nature* and *Medicine* magazines, Barbara D. Culliton, directs the program. Boston University's Science Journalism Program only requires "some science background"; its forty students receive an M.S. in science journalism after a one-year course. At NYU the Science and Environmental Reporting Program accepts fifteen new students each year; past faculty have included luminaries like Pulitzer Prize winner Natalie Angier and Dennis Overbye.

At the undergraduate level some twenty-five schools offer science communication courses, sequences, or programs, including the University of Missouri, Lehigh University, the University of Wisconsin, DePaul University, the University of Colorado, and Cornell University. Each has its own idea of the ideal curriculum. At Lehigh University's Science and Environmental Writing Program, directed by Sharon Friedman, undergraduates take "an awful lot of science and science philosophy." At Cornell, Wisconsin, and other schools the emphasis is on the history of science. Some programs focus on a particular field—Colorado on environment, the University of Texas on agronomy.

Science writers themselves disagree on the value of the science writing programs. "As a literature major I have a broader perspective than the scientists I cover," says Natalie Angier, whose master's is in the medieval period. "I don't think these graduates know what a news story is," adds Charlie Petit, a longtime science reporter at the San Francisco *Chronicle*. For their part, graduates, especially of Santa Cruz, tend to wax rhapsodic about the programs, as do their editors, like Ellis Rubinstein of *Science*.

Many of the new generation of writers in this collection, including Dennis Overbye, Gary Taubes, Shannon Brownlee, and Natalie Angier, learned their craft at *Discover* magazine in the early and mid-1980s. Most agree the experience, traumatic as it was ("It was masthead roulette," says Overbye), outstripped that of any classroom.

The Masks of Science

In the end the tensions between science and journalism are inevitable because the tensions within science itself are so critically important. "Science thrives on anomaly, inconsistency, controversy and doubt," wrote scientist Christian Von Baeyer. Journalism, to use Ward Just's simile, is like the drunk man at a baseball game who is one step behind the action but nevertheless obnoxiously cheers and boos. The publicists' trade in titillation masks the most basic truth of science research: Mostly it's boring, lonely, incredibly difficult, and tentative.

Science coverage at its best reminds us that personality and the painful processes of cognition and competition are as much a part of science as lab mice and white coats. Many writers relish the challenge. "It's not the same old corruption story with new names," says Charlie Petit. "What's new in science is what's new in human experience." At its worst it can overplay bad research and miss incredible lapses. When media coverage captures the real sweat of brilliant research, though, it addresses the ultimate questions and restores the childlike wonder of the grand detective story. "It's a field full of egos and drama and conflict," says Petit. "What more could you want?"

1

TIMOTHY FERRIS

The Interpreter

From *The Mind's Sky*, Bantam Books,
1992

As his book titles suggest, Timothy Ferris is a born story-teller. In works like The Red Limit: The Search for the Edge of the Universe *(1977),* Galaxies *(1980),* Space Shots: The Beauty of Nature Beyond Earth *(1984), and* Coming of Age in the Milky Way *(1988), he became one of the first writers to mine gold from the difficult material of astronomy journals and conferences. Beginning with the idea that "there's more to this world than* this *world, and more to this world than we know," his work invokes myth and the mind in conveying a love for the universe "about which we still know only an infinitesimal amount."*

Born in 1944 in Miami, Florida, he is one of the newer science writers who was not trained in science. He attended Northwestern University, where he majored in English and enrolled in law school for a year. Heading to New York, he worked as a reporter for United Press International and the New York Post *before becoming an editor at* Rolling Stone *and then taking an academic appointment at the University of California at Berkeley. With roots firmly in literary journalism, his focus on astronomy was a return to his joy with a telescope at nine years old. His writing has earned numerous honors, including the American Institute of Physics Prize, an American Association for the Advancement of Science–Westinghouse Writing Award, a Guggenheim fellowship, and a Pulitzer Prize nomination.*

A pioneer in the new science writing, Ferris is not happy with the most recent trends in the field. Though he is not a science critic or investigator, he dislikes the recent trend toward packaged and rehearsed press conferences, literary deals, and "too much mutuality between writers and scientists." In his view, the publishing world is corrupting science to some degree. Big literary advances have "caused some scientists to put a price tag on their discoveries, in something like the way that witnesses to news events expect to be paid by the tabloids for their stories."

Still he is sanguine about the field as a whole. "The scientific community is a dream for a reporter to cover," he says, "because it is the opposite of secretive; it operates on maximum free exchange of information."

In The Mind's Sky he turns the journey inward, capturing a cultural moment when our greatest adventures seem to be both into the mind and outward into the cosmos. It began with an assignment to cover a conference on the search for extraterrestrial intelligence but moved quickly to a study of the "nature of intelligence itself." In "The Interpreter" he looks at recent work on the multiple and often completely unknown functions and structures of the mind, comparing them to the multiple structures of our world.

WHEN I THINK OF THE RELATIONSHIP BETWEEN the universe and the human brain an image that comes to mind is that of a tree—not just its glorious crown of branches but also its system of roots, which may extend as far into the earth as the branches spread to the sky. To me, the branches symbolize the observed universe, while the roots symbolize the brain. Both systems are constantly growing and evolving, and they depend on each other.

One might object that this makes too much of the roots: The brain, after all, is far less complex and extensive than the universe, which can get along fine without us. But the symmetry of the metaphor is preserved if we think of the branches as referring to the *perceived* universe. *That* universe exists only so long as there is someone to perceive it. Moreover, it is the only universe we can ever know. Neither we nor any other thinking beings can comprehend any more of the universe than what we can make of it in our minds. In that sense, roots and branches—mind and cosmos—are mutually dependent and forever equal.

They are symmetrical, too, in that we tend to think of the universe and the brain as each being one thing. Why we should do so intrigues me, and the next chapter investigates the concept of the universe as a unified whole. Here I want to examine the assumption that each of us has but one brain.

Like most people I think of myself as of one mind. I say, "I have made up my mind," not, "I have made up my minds." In this I have plenty of company; so universal is the doctrine of "one man, one mind" that it constitutes a hallmark of mental health; to act as if you were of *several* minds is to risk commitment to a mental ward. As the American brain researcher Michael Gazzaniga writes, "The strong subjective sense we all possess of ourselves is that we are a single, unified, conscious agent controlling life's events with a singular, integrated purpose."

And yet, as Gazzaniga adds, "it is not true." His research and that of many colleagues reveals that the brain is by no means monolithic, but consists of many different modules—Gazzaniga calls them "programs"—that function more or less independently. How many programs are there? Nobody knows. Some estimate the number at a dozen or so. Gazzaniga thinks it may be as high as a hundred or more. Nobody who has studied the brain thinks the number is one.

Now you may have noticed that I am indulging in a bit of sleight of hand here, by saying "mind" when I refer to the sense of personal unity that each mentally healthy person possesses, and "brain" when I claim that we contain multitudes. And this, the mind-brain question, is indeed the crux of the problem.

Brain is easy to define: It is the wet, oatmeal-colored organ, weighing about three pounds, that resides inside the skull, along with such appurtenances (the eye, the spinal cord) as the neurologists see fit to include in their concept of the brain. Its physical multiplicity is unquestionable: Anatomists have identified hundreds of brain parts, on which they have bestowed enough bewildering names to give medical students migraine headaches—the frontal lobes, the parietal and occipital lobes, motor and sensory cortex, Wernicke's area, Broca's area, the cingulate gyrus, the pulvinar, the cerebral aqueduct and peduncle, the pineal body, the cerebellorubrothalamic tract, the commissure of fornix, the nucleus of Darkschewitsch, the island of Reil, Ammon's horn, and the interstitial nucleus of Cajal.

One way to bring order to the complexity of the brain is to study how it has evolved over time, a process that is to some extent recapitulated in the growth of the human embryo. This research has established that the brain stem—the bulb where the brain meets the spine—is the oldest part, with the midbrain and higher brain having been built atop it in something like the way that the newer buildings of an ancient city are constructed on the foundations of the old. This perspective informs the "triune brain" paradigm, propounded by the American neuroscientist Paul MacLean, which divides the brain into three systems: At the base resides the "reptilian complex," responsible for aggression, territoriality, and ritual; above that is found the limbic system, seat of powerful emotions, sexual instincts, and the sense of smell; and over the top arches the neocortex, the most recent and most distinctly human system, generator of language and geometry, "the mother of invention and father of abstract thought," in MacLean's words.

Mind is a slipperier concept. A statement of its various definitions takes up three full pages of the *Oxford English Dictionary*. For our purposes we can define "mind" as the subject of consciousness—the totality of thoughts, feelings, and sensations presented by the brain to that segment of it that is conscious. But as we will see, consciousness forms a much smaller part of the operations of the brain than was once supposed. Mind is not the all-knowing monarch of the brain, but a little circle of firelight in a dark, Australia-sized continent where the unconscious brain processes carry on.

Freud, the Magellan of the subconscious, was the first to appreciate this. Whatever may have been the limitations of his analysis of the unconscious, Freud appreciated its vast extent and called attention to its veiled influences on the mind. These influences highlight the curious question of how and why, given that the brain is multipartite, it represents itself to the mind as unified. Were our conscious selves perfectly unified, we would feel justified in concluding that the brain for all the disparity of its parts is in truth a fully unified system. But we find, instead, that our sense of personal unity and command over the brain is an imperfect illusion, like the mechanical regent constructed by the Wizard of Oz to impress his subjects. Evidence of an underlying multiplicity keeps peeking from behind the scrim, and what it reveals is that each of us, like the wider universe, is made of many different entities.

This strange circumstance—that one's mind neither controls nor comprehends most of what goes on in one's brain—is emphasized in the results of two recent experiments. One was conducted by Benjamin Libet, a neurophysiologist at the School of Medicine of the University of California at San Francisco. The other was pioneered by Roger Sperry and his colleagues at the California Institute of Technology and expanded upon by Sperry's students, Gazzaniga among them.

Libet asked the subjects of his experiments simply to flex one finger. To do so would seem to be a purely volitional act, one that the conscious mind orders and the rest of the nervous system carries out. But Libet's results proved otherwise.

Libet wired up his subjects with electrodes that measure brain activity, and seated them in full view of a rapidly rotating clock hand that enabled them to note exactly when they "ordered" their finger to flex. Libet could then mark three events in time: The onset of increased brain activity recorded by the electrodes, the flexing of the finger, and the point at which each subject had consciously willed his finger to flex.

What Libet found was that in each instance, a flurry of brain activity took place a fraction of a second *before* the "order" to flex the finger was dispatched by the conscious mind. "In other words," says Libet, "their neurons were firing a third of a second before they were even conscious of the desire to act. Hence, it appeared the brain had begun preparing for movement long before the mind had 'decided' to do anything."

The illusion of conscious control is maintained, Libet notes, because another mechanism in the brain delays the sensation of the finger moving, so that the conscious mind continues to think that it has first decreed the action, then felt the muscles act. Actually, by the time the mind orders the finger to flex, the impulse has already been dispatched. All the mind gets is a last-minute opportunity to veto the decision: I can stop my finger from flexing by sending an intercept command that overtakes and interrupts the original command and thus keeps my finger immobile. (This is what happens when you reach for a plate in the kitchen, then stop yourself upon remembering that the plate is hot.) The mind is thus permitted to sustain the flattering illusion that it controls the game. In actuality it is playing catch-up ball.

It is not difficult to conjecture *why* we should have evolved the pleasing if illusory conviction that we both control and understand more of the brain than we do: He who hesitates is lost, and I can act more quickly and decisively if I imagine that "I"—my mind—is running the show. But *how* does the brain so constantly and consistently fool the mind?

Light was shed on this question in experiments conducted by Sperry, Gazzaniga, and others on what are called "split-brain" patients. The cerebrum—the seat of thought and voluntary action—is divided into two lobes or hemispheres. In most individuals, the left cerebral hemisphere processes visual information from the right side of each eye's field of view, and controls the right side of the body, while the right hemisphere performs the same functions for the left side. Communication between the two hemispheres is handled by the corpus callosum, a bundle of over two hundred million nerve fibers. Sufferers from *grand mal* epilepsy may find relief through a surgical procedure in which the corpus callosum is cut, terminating communication between the right and left sides of the higher brain. Typically these individuals go on to lead normal lives, with few obvious side effects. But careful studies of their perceptions and actions have taught scientists a great deal about how the brain works.

In the 1950s, Sperry and his colleagues flashed pictures on a screen in such a way that their subjects could see them on only one side of their field of view. This apparatus could, for example, show a picture to the right brain while keeping the left brain in the dark. In a normal individual this would make little difference; the corpus callosum, a high-bandwidth transmission channel that shuttles information back and forth between lobes, would inform the left brain of what the right brain had seen. But a split-brain patient has lost the use of the corpus callosum; consequently his left brain has little or no way of knowing what the right brain has seen.

This made it possible, by studying split-brain patients, to identify certain functions as localized in one or the other hemisphere. Language, for instance, turned out to be a function primarily of the left brain. When a word is flashed to the right hemisphere of a split-brain patient, she cannot tell the researcher what the word was. The left brain, which handles speech, does not know what to say, because it has not seen the word. The right brain knows, but cannot speak. It can, however, answer questions in other ways. In one experiment, a subject's right brain was shown a picture of an apple; he could not say what he had been shown, but when his left hand (the hand controlled by the right brain) was given several hidden objects to choose from, it picked the apple.

Generalizations about the proclivities of the right and left cerebral hemispheres—adept, respectively, at patterns and words—spread from Sperry's laboratories to become part of the broader culture, where they were sometimes put to rather facile uses. Writers were declared to be "left-brain" types, painters to be "right-brain" dominated. Golfers and tennis players were trained to engage their right brain functions in order to play more naturally and gracefully. School administrators endeavored to address the supposedly neglected right brain by putting more stress on arts and crafts.

But the implications of localized brain functions can also help us understand the unity of mind. The split-brain experiments indicate that the brain is made up of many modules that operate more or less independently, and that the function of the mind is not so much to tell the other units what to do as to try to make some coherent sense out of what they already have chosen to do.

This was where Gazzaniga came in. He worked with split-brain patients whose right hemispheres had sufficient linguistic facility to understand simple commands. (Some people, especially the left-handed, distribute part of their language processing to the right hemisphere.) When a command—"Walk!"—was flashed to such a patient's right brain, he got up and began to walk out of the room. The remarkable thing is that when asked, the patient invariably came up with a rational though bogus explanation for his actions. Asked, "Where are you going?" a typical response was something like, "Uh, I'm going to get a Coke."

This behavior calls to mind a similar phenomenon often observed in connection with hypnosis. "Under hypnosis the patient is given a post-hypnotic suggestion," writes the philosopher John Searle, of the University of California, Berkeley. "You can tell him, for example, to do some fairly trivial, harmless thing, such as, let's say, crawl around on the floor. After the patient comes out of hypnosis, he might be engaging in conversation, sitting, drinking coffee, when suddenly he says something like, 'What a fascinating floor in this room!' or 'I want to check out this rug,' or 'I'm thinking of investing in floor coverings and I'd like to investigate this floor.' He then proceeds to crawl around on the floor.

"Now the interest of these cases," Searle notes, "is that the patient always gives some more or less adequate reason for doing what he does." We rationalize our actions, explaining them in terms we ourselves accept as true, even when our conscious mind is ignorant of the motives behind them. The posthypnotic subject does not know why he is crawling around on the floor; this knowledge was blocked from him under hypnosis. Gazzaniga's split-brain patients do not know, either, why they suddenly get up and walk away, communications having been severed between the right hemisphere, which received the command, and the left hemisphere, which is called upon to account for it. Yet all these subjects readily explain their behavior. And evidently they *believe* the explanation, even though the experimenter can tell that it's a fabrication.

The implication seems clear that there is a program in the brain responsible for presenting the mind with plausible explanations for actions, and that it acts, so to speak, unscrupulously, blithely explaining matters about which it is uninformed. Gazzaniga calls this program "the interpreter," and he notes that its functioning accounts for the embarrassing fact that we all from time to time hear ourselves saying something patently false. "The realization that the mind has a modular organization suggests that some of our behavior might have no origins in our conscious thought process," Gazzaniga writes. "For example, we just happen to eat frogs' legs for the first time. . . . While the interpreter does not actually know why there was an impulse to consume frogs' legs it might hypothesize, 'Because I want to learn about French food.' " Who among us has not uttered such a lame, silly phrase, and wondered where it came from? Gazzaniga's answer is that it comes from the interpreter program.

The interpreter may be seen at work in the phenomenon of cognitive dissonance. Long remarked upon by psychologists, cognitive dissonance occurs when we find ourselves acting in ways that contradict our moral precepts, and seek to explain away the disparity. In one oft-cited study, students who said they deplored cheating were given an examination under conditions in which it was easy to cheat; those who succumbed to temptation and cheated, when queried anew about their ethical precepts, expressed less condemnatory attitudes toward cheating than they had before. Gazzaniga's explanation is that since much of our behavior is not controlled by the conscious mind in the first place, the interpreter program often is called upon to put a good face on dissonant behavior, and does so by presenting the conscious mind with a self-serving rationale for what we have done.

Gazzaniga's results indicate that the interpreter is located in the left cerebral hemisphere, near the speech center. This makes sense, in that language is the great explainer—and counterfeiter—of human motives and actions. In the twentieth century we have seen the interpreter working overtime, turning out reams of Orwellian doublespeak, from the Nazis who put a sign above the death camp gates reading "Obedience to the Law is Freedom," to the military publicist who coined the term "preemptive response" to describe the bombing of Vietnamese cities. Gazzaniga's research suggests that sophistry and propaganda succeed because they employ techniques that the interpreter has been using all along to preen and persuade our vain and limited minds. "Language," says Gazzaniga, "is merely the press agent for these other variables of cognition."

We are confronted, then, with the prospect that the sense of unity and control that the conscious mind presents to each mentally healthy individual is an illusion. (In this sense, the crazy person who hears a multitude of competing voices in his mind is saner than the rest of us, just as poets have been saying for centuries.) The brain is not unified, nor is the mind in control; it only seems that way, thanks to the ceaseless public relations efforts of the interpreter—and, perhaps, of other similar programs not yet identified. The mind may rule the self, but it is a constitutional monarch; presented with decisions *already made* elsewhere in the brain, it must try somehow to put on a good show of their adding up to some coordinated, sensible pattern. Functionally it resembles Ronald Reagan's presidency: It acts as if it were in control, and thinks it is in control, and believes it has good reasons for what it does, when in actuality it is often just mouthing soothing rationalizations while obeying the orders of unseen agencies hidden offstage.

The brain is analogous to a computer in that it disguises a multiplicity of operations behind a unified facade. The computer on which I am typing this sentence is busy doing many things at once—one part of it is keeping track of time, another is searching sectors in one of its disc drives, another is moving blocks of data here and there in its memory—but the image it paints on the screen is coherent and unitary, like the picture presented to the mind by the brain. At the moment, that image replicates black letters inked on white paper. If I press a few keys to access another program, the image will change to replicate a chess board, the stars over Padua on a summer night in the year 1692, or an air battle over the Pacific in 1942. In every instance the unified image is a scrim, presented by a program that in turn interfaces with other programs. The brain similarly renders the multiple functions of its several programs into a pleasing if illusory unity.

And this, I suspect, could describe the psychology of the galaxy-wide computer network I was describing earlier in this book. The network might regard itself as intelligent, but most of what it knows would have come from agencies that it could never really understand—the living, thinking beings on the many worlds that had contributed knowledge to the network. In much the same way, our minds rely upon entities within the brain that *we* do not understand. Though the network might think it *wanted* to bring new worlds into contact and to establish communications links with other galaxies, in reality it merely had been programmed to do so—just as we, for all we know, are carrying out instructions coded in our genes, their message and intent a mystery to us.

Perhaps that is the fate of all intelligence, everywhere—to act in ways it thinks are volitional, while never knowing whether instead it actually is playing a role in some unglimpsed master plan. I wonder how many minds, from here to the galaxies of the Hydra Supercluster, have asked themselves the same question: Are we free agents who seek to learn about the universe, or are we a means by which the universe seeks to learn about itself?

2

NATALIE ANGIER

Busy as a Bee? Then Who's Doing the Work?

The *New York Times*,
July 30, 1991

A science reporter who has been at the New York Times *since 1990, Natalie Angier specializes in what she calls "conceptual breakthrough stories." She follows professional science journals closely until she sees the same subject mentioned in four or five different studies. "Then I go to work," she says.*

This is a common practice among science writers. What separates Angier, who has won both Pulitzer and American Association for the Advancement of Science–Westinghouse Writing prizes, is the elegant style she brings to her trend pieces. She generally does not open with a conventional narrative lead or news hook but with a meditative philosophical statement laced with a wry wit.

Such an unusual style—comparable to that of the late scientist and essayist Lewis Thomas—stems in part from her years as an English major at Barnard College, from which she graduated in 1978. At first Angier planned to pursue a Ph.D. in medieval literature. "I had been thinking of science though for a long time, taking courses in calculus and physics as a mental discipline and incorporating science images in poetry I was writing." Her first job out of school was as a technical writer at Texas Instruments. She then landed an entry-level position as Discover *magazine was getting its start, entering one of the key training grounds for writers in this volume. She focused on biology, which became her specialty, because the magazine already had a mathematics and physics reporter.*

She left there to write for Time *magazine and to author a book,* Natural Obsessions: The Search for the Oncogene *(1988), which announced Angier as one of the new journalists of science, capturing the frantic life of a biomedical research team and charting her own relation to the group. She was teaching science writing in the graduate journalism program at New York University when she landed her position at the* New York Times. *As with many of the newer science writers, her models are Watson's* The Double Helix *and Tracy Kidder's* The Soul of a New Machine, *as well as the work of the late* New Yorker *writer who perfected the medical detective story, Berton Roueché.*

"Busy as a Bee?" was among three Angier stories named winners of the AAAS–Westinghouse Writing Award in 1992. "I consider it one of my great accomplishments," she says, because her approach to the topic differed from her usual method. "I came up with the idea in midsummer because I was feeling very lazy. Then I had to go out and report it, which in this case was very difficult." She recalled the work on ants being done by Dr. Gene Robinson at the University of Illinois–Champaign, who in turn led her to Dr. Paul Sherman, who pointed out a scholarly paper done on the subject by Dr. Joan Herbers at the University of Vermont. In a sense Angier contributed to the development of scientific theory with this story.

Angier does get criticized for the artfulness of her style. "The scientists mostly like the pieces," she notes, "although I did get flack for the anthropomorphism. Critics said, you can't call animal inactivity laziness. You're seeing a lot of controversy on anthropomorphosis in various journals lately."

Making it, in a sense, the next story for Angier to cover.

I N THESE LANGUID MIDSUMMER DAYS, HUMANS who feel the urge to take it easy but remain burdened by a recalcitrant work ethic might do well to consider that laziness is perfectly natural, perfectly sensible and shared by nearly every other species on the planet.

Contrary to the old fables about the unflagging industriousness of ants, bees, beavers and the like, field biologists engaged in a new specialty known as time budget analysis are discovering that the great majority of creatures spend most of their time doing nothing much at all.

They eat when they must or can. They court and breed when driven by seasonal impulses. Some species build a makeshift shelter now and again, while others fulfill the occasional social obligation, like picking out fleas from a fellow creature's fur.

But more often than not, animals across the phylogenetic spectrum will thumb a proboscis at biblical injunctions to labor and proceed to engage in any number of inactive activities: sitting, sprawling, dozing, rocking back and forth, ambling around in desultory circles.

"If you follow an organism in the field for extended periods of time, and catalogue every type of activity for every moment of the day, you can't help but come to the conclusion, by George, this organism isn't doing much, is it?" said Dr. Joan Herbers, a zoologist at the University of Vermont, who has written comparative reports of laziness in animals. "Being lazy is almost universal."

In fact, compared with other creatures, human beings spend anywhere from two to four times as many hours working, particularly if family, household and social duties are taken into account.

But lest people feel smug about their diligence, evolutionary biologists are discovering that animal inactivity is almost never born of aimless indolence, but instead serves a broad variety of purposes. Some animals sit around to conserve precious calories, others to improve digestion of the calories they have consumed. Some do it to stay cool, others to keep warm. Predators and prey alike are best camouflaged when they are not fidgeting or fussing. Some creatures linger quietly in their territory to guard it, and others stay home to avoid being cannibalized by their neighbors.

So while there may not be a specific gene for laziness, there is always a good excuse.

"When you just see an animal that looks like it's in repose, you may be looking at any number of very adaptive features," said Dr. Paul Sherman of Cornell University in Ithaca, N.Y. "You can't say it's simply doing nothing, and you can't always predict from common sense alone what the apparent rest is all about."

So diverse are the possible reasons for laziness that some biologists are beginning to shift the focus of their research. Rather than observing the behavior of animals in action, as field researchers historically have, they are attempting to understand the many factors that lie behind animal inertia. They hope that by learning when and why an animal chooses inactivity, they can better understand key mysteries of ecology, like the distribution of different species in a particular environment and how animals survive harsh settings and lean times.

"In the past, field biologists focused on movement, foraging, mating behavior," said Dr. Herbers. "Now they're worrying about why animals sit still."

How They Do It

A Repertory of Resting

Animals certainly give their researchers much to fret over. Dr. Craig Packer and Dr. Anne Pusey, zoologists with the University of Minnesota in Minneapolis, have studied lions in the Serengeti since the 1970's, and they said nearly all of that time has been spent staring through binoculars at tawny heaps of fur, the pride's collective immobility broken only by the intermittent twitch of an ear.

"A lion can lie in the same spot, without budging, for 12 hours at a stretch," said Dr. Pusey. "They're active on their feet maybe two or three hours a day." In that brief spate of effort, they are likely to be either hunting or devouring the booty of that hunt, which is one reason they need so much downtime.

"A lion can eat an enormous amount in one sitting," maybe 70 pounds of meat, said Dr. Pusey. "Their bellies get extremely fat, and they look incredibly uncomfortable and incredibly immobile, lying on their backs and panting in the heat."

Monkeys are commonly thought of as nature's indefatigable acrobats, but many species sit around as much as three-quarters of the day, not to mention the 12 hours of the night they usually spend sleeping.

"MONKEYS WERE STILL SLEEPING"

Dr. Frans de Waal, a primatologist at the Yerkes Regional Primate Center in Atlanta and author of *Peacemaking Among Primates*, said that he was amused to discover the lax habits of the woolly spider monkey, which he observed in Brazil with Dr. Karen Stryer. One morning the two researchers awoke before dawn to get out to a distant observation site by 7 A.M., when they assumed the monkeys would begin their day's foraging.

"We were sitting there and sitting there," said Dr. de Waal. "By 11 o'clock, the monkeys were still sleeping, at which point I fell asleep myself."

Hummingbirds are the world's most vigorous and energy-intensive fliers—when they are flying. The birds turn out to spend 80 percent of their day motionless on a twig; at night, they sleep.

Beavers are thought to bustle about so singlemindedly that their name is often used as a synonym for work. But beavers emerge from the safe haven of their lodge to gather food or to patch up their dam for only five hours a day, give or take a few intermissions. "Even when they're supposed to be most active, they'll retreat back into the lodge for long periods of time, and rest," said Dr. Gerald E. Svendsen, a zoologist at Ohio University in Athens who studies beavers.

11 MONTHS OF IMMOBILITY

The spade-foot toad of the southwestern desert burrows three feet underground and refuses to budge for 11 months of the year. In that time it does not eat, drink or excrete waste, all the while conserving energy by turning down its core metabolism to one-fifth of what it is during its single active month. "If you find one of these dormant toads, you've got it," said Dr. Vaughan H. Shoemaker, a zoologist at the University of California at Riverside. "It's just sitting in the soil like a rock or a potato."

Even the busy bees or worker ants of Aesopian fame dedicate only about 20 percent of the day to doing chores like gathering nectar or tidying up the nest. Otherwise, the insects stay still. "They seem to have run out of work to do," said Dr. Gene E. Robinson, an entomologist at the University of Illinois in Urbana–Champaign. "They really do look lazy."

WHY THEY DO IT

Cost-Benefit Study Shows Rest Is Best

In his view, the myth of the tireless social insect probably arose from observations of entire hives or anthills, which are little galaxies of ceaseless activity. "Human fascination with the industriousness of social insects probably comes from considering whole colonies rather than from considering what individuals in those colonies do," he said. "But since we've been tagging individuals to see what each bee does, we've found that any individual has a lot of surplus time."

Biologists studying animals at rest turn to sophisticated mathematical models resembling those used by economists, which take into account an animal's energy demands, fertility rate, the relative abundance and location of food and water, weather conditions and other factors. They do extensive cost-benefit analyses, asking questions like: How high is the cost of foraging compared to the potential calories that may be gained?

THE COST OF MOVING

Such a calculation involves not only a measure of how much more energy an animal burns as it rummages about relative to what it would spend resting, but also a consideration of, for example, how hot it will become in motion, and how much of its stored water will then be needed to evaporate away heat to cool the body. Overheating can be a deadly threat for many animals.

When they complete their computations, biologists usually end up respecting an animal's decision to lie low.

"Let's say a moose spends so much time foraging that its body temperature rises close to the lethal maximum," said Dr. Gary E. Belovsky, associate professor of wildlife ecology at the University of Michigan in Ann Arbor. "And let's say a wolf comes along and chases it. Well, that raises the moose's body temperature further, and it's likely to drop over dead. The moose must stay cool if it is to survive."

Some scientists strenuously object to the use of the term laziness to describe any animal behavior, which they say implies some wilful shirking of a task that would improve the animal's lot in life if it were done.

"Animals are inactive when they have to be," said Dr. Belovsky. "It's not as though they're choosing laziness when they'd be better off doing something productive."

For example, moose are ruminants, like cattle, and must stay fairly still while digesting food, he said. For every hour of grazing on vegetation, he said, the moose needs four hours to metabolize its food. "It has no other option but to be at rest," he said.

FLYING IS SO DRAINING

Researchers who have looked at hummingbird behavior have also concluded that the tiny birds are perfectly justified in taking frequent breaks. To hover in midair while sipping from long-tubed flowers, they must beat their wings in elaborate figure-eight patterns at a rate of 60 times a second.

"The cost of their flight is among the greatest of any type of movement in the animal kingdom," said Dr. Frank B. Gill, curator of ornithology at the Academy of Natural Sciences of Philadelphia. "They burn more fuel in calories per gram of body weight when flying than anything else ever studied."

Flying is so draining that many hummingbirds and their African relatives, the sunbirds, are better off staying motionless unless the food they can obtain is very rich indeed. To help assure that they can get nectar without having to travel too far for their dinner, sunbirds will choose a territory and stand around on the perimeter, waiting for the flowers within to become plump with nectar.

How They Benefit

Conserving Water and Heat

For some creatures, immobility carries so many benefits that they become almost Buddha-like in their stillness. The fringe-toed lizard, which lives in the desert of the southwest United States, sits motionless just below the surface of the sand for hours, with nothing sticking up but its eyes. As the lizards sit, the sand warms and invigorates them. "They're ready to lurch out at anything edible that passes by, like a butterfly," said Dr. Philip Brownell, a biologist at Oregon State University in Corvallis.

And should it see a predatory snake approaching, the lizard can further immobilize itself by suppressing its breathing. "The lizard just shuts off its engines," Dr. Brownell said.

What is more, by staying snug in its sandy blanket, the lizard cuts down on water loss, a constant threat to desert creatures.

In a harsh place like the desert, most animals spend most of the time waiting for water and coolness. Spadefoot toads come out only in July, when the annual rains bring insects to feed on. Male and female toads meet and mate the very first night they emerge from their rock-like state, and they then begin eating enough to put on an extra 30 percent in body fat required to make it through their dormant 11 months.

Several hundred species of mammals go into hibernation each winter, cutting down on energy expenditure by dramatically lowering their metabolic rates. In hibernating ground squirrels, for example, the heart rate slows to only one or two beats a minute, and the body temperature goes down to near freezing. For herbivores, winter hibernation makes sense. "There's nothing for you to eat, the weather's bad, you can't reproduce, and there are still predators trying to eat you," said Dr. Sherman. "The best thing to do is go into suspended animation."

WHEN THEY MOVE

Vigilant Resters Spring to Life

But sometimes a biologist is stumped over apparent indolence that cannot be explained by obvious things like inclement weather. Dr. Sherman has been studying the naked mole rat, a peculiar social mammal that spends its entire life underground. He long wondered why the largest mole rats in a group did the least and seemed to sleep the most, but he found out one day when he introduced a snake into the colony he had set up in his lab.

"The big ones instantly sprang into action, and attacked the snake," he said. "We'd thought they were sleeping, but they were just maintaining quiet vigilance."

Such a need for vigilance may help explain why bees and ants spend so much time resting. Dr. Robinson recently has learned that honeybees have a soldier caste; members do little or nothing around the hive but are the first to act should the hive be disturbed. "They're like a standing army," he said. "They're hanging around the colony, not doing anything in particular, but they can be immediately mobilized."

Other bees and ants may be saving their energy for a big job, like the discovery of an abundant new source of food, which requires overtime effort to harvest it, or the intermittent splitting of one hive into two, which suddenly leaves fewer workers to do the same tasks. "A colony has a labor force bigger than it really needs to get through those critical episodes," said Dr. Robinson.

New studies show that social insects cannot afford to waste their energy on non-critical activities. It turns out ants and bees are born with a set amount of energy to de-vote to their colony, which for reasons that remain myste-rious seems to have less to do with the amount of food they eat than with an inborn genetic program. "They're like batteries," said Dr. Peter Nonacs, who studies ants with Dr. Edward O. Wilson at Harvard University. "They have a fixed amount of energy in them, which they can use up quickly or slowly. The harder they work, the quicker they die." With that knowledge, Dr. Nonacs says he now has great sympathy when he comes upon an ant in repose.

And perhaps biologists who study inactivity can even lend luster to the much-maligned creature that gave lazi-ness its most evocative term: the sloth. Found throughout Central and South America, the sloth hangs from trees by its long rubbery limbs, sleeping 15 hours a day and moving so infrequently that two species of algae grow on its coat and between its claws. A newborn sloth sits atop its moth-er's belly and is so loathe to move that it freely defecates and urinates onto her fur, which she will only intermit-tently bother to clean.

But lest such sluggishness seem almost perverse, the sloth is suited to its niche. By moving so slowly, it stays re-markably inconspicuous to predators. Even its fungal coat serves a camouflaging purpose. With the algae glinting greenish-blue in the sunlight, the sloth resembles the hanging plant it has very nearly become.

3

JIM KELLY

How to Get Ahead in Science? Simple.

Houston *Press*,
August 15, 1991

Jim Kelly faced problems all science writers encounter at one time when he wrote "How to Get Ahead in Science? Simple." He abhorred chemistry, though he had spent two years as a Rice University engineering major. He had less than two weeks before deadline. He was intimidated by his subject, the Rice "legend," chemist Rick Smalley. Then, as a final distraction, his parents dropped in for a visit as he was in the middle of writing the piece.

"It was a labor of terror," says Kelly, who was a twenty-three-year-old copy editor at the small alternative newspaper the Houston Press *at the time he wrote the piece. He had heard of Smalley through the alumni grapevine and had proposed the subject a month earlier. When his editor told him their cover story had fallen through, Kelly had his first major assignment. No one realized the result would be a brilliant snapshot of a chemistry invention—the "science story of 1991," according to* Newsweek. *Perhaps it was the terror of a talented young writer that made the piece a winner of a 1992 American Association for the Advancement of Science–Westinghouse Writing Award.*

Kelly's first challenge was to understand the material.

Talking with a scientist who reminded him most of all of Lenin in his appearance and dictatorial authority, Kelly says, "was like finding myself in Chemistry 101 at midterm, realizing I knew nothing of what was going on. Worse, my mind kept wandering." Kelly's solution was as ingenuous as some of those practiced by Dr. Smalley. He used a tape recorder, as most science writers do, and carefully went over each word afterward, verifying his understanding with other sources. As he sat with Smalley, he studied his office, noting the details of the man reflected in his surroundings that made the scientist come alive—and gave the article its unique urgency.

As inspiration for his writing, Kelly recalls an undergraduate course: the history of science, taught by Albert Van Helden. Most of the students in the class were science majors taking it pass-fail to fill their humanities requirement. "The best assignment was writing a weekly review of a new science book," says Kelly, who became an English major, like Angier and Ferris. "I was encouraged to indulge myself in all kinds of science writing and to experiment in form."

Now a freelancer based in Florida, Kelly says the heart of his article, the beery night when Smalley fashioned a geodesic dome out of his son's construction paper, sent Kelly back many times to a drawing pad to figure out the science. "The scene was kind of a set performance Smalley gave. I really struggled to write it," he says. In that scene, as in the rest of the article, Kelly captures the strange link of intense competition and capacity for loopy and indirect thought—using his son's soccer ball—that makes for a great inventor.

EVER SINCE THE BUCKYBALL STORY BROKE BIG last year, Rice University chemist Rick Smalley has been getting the phone calls. Rick, they say, this is Jamie in

Minnesota, and I saw this article. I just wanted you to know that I've *dreamed* about this molecule and now I can see it. And Smalley, whose job it is in a sense to dream about molecules, finds himself talking to a complete stranger about the one he discovered by accident.

Officially, the molecule is called buckminsterfullerene, in honor of the eccentric futurist-inventor R. Buckminster Fuller, and it fascinates not only the Jamies of this world but the Paul Chus as well. The story of its discovery is a kind of parable of science, a strange juxtaposition of powerful lasers and paper models taped together at midnight, of Monty Python hijinks in the lab and transcendent ideas argued over tacos and enchiladas. It's also the story of Rick Smalley—a reluctant investigator who found himself swept by serendipity into the discovery of a lifetime.

Smalley calls the molecule, rather affectionately, bucky. The nickname plays down the significance of his discovery. What he found in 1985, with help from Harry Kroto of the University of Sussex and Rice's Robert Curl, was nothing less than the third molecular form of the element carbon, the other two being diamond and graphite. What gets people excited about the buckyball is its shape: it's round, with sixty atoms of carbon arranged in a structure of hexagons and pentagons that resembles nothing so much as a soccer ball, or a geodesic dome—like those designed by Buckminster Fuller.

Fuller expected big things from his domes; he once proposed air-conditioning all of New York by enclosing the city in one. These days, bucky's getting an even bigger buildup, driven by a breakthrough last year that made it available in quantities large enough for chemists to work with. It's extraordinarily stable and impervious to radiation and chemical destruction, they say, an entirely new molecule with possible applications across the board. New semiconductors for computers, new medicines, super-lubricants, super-batteries, affordable solar cells, superconductors— you name it, the buckyball *might* make it. As far as the layperson's scientific press is concerned, it's this year's molecule, playing big in places like *Discover* and *Popular Science* and even popping up in the *Wall Street Journal.*

More substantial is the attention recorded in a set of thick black three-ring binders on Smalley's desk, labeled Bucky I, II, III, IV and V—a bibliography of scientific papers Smalley's been keeping on bucky. The 48-year-old chemist has added more than 200 entries since the beginning of this year—tracing what amounts to a scientific feeding frenzy, and one in which he himself is generally acknowledged to be the biggest fish in the water.

Smalley's office is buckminsterfullerene central. The signs of bucky are all over the place—a picture of the Thinker meditating on a soccer ball posted on his open door, a giant plastic buckyball model on a steel pedestal, a clipping from the *New York Times* with an illustration of a certain new carbon molecule. On a work table there's a little wind-up walking soccer ball. A computer screen shows white objects shooting out of a central focus, and at first *they* look like soccer balls—but then you realize that it's a standard screen-saver starfield, with an occasional spaceship thrown in.

"The thought that in 1985 or 1990 you could wake up in the morning and find that somehow a new form of carbon has been discovered through something you did," Smalley says quietly, his beard and high forehead making him look something like a taller, fairer Lenin in jeans and loafers, "is just ridiculous."

But that, as it turns out, is just what Smalley did.

In 1984—one year before bucky—Rick Smalley was, as he puts it, "having a tremendously fun time" studying exotic clusters of atoms with a machine that goes by the jawbreaking moniker of the "laser supersonic cluster beam apparatus." "App Two," as it's known for short, is a hulking assemblage of steel cylinders, pumps, lasers and copper tubing that dominates an entire end of Smalley's high-tech salvage yard of a lab. It looks a bit like a primitive steam engine. This ungainly contraption uses a puff of helium gas to cool and condense individual atoms—blasted off a sample of silicon or germanium or *whatever* heated to 10,000 degrees Celsius by a laser pulse five-billionths of a second long—into unusual, highly reactive clusters not normally found in nature. "At the time we didn't know how long into the gas pulse we would have to wait until things really got cold," Smalley says, "so I looked in the catalog and I got the biggest vacuum pump that I could fit in the room without drilling a hole in the floor."

Smalley designed App Two to probe the chemistry not of molecules (those familiar stable combinations of atoms everyone has drummed into their heads in high school) but of what he calls "stuff"—raw hunks of matter, so hungry for other material to combine with that their survival depends upon isolation from the container holding them. App Two does that job, making clusters of silicon, say, or gallium arsenide (big names in the semiconductor and computer business, those two), shooting them into a vacuum chamber on a pulse of non-reactive helium and studying them on the fly.

When Smalley and his students built App Two in the early '80s it was unique (although its design was quickly cloned for similar machines at Exxon Research and Bell Labs), and rather famous in certain circles. One of those intrigued by its potential was a rather intense British chemist named Harry Kroto, who saw in Smalley's "gadget" the answer to a problem he'd been thinking about for some time.

It seemed Kroto, who specialized in interstellar chemistry, was on the unpopular side of a debate about the origin of long chains of carbon atoms he had helped detect in the space between the stars. It was his opinion that these "carbon batons" had been formed in red giant stars—enormous, ancient suns, swollen with age (it's believed our own sun will become one in a few billion years) and known to be loaded with carbon. There was no way for Kroto to bring a red giant to his lab at the University of Sussex; but if he could get access to the instantaneous and very tiny inferno produced by the laser on Smalley's beam machine he could simulate a red giant on the surface of a graphite sample, and see if any carbon chains were produced.

There was only one problem: Smalley wasn't interested. He didn't want to run carbon in App Two. Pure carbon was dull stuff; it lacked the sex appeal of semiconductors and exotic metals like platinum and iridium (tiny clusters of which perform a dimly understood chemical black magic in your car's catalytic converter). We'll do carbon if we get around to it, Smalley told Kroto. When Kroto called back the following year to press the issue—he could be in Houston in late August if Smalley would run carbon, he said—the Rice chemist was even more reluctant. A team at Exxon had just done similar work with their clone of App Two, and Smalley didn't want to step on their toes. In the end, though, Kroto's persistence—and his certainty that something exiting would pop up if they zapped carbon with a laser—prevailed. Nobody, of course, expected anything quite as exciting as what he and Smalley's Rice team would find.

Some people can tell you exactly where they were when John F. Kennedy was shot; Rick Smalley can give you an almost exact chronology of the events that followed Harry Kroto's arrival at Rice on August 30, 1985. The dark-haired Englishman in his late forties charged into Smalley's office at eight o'clock on a Friday morning. Apparently unaffected by jet lag—he'd arrived the night before—he commandeered the blackboard for four hours to draw diagrams of red giants and explain how his carbon chains could answer all the questions of astrophysics. Kroto got good news in the next couple of days—Smalley's graduate students Jim Heath and Sean O'Brien were zapping graphite and getting results consistent with the production of long chains of carbon molecules.

Grad students are the Sherpas of the scientific world; they do the grunt work, building experiments and taking the data that eventually carries the professor they work for to the summit of publication. In exchange for long hours in the lab they get their names on the papers they help to produce and move just a little bit closer to their degrees. And if they're lucky—*really* lucky—they get something else: a first glimpse of discovery.

In O'Brien and Heath's case, the glimpse was a "flagpole" in the data on the number of atoms in the clusters produced by App Two, a sudden, sharp spike on a graph showing unusual amounts of 60-atom carbon clusters being produced by the machine. By the Wednesday night after Kroto's arrival it was obvious that App Two was making more 60-atom clusters of carbon than anything else— something Smalley found intriguing.

For the next week Smalley, Kroto and Rice professor Robert Curl argued the mystery back and forth. They argued it in Smalley's office; they argued it at Jim Goode's taqueria on Kirby, which the Englishman thought had the best Mexican food he'd ever tasted. The most likely thing, they thought, was the least exciting: that they were just making little chunks of graphite, flat sheets of carbon atoms arranged in hexagonal "chickenwire" patterns. But if that were the case, the number of atoms in each cluster should have been random, since any number of loose carbon atoms could easily hook up to the edges of the graphite sheets. Somehow, something was imposing a pattern on the formation of the clusters. "We couldn't figure out a really compelling reason why they would have an even number of atoms," Smalley says, "and certainly we couldn't figure out why 60 would be special."

Maybe, Smalley and Kroto started to think, the carbon-atom sheets somehow curved around to form a closed surface like that on one of Buckminster Fuller's geodesic domes—the details of which none of them could recall exactly, except that they involved hexagons.

"We were saying, well what would you call this molecule?" Smalley says. "And we said 'It's ... *buckminsterfullerene!*'—in the sort of jargon you would use in *Monty Python's Flying Circus*."

Curl—a gray-bearded, gnomish-looking man in his late fifties—was skeptical; it may have been that the silliness of his younger colleagues was a bit too much fun for him.

Only a few days remained in Kroto's stay at Rice. Kroto and Smalley agreed that some more serious stab at explaining the strange results they'd come up with had to be made. After an early dinner at Goode Co., Smalley and Jim Heath resolved to try to figure out the structure that night at home. Heath's attempt—made with the assistance of his wife, Carmen, and involving gummy bears and toothpicks—ended in sticky frustration. Smalley tried for a few hours to model the molecule graphically on his computer, then gave up and began cutting paper hexagons out of a legal pad. Try as he might, cheating by overlapping the edges, Smalley still couldn't get the hexagons to close up into the proper shape.

"There was no way you could get 'em to work out,"

Smalley says. "Right about this time—it was about eleven o'clock at night—my wife comes in and says, 'Time to go to bed,' and I snarl at her. This whole great idea has just *died*. I said, 'Not now. Leave me alone.' "

Smalley got up to get a beer and sat down "to try to calm down a bit." Then he remembered something Kroto had said about building a geodesic dome for his children. Somehow, Kroto thought, there were *pentagons* involved. Pentagonal arrangements of carbon atoms are not unknown in chemistry, just less common than hexagonal ones.

Smalley cut out a paper pentagon and taped the hexagons around it. In order to connect their edges he *had* to bend them up into a bowl. Adding more pentagons and surrounding them with hexagons, he realized he was building a ball-like object that would have . . . 60 vertices when it was finished. Sixty positions that could be occupied by carbon atoms. Hours later, with trembling hands, he patched in a final pentagon and dropped the paper model of the buckyball on the floor.

It bounced.

The next morning, on the long drive to work from his home near Sugarland, Smalley used his car phone to call Curl and tell him to bring the group together in his office. Coming in the office door, he tossed the paper ball on a coffee table in front of them. Kroto was immediately taken with the structure, recognizing it as a smaller version of the dome he'd made for his children. While Kroto and Curl checked to see that the model had the proper number and kind of chemical bonds, Smalley called Bill Veech, the head of the Rice math department, to ask him what the shape he'd stumbled on was called.

"I could explain this to you in a number of ways," Veech said, "but what you've got there, boys, is a soccer ball."

*   *   *

For five frustrating years after he discovered it, Smalley never actually saw a sample of buckminsterfullerene. No matter how much graphite his team vaporized, they couldn't come up with more than the smallest amounts of bucky—enough to study with the special equipment at the Rice lab, but far too little to see or do the kind of complicated hands-on chemistry Smalley and other people wanted to do. Then, in September 1990, Donald Huffman of the University of Arizona and Wolfgang Krätschmer of the Max Planck Institute in Heidelberg, Germany, announced that they'd come up with a way to make large amounts of what had come to be called "fullerenes," the family of closed carbon clusters of which bucky was the most stable and common member. Interested, like Kroto, in interstellar carbon, the pair had been making carbon clusters by passing a strong electric current through a pair of barely touching graphite rods. Mixed in with the soot produced by the process was an incredibly large amount of buckminsterfullerene—milligrams of it, more than anybody had ever seen before.

This summer Jan Fure, a Rice undergraduate from Norway, is making buckyballs eight hours a day in Smalley's lab, his skinny bare legs sticking out from the bottom of a soot-smudged lab coat as he moves around, making adjustments to a machine that looks positively medieval next to the sleek lasers on the table beside it. Smalley's improvement on the Huffman-Krätschmer apparatus sucks bucky-containing soot off an electric arc between two half-inch carbon rods with the familiar scream of a Sears Kenmore vacuum cleaner—the motor, in fact, came from Smalley's vacuum. One of science's charming ironies is that the makeshift process at the root of great discoveries—think of Franklin and his kite—so often involves such low-tech everyday items. It's Fure's job to empty the soot out of the Kenmore vacuum-cleaner bags used to collect it.

Most researchers don't have access to their own buckyball-making machine, but a lot of people want the stuff. Within six months of the publication of Huffman and Krätschmer's results, two companies were selling buckyballs for research use, one of them the Houston-based Texas Fullerenes Corporation, founded by Smalley's graduate student Lila Anderson. "We have clients who range from locals over at UH to Japanese, Germans and Swedes—I just sent an order to Switzerland yesterday," Anderson says. She gives universities a 50 percent discount, but everybody else pays $20 a gram for her fullerene-rich soot.

"You have this repertoire of molecules," says Bell Labs' Robert Haddon, one of Anderson's customers, explaining the research frenzy that bucky's availability touched off. "To have something so alien as C-60 appear . . . it's almost as if an alien landed on the planet."

In May, the Bell Labs team announced that they'd taught the alien a new trick: they'd made a buckminster-fullerene superconductor by "doping" a thin film of buckyballs with potassium. While not capable of passing electricity without resistance at as high a temperature as the superconductors pioneered by the University of Houston's Paul Chu, buckyball superconductors have other properties that might make it easier to fashion wires and thin shells from them.

A phone call to Chu found him up to his eyeballs in buckyballs, but able only to hint at the source of his fascination with the material. He has, he says, found something "extremely unusual," which has "device implications as well as scientific ones," but he's hesitant to talk about it; he's awaiting word from the British journal *Nature* on whether or not a paper he's submitted on the subject will be accepted for publication. "For six weeks we were work-ing day and night to see if this is real—because it's too wild," says the secretive Chu, without offering much fur-ther explanation of the discovery he thinks he's made.

Earthling chemists have created a new language to deal with the space invader. "Fuzzyballs" are buckyballs bonded to organic compounds; "Mrs. Bucky" is the rugby-ball-shaped C-70 cluster, the next most common found; a "dopeyball" is a buckyball which has been "doped"—modified by placing an atom from a different element at its center or in place of a carbon in the cage. The name game is complicated by the fact that many of the terms of organic chemistry were developed to deal with two-dimensional molecules and can't be applied to spherical, 3-D bucky. "Here's a molecule that's going to start a whole new class of organic molecules," says Bob Haufler, one of Smalley's graduate students. "And we don't even have a nomenclature to talk about it yet."

Haufler, who says he's in Smalley's lab from 8 A.M. to 11 A.M. daily ("The Chinese students work harder"), makes a comparison you hear a lot from people asked to specu-late about bucky's importance. Bucky today, he says, is a lot like the molecule benzene was when it was discovered in the early 19th century. "You start with benzene, you add one thing and you can make aspirin," Haufler says. "You add another and you make Tylenol." An enormous number of man-made compounds employ the flat, six-cornered benzene ring—but the buckyball has 60 corners, arranged three-dimensionally, thus theoretically opening up an even bigger number of new possibilities.

Smalley is more careful when the benzene question is raised. "Basically, that molecule led to the development of organic chemistry," he says cautiously, as if unwilling to make exaggerated claims for himself. "We suspect that bucky is not going to have quite that impact. But at times, when you've got enough beers in you, you can start thinking global thoughts like that."

What brings someone to the position where they can entertain global thoughts? In Rick Smalley's case it started inauspiciously enough in the basement of his family's house in Kansas City, Missouri. A shy and introverted youngster, he spent a lot of time alone down in his father's woodworking shop, making things—an experience that probably prepared him better than anything else for the lab. Certainly it did a better job than his early academic career. Smalley was a mediocre student through his junior year in high school (he remembers playing hooky 45 days in fifth grade); he wanted to become an architect, but with his grades he couldn't hope to be much more than a draftsman.

Then the launch of Sputnik knocked him out of his parking orbit and onto a new trajectory. "At that time it was the most romantic thing you could possibly do, to go into science and engineering, because of Sputnik," he says. "So all my buddies and I wanted to be engineers, and we all wondered whether we'd ever become something like that."

Once he got into a chemistry class, Smalley went into academic overdrive. Competing with an older sister, he aced the course. The following year, as a senior, Smalley also did well in physics and found that despite a "pretty abysmal" grade average he had a chance to go to college after all. The choice of majors was obvious, he jokes: "The only thing I ever got an A in was chemistry."

It's proven a fruitful and fulfilling field for Smalley. Almost defensively, he points out that stumbling over the buckyball was not his first success; he has been doing notable work ever since graduate school, building and doing experiments with fantastic machines like App Two.

"He's a machine-builder beyond anybody else around," says UCLA's Robert Whetten, a younger competitor in the buckyball game. Despite disagreements in the past six years, Whetten deeply respects Smalley, pointing to his status as a pioneer in the field.

Luck has a lot to do with pioneering. But even more important is the ability to capitalize on luck—having the tools, both physical and mental, to make something of what fortune tosses you. Rick Smalley has both, in spades.

This morning Smalley wears new Nikes, bright white and purple and reddish-pink. It's an exciting day for his group; they're gathered in his office to discuss the possibility that they've been the first to make large amounts of dopeyballs—specifically, a variety made with boron called "borobucky." Smalley's at the blackboard, kidding with his students as they try to explain the appearance of potassium—which wasn't supposed to be involved in the process—in the analysis of the samples.

"Is that right?" he says, his voice constricted into a Monty Python falsetto. "Oh, how nice." A Chinese woman named Yan Chai takes the board. Smalley sits down, pulling strawberry candy from a red soccer-ball-shaped jar. He retains control of the discussion, making suggestions and shooting down hypotheses. "We've now proved there really are angels," he says, after one particularly far-fetched suggestion is made. There's a confusion of responses, dominated by the voice of graduate student Lai-Sheng Wang from the couch. "I'll bet any amount of money," Wang says. "I don't believe there's potassium in there."

Smalley practically jumps across the room to his brief-case, pulling out a ten-dollar bill. "Who's gonna hold this money?" he asks.

Later, the meeting over and the mysterious potassium

possibly explained as a result of contamination in the doping apparatus, Smalley ruminates on the significance of what his group has come up with. If their results are correct, they've not only managed to put atoms of boron in the buckyball's outer cage but also—accidentally—"shrink-wrapped" potassium in the molecule's center. They've made dopeyballs before, but never in such quantities; the dopeyball is in the same place buckyball was in 1985: unavailable in the quantities needed for large-scale research. "Oh, shit," Smalley says, softly. "If this is real, it's big. It's the answer to all my questions about what I'm going to talk about for the next six months. It makes sense. But is it real? Is it real?"

Is it real? It's a question Smalley's been asking himself all his academic life. If he has found a way to isolate a whole lot of dopeyballs, he's opened the door to a world of customized bucky—buckyballs modified with the addition of other elements, each having different and possibly very useful properties. An esoteric-sounding accomplishment, to be sure, but a major one, the kind of thing that has kept Smalley in the buckyball game.

He lives closer to work now, a four-minute walk from his office. The way things are going at the moment, he sometimes can't tell one from the other; he's working even in his sleep, waking up at three in the morning trying to figure things out. He gets offers from entrepreneurs about once a week, and he tells them all to call him back next year; things are moving too fast now. There's no time for the complications of business, and no room in his head for the partitions he'd have to build to protect corporate secrets.

But underneath Smalley's bucky-driven excitement there's a certain uneasiness. More and more he's become identified with the buckyball—and the time is coming, he thinks, when he'll leave it behind for something new,

something with room for a pioneer. He turns down students who come to him expressly to study buckminsterfullerene, telling them he's not sure whether he'll even be
working on it in two years.

"If you look at Rick's career, he does this for seven or
eight years, and then he turns around and does *this* for
seven or eight years," says Bob Haufler. "I think a change
is soon to come."

That change raises an inevitable question, and one
Smalley admits he's nervous about. Can he top bucky?

"I don't know," says Smalley. "Probably not. Simply put,
bucky is a lot more important and transcendent than anything I've ever worked with. This is the third form of carbon, and 17 zillion years from now there'll still be
diamond, graphite and bucky."

4

PAUL HOFFMAN

The Man Who Loves Only Numbers

The Atlantic Monthly,
November 1987

*There are two ways you can write about mathematics—
focus on the personality of the mathematician or focus on
the beauty of the math. If you choose the latter, you will
probably have to resort to all sorts of cute, quick simplifica-
tions that do little to portray the full elegance of a proof or
theorem or to convey the spiritual and universal beauty of
numbers.*

*In "The Man Who Loves Only Numbers," winner of a
National Magazine Award for Feature Writing in 1988,
Paul Hoffman found a subject and style that unified both
approaches. And he did it without sacrificing the elegance
and simplicity of the mathematics practiced by Hungarian
Paul Erdös. Hoffman even works into the article some of the
major political crises of the twentieth century. Erdös, who
was Jewish, barely escaped a Nazi concentration camp—
only to be barred for years from entering the United States
because his home had been overrun by the Russian commu-
nists. It's perhaps understandable why Erdös called God the
"Supreme Fascist" but harder to understand why he so fer-
vently believed in the "SF," or in children whom he referred
to as "epsilons," or in numbers, which he considered his
own children.*

As the longtime president and editor-in-chief of Dis-cover and a correspondent for the "McNeil-Lehrer News Hour," Paul Hoffman is one of the most influential science writers and editors in the country. Born in 1956, he attended Harvard University as an undergraduate. There he was in-spired by a freshman lecture course on relativity to pursue science writing as a career. He went on to become the senior editor of Scientific American *and to write a popular col-umn for* Science Digest *called "Dr. Crypton," posing new puzzles and paradoxes in every issue. A past contributor to* The Atlantic *and* Smithsonian, *he is the author of* Archi-medes' Revenge: The Joys and Perils of Mathematics *(1986).*

I T IS DINNERTIME IN GREENBROOK, NEW JERSEY, and Paul Erdös, seventy-four, has lost four mathematical colleagues, who are sitting fifty feet in front of him, sip-ping green tea. Squinting, Erdös scans the tables of the small Japanese restaurant, one arm held out to the side like a scarecrow's. He is angry with himself for letting his friends slip out of sight. His mistake was to pause at the coat check while they charged ahead. His arm is flapping wildly now, and he is coughing. "I don't understand why the SF has seen fit to send me a cold," he wheezes. (The SF is the Supreme Fascist, the Number-One Guy Up There, God, who is always tormenting Erdös by hiding his glasses, stealing his Hungarian passport, or, worse yet, keeping to Himself the elegant solutions to all sorts of in-triguing mathematical problems.) "The SF created us to enjoy our suffering," Erdös says. "The sooner we die, the sooner we defy His plans."

Erdös still does not see his friends, but his anger dissipates—his arm drops to his side—as he hears the high-pitched squeal of a small boy, who is dining with his parents. "An epsilon!" Erdös says. (*Epsilon* is Erdös's word for a small child; in mathematics that Greek letter is used to represent small quantities.) Erdös moves slowly toward the child, navigating not so much by sight as by the sound of the boy's voice. "Hello," he says, as he reaches into his ratty gray overcoat and extracts a bottle of Benzedrine. He tosses the bottle into the air and catches it at the last second. The epsilon is not at all amused, but, perhaps to be polite, his parents make a big production of applauding. Erdös repeats the trick a few more times, and then he is rescued by one of his confederates, Ronald Graham, the director of the Mathematical Sciences Research Center at AT&T Bell Laboratories, who calls him over to the table where he and Erdös's other friends are waiting.

The waitress arrives, and Erdös, after inquiring about each item on the long menu, orders fried squid balls. While the waitress takes the rest of the orders, Erdös turns over his placemat and draws a tiny sketch vaguely resembling a rocket passing through a hula hoop. His four dining companions lean forward to get a better view of the world's most prolific mathematician plying his craft. "There are still many edges that will destroy chromatic number three," Erdös says. "This edge destroys bipartiteness." With that pronouncement Erdös closes his eyes and seems to fall asleep.

Mathematicians, unlike other scientists, require no laboratory equipment. A Japanese restaurant is as good a place as any to do mathematics. Mathematicians need only peace of mind and, occasionally, paper and pencil. "That's the beauty of it," Graham says. "You can lie back, close your eyes, and work. Who knows what problem Paul's thinking about now?"

Erdös has thought about more problems than any other

mathematician in history. He has written or co-authored more than 1,000 papers, many of them monumental, and all of them substantial. In the past year alone he has published fifty papers, which is more than most good mathematicians write in a lifetime. He has shown that mathematics is not just a young man's game.

Erdös (pronounced "air-dish") has structured his life to maximize the amount of time he has for mathematics. He has no wife or children, no job, no hobbies, not even a home, to tie him down. He lives out of a shabby suitcase and a drab orange plastic bag from Centrum Aruhaz ("Central Warehouse"), a large department store in Budapest. In a never-ending search for good mathematical problems and fresh mathematical talent, Erdös crisscrosses four continents at a frenzied pace, moving from one university or research center to the next. His modus operandi is to show up on the doorstep of an esteemed mathematician, declare, "My brain is open," work with his host for a day or two, until he's bored or his host is run down, and then move on to another home. Erdös's motto is not "Other cities, other maidens" but "Another roof, another proof." He has done mathematics since he was three, but for the past sixteen years, since the death of his mother, he has put in nineteen-hour days, keeping himself fortified with ten to twenty milligrams of Benzedrine or Ritalin, strong espresso, and caffeine tablets. "A mathematician," Erdös is fond of saying, "is a machine for turning coffee into theorems." When friends urge him to slow down, he always has the same response: "There'll be plenty of time to rest in the grave."

Erdös lets nothing stand in the way of mathematical progress. When the name of a colleague in California comes up at breakfast in New Jersey, Erdös remembers a mathematical result he wants to share with him. He heads toward the phone and starts to dial. His host interrupts him, pointing out that it's 5:00 A.M. on the West Coast.

"Good," Erdös says, "that means he'll be home." When challenged further in situations like this, Erdös has been known to respond, "Louis the Fourteenth said, 'I am the state'; Trotsky could have said, 'I am society'; and I say, 'I am reality.' " No one who knows him would argue. "Erdös has a childlike tendency to make his reality overtake yours," a friend says. "And he's not an easy houseguest. But we all want him around—for his mind. We all save problems up for him." To communicate with Erdös you must learn his language—not just "the SF" and "epsilon" but also "bosses" (women), "slaves" (men), "captured" (married), "liberated" (divorced), "recaptured" (remarried), "noise" (music), "poison" (alcohol), "preaching" (giving a mathematics lecture), "Sam" (the United States), and "Joe" (the Soviet Union). When he says someone has "died," Erdös means that the person has stopped doing mathematics. When he says someone has "left," the person has died.

At five foot six, 130 pounds, Erdös has the wizened, cadaverous look of a drug addict, but friends insist that he was frail and gaunt long before he started taking amphetamines. His hair is white, and corkscrew-shaped whiskers shoot out at odd angles from his face. He usually wears a gray pin-striped jacket, dark trousers, a red or mustard shirt or pajama top, and peculiar pockmarked Hungarian leather shoes, made specially for his flat feet and weak tendons. His whole wardrobe fits into his one small suitcase, with plenty of room left for his dinosaur of a radio. He has so few clothes that his hosts find themselves washing his socks and underwear several times a week. "He could buy more," one of his colleagues says, "or he could wash them himself. I mean, it takes zero IQ to learn how to operate a washing machine." But if it's not mathematics, Erdös won't be bothered. "Some French socialist said that private property was theft," Erdös recalls. "I say that private property is a nuisance."

All of his clothes, including his socks and custom-made underwear, are silk, because he has an undiagnosed skin condition that is aggravated by other kinds of fabric. He doesn't like people to touch him. If you extend your hand, he won't shake it. Instead, he limply flops his hand on top of yours. "He hates it if I kiss him," says Magda Fredro, sixty-six, a first cousin who is otherwise very close to him. "And he washes his hands fifty times a day. He gets water everywhere. It's hell on the bathroom floor."

Although Erdös avoids physical intimacy, and has apparently always been celibate, he is friendly and compassionate. "He exists on a web of trust," says Aaron Meyerowitz, a mathematician at Florida Atlantic University. "When I was a graduate student and we had never met before, I gave him a ride. I didn't know the route and asked him if he wanted to navigate with a map. He didn't want to. He just trusted that I, a total stranger, would get him there." What little money he receives in stipends or lecture fees he gives away to relatives, colleagues, or graduate students. A few years ago he won the prestigious Wolf prize, the most lucrative award in mathematics. He contributed most of the $50,000 he received to a scholarship in Israel in the name of his parents. "I kept only seven hundred and twenty dollars," Erdös says, "and I remember someone commenting that for me even that was a lot of money to keep." The two times he lectured in India he had the fee sent to a woman he has never met, the widow of Srinivasa Ramanujan, a legendary mathematical prodigy who died of tuberculosis at the age of thirty-two. Whenever Erdös learns of a good cause—a struggling classical-music radio station, a fledgling Native American movement—he promptly makes a small donation.

Erdös was born in Budapest on March 26, 1913, the son of two high school mathematics teachers. While his mother,

Anna, was in the hospital giving birth to him, her two daughters, ages three and five, contracted septic scarlet fever and died within the day. "It was something my mother didn't like to talk about," Erdös says. "Their names were Clara and Magda, I think." Of the three children, the girls were considered to be the smart ones.

When Erdös was one and a half, his father, Lajos, was captured in a Russian offensive and sent to Siberia for six years. Erdös's mother kept him out of school, fearing that it was the source of childhood contagions. He stayed home until high school, and even then he went only every other year, because his mother kept changing her mind.

Erdös was a mathematical prodigy. At three he could multiply three-digit numbers in his head. At four he discovered negative numbers. "I told my mother," he recalls, "that if you take two hundred and fifty from a hundred you get minus a hundred and fifty." He knew then that he wanted to be a mathematician, although he would pay attention to his tutorials in history, politics, and biology. As soon as he could read, his mother plied him with medical literature, which he eagerly studied. She apparently had vague hopes that he might become a doctor.

When Erdös was seventeen, he entered the University of Budapest; he was graduated four years later with a Ph.D. in mathematics. In October of 1934 he went to Manchester, England, for a four-year postdoctoral fellowship. "I left Hungary for political reasons," Erdös says. "I was Jewish, and Hungary was a semi-fascist country. But I was very homesick, so I went back three times a year, for Easter, Christmas, and the summer. In March, 1938, Hitler went into Austria, and it was too dangerous for me to return to Hungary in the spring. I did slip back in during the summer. But on September 3, 1938, I didn't like the news—the Czech crisis—so I went back to England that evening and was on my way to the United States three and a half weeks later. The Nazis ended up murdering four of my mother's five brothers and sisters, and my father died of a heart attack in 1942.

"Then my problems started with Sam and Joe. I didn't want to return to Hungary because of Joe. In 1954 I was invited to an international mathematics conference in Amsterdam. Sam didn't want to give me a re-entry permit. It was the McCarthy era. The immigration officials asked me all sorts of silly questions. 'Have you read Marx, Engels, or Stalin?' 'No,' I said. 'What do you think of Marx?' they pressed. 'I'm not competent to judge,' I said, 'but no doubt he was a great man.' So they denied me a re-entry visa. I had the classic American reaction: I left. I ended up mostly in Israel. In the 1960s Sam decided it was okay for me to return."

In 1964 his mother, at the age of eighty-four, started traveling with him. For the next seven years she accompanied him everywhere except to India, which she avoided because of her fear of disease. His mother hated traveling—she knew barely a word of English, and he traveled regularly to English-speaking countries—but she wanted to be with him. Wherever he did mathematics, she sat quietly, basking in his genius. They ate every meal together, and at night he held her hand until she fell asleep. "She saw in Paul the world," Fredro says. "He was her God, her everything. They stayed with me in 1968 or 1969. When they were together, I was nobody. It was like I didn't exist. That hurt me a lot, because I was very close to her. She was my aunt, and when I got out of Auschwitz, I went first to her home. She fed me and bathed me and clothed me and made me a human being again."

In 1971 Erdös's mother died of a bleeding ulcer in Calgary, Canada, where Erdös was giving a lecture. Apparently, she had been misdiagnosed, and her life might otherwise have been saved. Soon afterward Erdös started taking a lot of pills, first anti-depressants and then amphet-amines. As one of Hungary's leading scientists, he had no trouble getting sympathetic Hungarian doctors to pre-scribe drugs. "I was very depressed," Erdös says, "and Paul Turán, an old friend, reminded me, 'A strong fortress is our mathematics.'" Erdös took the advice to heart and started putting in nineteen-hour days, churning out papers that would change the course of mathematical history. Still, math proved more of a sieve than a fortress. Ten years later, one day when Erdös was looking particularly gloomy, a friend asked him what was wrong. "Haven't you heard?" he replied. "My mother has left." Even today he never sleeps in the apartment that they once shared in Bu-dapest, using it only to house visitors; he stays in a guest suite at the Hungarian Academy of Sciences.

Long before his mother died, Erdös became preoccu-pied with his own mortality. "My second great discovery [the first being negative numbers]," he says, "was death. Children don't think they're ever going to die. I was like that too, until I was four. I was in a shop with my mother and suddenly I realized I was wrong. I started to cry. I knew I would die. From then on I've always wanted to be younger. In 1970 I preached in Los Angeles on 'my first two-and-a-half billion years in mathematics.' When I was a child, the earth was said to be two billion years old. Now scientists say it's four and a half billion. So that makes me two-and-a-half billion. The students at the lecture drew a time line that showed me riding a dinosaur. I was asked, 'How were the dinosaurs?' Later, the right answer oc-curred to me: You know, I don't remember, because an old man only remembers the very early years, and the di-nosaurs were born yesterday, only a hundred million years ago."

In the early 1970s Erdös started appending the initials P.G.O.M. to his name, which stand for Poor Great Old

Man. When he turned sixty, he became P.G.O.M.L.D., the L.D. for Living Dead. At sixty-five he graduated to P.G.O.M.L.D.A.D., the A.D. for Archaeological Discovery. At seventy he became P.G.O.M.L.D.A.D.L.D., the L.D. for Legally Dead. And he plans next year, at seventy-five, to be P.G.O.M.L.D.A.D.L.D.C.D., the C.D. for Counts Dead. He explains, "The Hungarian Academy of Sciences has two hundred members. When you turn seventy-five, you can stay in the academy with full privileges, but you no longer count as a member. That's why the C.D. Of course, maybe I won't have to face that emergency. They are planning an international conference for my seventy-fifth birthday. It may have to be for my memory. I'm miserably old. I'm really not well. I don't understand what's happening to my body—maybe the final solution."

When Paul Turán, the man who had counseled, "A strong fortress is our mathematics," died in 1976, Erdös had an image of the SF assessing the work he had done with his collaborators. On one side of a balance the SF would place the papers Erdös had co-authored with the dead, on the other side the papers written with the living. "When the dead side tips the balance," Erdös says, "I must die too." He pauses for a moment and then adds, "It's just a joke of mine."

Perhaps. But Erdös vigorously seeks out new, young collaborators and ends many working sessions with the remark, "We'll continue tomorrow, if I live." With more than 250 co-authors, Erdös has collaborated with more people than any other mathematician in history. Those lucky 250 are said to have "an Erdös number of 1," a coveted code phrase in the mathematics world for having written a paper with the master himself. If your Erdös number is 2, it means you have worked with someone who has worked with Erdös. If your Erdös number is 3, you have worked with someone who has worked with someone who has worked with Erdös. The mathematical literature is peppered with tongue-in-cheek papers probing the properties of Erdös numbers. Einstein had an Erdös number of 2, and the highest known Erdös number is 7.

Since 1954 Erdös has been spurring on his collaborators by putting out contracts on problems he hasn't been able to solve. The outstanding rewards total about $10,000, and range from $10 to $3,000, reflecting his judgment of the problems' difficulty. "I've had to pay out three or four thousand dollars," Erdös says. "Someone once asked me what would happen if all the problems were solved at once. Could I pay? Of course I couldn't. But what would happen to the strongest bank if all the creditors asked for their money back? The bank would surely go broke. A run on the bank is much more likely than solutions to all my problems."

Though he is confident of his skill with mathematics, outside that arcane world Erdös is very nearly helpless. Since his mother's death the responsibility of looking after him has fallen chiefly to Ronald Graham, who spends almost as much time handling Erdös's affairs as he does overseeing the seventy mathematicians, statisticians, and computer scientists at Bell Labs. Graham is the one who calls Washington when the SF steals Erdös's visa, and, he says, "the SF is striking with increasing frequency these days." Graham also manages Erdös's money, and was forced to become an expert on currency exchange rates because honoraria from Erdös's lectures dribble in from four continents. "I sign his name on checks and deposit them," Graham says. "I've been doing this so long I doubt the bank would cash a check if he endorsed it himself."

On the wall of Graham's office, in Murray Hill, New

Jersey, is a sign: ANYONE WHO CANNOT COPE WITH MATHE-
MATICS IS NOT FULLY HUMAN. AT BEST HE IS A TOLERABLE
SUBHUMAN WHO HAS LEARNED TO WEAR SHOES, BATHE, AND
NOT MAKE MESSES IN THE HOUSE. Near the sign is the
"Erdös room," a closet full of filing cabinets containing
copies of Erdös's 1,000-plus articles. "Since he has no
home," Graham says, "he depends on me to keep his papers. He's always asking me to send some of them to one
person or another." Graham also handles all of Erdös's incoming correspondence, which is no small task, because
many of Erdös's mathematical collaborations take place by
mail. Last year Erdös sent out 1,500 letters, none of which
dwelt on subjects other than mathematics. "I am in Australia," a typical letter begins. "Tomorrow I leave for Hungary. Let k be the largest integer. . . ."

Graham has had less success influencing Erdös's health.
"He badly needs a cataract operation," Graham says. "I've
been trying to persuade him to schedule it. But he refuses,
because he'd be laid up for a week and he doesn't want to
miss even seven days of working with mathematicians.
He's afraid of being old and helpless and senile." Like all
of Erdös's friends, Graham is concerned about his drug-
taking. In 1979 Graham bet him $500 that he couldn't
stop taking amphetamines for a month. Erdös accepted
the challenge, and went cold turkey for thirty days. After
Graham paid up—and wrote the $500 off as a business
expense—Erdös said, "You've showed me I'm not an addict. But I didn't get any work done. I'd get up in the
morning and stare at a blank piece of paper. I'd have no
ideas, just like an ordinary person. You've set mathematics
back a month." He promptly resumed taking pills, and
mathematics has been the better for it.

Graham recently built an addition onto his house, in
Watchung, New Jersey, so that Erdös would have his own
bedroom and library for the thirty or so days he's there

each year. Erdös likes staying with Graham because the household contains a second strong mathematician, Graham's wife, Fan Chung, a Taiwanese émigré who is the director of mathematics at Bell Communications Research, a spinoff of Bell Labs that does research for the regional phone companies. When Graham won't play with him, Chung will, and the two have co-authored fifteen papers.

Graham and Erdös seem an unlikely pair. Although Graham is one of the world's leading mathematicians, he has not, like Erdös, forsaken body for mind. Indeed, he has pushed both to the limit. At six foot two, with blond hair, blue eyes, and chiseled features, Graham looks at least a decade younger than his fifty-two years. He is an accomplished trampolinist, and he put himself through college as a circus acrobat. He can juggle six balls and is a past president of the International Jugglers Association. He has bowled two 300 games, is vicious with a boomerang, and more than holds his own at tennis and Ping-Pong.

While Erdös can sit for hours, Graham is always moving. In the middle of solving a mathematical problem he'll spring into a handstand, grab stray objects and juggle them, or jump up and down on the super-springy pogo stick he keeps in his office. "You can do mathematics anywhere," Graham says. "I once had a flash of insight into a stubborn problem in the middle of a back somersault with a triple twist on my trampoline."

"If you add up Ron's mathematical theorems and his double somersaults," one of his colleagues says, "he'd surely have a record." Graham, in fact, does hold a world record—one no less peculiar. He is cited in the *Guinness Book of World Records* for having used the largest number in a mathematical proof. The number is incomprehensibly large. Mathematicians often try to suggest the magnitude of a large number by likening it to the number of atoms in the universe or the number of grains of sand in the Sahara. Graham's number has no such physical analogue. It can't even be expressed in familiar mathematical notation, as, say, the number 1 followed by a zillion zeroes. To cite it a special notation had to be invoked, in which exponents are heaped on exponents to form a staggering leaning tower of digits.

Besides staying on the cutting edge of mathematics and acrobatics, Graham has found time to learn Chinese and take up the piano. Neither his wife nor his co-workers understand how he does it. "It's easy," Graham says. "There are a hundred and sixty-eight hours in *every* week."

Erdös and Graham met in 1963 in Boulder, Colorado, at a conference on number theory, and they have been collaborating ever since, writing twenty-five papers and one book together. That meeting was also the first of many spirited athletic encounters the two have had. "I remember thinking when we met that he was kind of an old guy," Graham says, "and I was amazed that he beat me at Ping-Pong. That defeat got me to take up the game seriously." Graham bought a machine that served Ping-Pong balls at very high speeds and went on to become Ping-Pong champion of Bell Labs. "We still play occasionally," Graham says. "Paul loves challenges. I give him nineteen points and play sitting down. But his eyesight is so bad that I can just lob the ball high into the air and he'll lose track of it."

In recent years Erdös has come up with novel athletic contests at which he'd seem to have more of a chance, though he invariably loses. "Paul likes to imagine situations," Graham says. "For example, he wondered whether I could climb stairs twice as fast as he could. We decided to see. I ran a stopwatch as we both raced up twenty flights in an Atlanta hotel. When he got to the top, huffing, I punched the stopwatch but accidentally erased the times. I told him we'd have to do it again. 'We're *not* doing it again,' he grumbled, and stalked off.

"Another time, in Newark Airport, Erdös asked me how hard it was to go up a down escalator. I told him it could be done, and I demonstrated. 'That was harder than I thought,' I said. 'That looks easy,' he said. 'I'm sure you couldn't do it,' I said. 'That's ridiculous,' he said. 'Of course I can.' Erdös took about four steps up the escalator and then fell over on his stomach and slid down. People were staring at him. He was wearing this ratty coat and looked like he was a wino from the Bowery. He was indignant afterward."

Erdös and Graham are like an old married couple, happy as clams but bickering incessantly, following scripts they know by heart though they are baffling to outsiders. Many of these scripts center on food. When Erdös is feeling well, he gets up about 5:00 A.M. and starts banging around. He'd like Graham to make him breakfast, but Graham thinks he should make his own. Erdös loves grapefruit, and Graham stocks the refrigerator when he knows Erdös is coming. On a recent visit Erdös, as always, peeked into the refrigerator and saw the fruit. In fact, each knew that the other knew that the fruit was there.

"Do you have any grapefruit?" Erdös asked.

"I don't know," Graham replied. "Did you look?"

"I don't know where to look."

"How about the refrigerator?"

"Where in the refrigerator?"

"Well, just look."

Erdös found a grapefruit. He looked at it and looked at it and got a butter knife. "It can't be by chance," Graham explains, "that he so often uses the dull side of the knife, trying to force his way through. It'll be squirting like mad, all over himself and the kitchen. I'll say, 'Paul, don't you think you should use a sharper knife?' He'll say, 'It doesn't matter,' as the juice shoots across the room. At that point I give up and cut it for him."

In mathematics Erdös's style is one of intense curiosity, a style he brings to everything else he confronts. Part of his mathematical success stems from his willingness to ask fundamental questions, to ponder critically things that others have taken for granted. He also asks basic questions outside mathematics, but he never remembers the answers, and asks the same questions again and again. He'll point to a bowl of rice and ask what it is and how it's cooked. Graham will pretend he doesn't know; others at the table will patiently tell Erdös about rice. But a meal or two later Erdös will be served rice again, act as if he's never seen it, and ask the same questions.

Erdös's curiosity about food, like his approach to so many things, is merely theoretical. He'd never actually try to cook rice. In fact, he's never cooked anything at all, or even boiled water for tea. "I can make excellent cold cereal," he says, "and I could probably boil an egg, but I've never tried." Erdös was twenty-one when he buttered his first piece of bread, his mother or a domestic servant having always done it for him. "I remember clearly," he says. "I had just gone to England to study. It was tea time, and bread was served. I was too embarrassed to admit that I had never buttered it. I tried. It wasn't so hard." Only ten years before, at the age of eleven, he had tied his shoes for the first time.

His curiosity about driving is legendary in the mathematics community, although you'll never find him behind the wheel. He doesn't have a license and depends on a network of friends, known as Uncle Paul sitters, to chauffeur him around. But he's constantly asking what street he's on and questioning whether it's the right one. "He's not a nervous wreck," Graham says. "He just wants to know. Once he was driving with Paul Turán's widow, Vera Sós. She had just learned to drive, and Paul was doing his usual thing. 'What about this road?' 'What about that road?' 'Shouldn't we be over there?' Vera was distracted and she plowed into the side of a car that must have been going forty or fifty miles an hour. She totaled it, and vowed that she would never drive with Erdös again."

But outside mathematics Erdös's inquisitiveness is limited to necessities like eating and driving; he has no time for frivolities like sex, art, novels, or movies. Once in a while the mathematicians he stays with force him to join their families on non-mathematical outings, but he accompanies them only in body. "I took him to the Johnson Space Center to see rockets," one of his colleagues recalls, "but he didn't even look up." Another mathematician took him to see a mime troupe, but he fell asleep before the performance started. A colleague whose wife is a curator at the Museum of Modern Art dragged Erdös to MOMA. "We showed him Matisse, but he would have nothing to do with it. After a few minutes we ended up sitting in the sculpture garden doing mathematics." Erdös hasn't read a novel since the 1940s, and thirty years have passed since he last saw a movie, *Cold Days*, the story of a 1942 atrocity in Novasad, Yugoslavia, in which Hungarians brutally drowned a few thousand Jews and Russians.

Erdös is a mathematical monk. He has renounced physical pleasure and material possessions for an ascetic, contemplative life, a life devoted to a single narrow mission: uncovering mathematical truth. What is this mathematics that could possibly be so diverting and consuming?

"There's an old debate," Erdös says, "about whether you create mathematics or just discover it. In other words, are the truths already there, even if we don't yet know them? If you believe in God, the answer is obvious. Mathematical truths are there in the SF's mind, and you just rediscover them. Remember the limericks:

There was a young man who said, 'God,
It has always struck me as odd
That the sycamore tree
Simply ceases to be
When there's no one about in the quad.'

'Dear Sir, Your astonishment's odd;
I am always about in the quad:
And that's why the tree
Will continue to be,
Since observed by,
Yours faithfully, God.'

"I'm not qualified to say whether or not God exists. I kind of doubt He does. Nevertheless, I'm always saying that the SF has this transfinite Book—transfinite being a concept in mathematics that is larger than infinite—that contains the best proofs of all mathematical theorems, proofs that are elegant and perfect." The strongest compliment Erdös can give to a colleague's work is to say, "It's straight from the Book."

"I was once introducing Erdös at a lecture," says Joel Spencer, a mathematician at SUNY at Stony Brook who has worked with Erdös since 1970. "And I started to talk about his idea of God and the Book. He interrupted me and said, 'You don't have to believe in God, but you should believe in the Book.' Erdös has made me and other mathematicians recognize the importance of what we do. Mathematics is there. It's beautiful. It's this jewel we uncover."

That mathematics could be a jewel may come as a surprise to those of us who struggled with multiplication tables as kids and now need help completing W-4 forms. Mathematics is a misunderstood and even maligned discipline. It's not the brute computations they drilled into us in grade school. It's not the science of reckoning. Mathematicians do not spend their time thinking up cleverer ways of multiplying, faster methods of adding, better schemes for extracting cube roots. Even those drawn to the subject have had misconceptions. "I always wanted to be a mathematician," Spencer says, "even before I knew what mathematicians did. My father was a CPA, and I loved numbers. I thought mathematics was about adding up longer and longer lists. I found out what it really was in high school. I'd undoubtedly be a lot richer now if I were making my living adding up long lists of numbers."

Erdös's cousin Magda Fredro hasn't the slightest idea what he does, even though she has known him for sixty years and has accompanied him on mathematical sojourns from Florida to Israel. "Tell me, what is this about?" she asked me, flipping through her copy of Erdös's book *The Art of Counting*. "It looks like Chinese. Also, tell me, how famous and brilliant is he? I know so little about him. He once looked up six phone numbers. Then we talked for half an hour before he phoned them all, from memory. More than all his scientific work, that impressed me."

For Erdös, Graham, and their colleagues, mathematics is order and beauty at its purest, order that transcends the physical world. When Euclid, the Greek geometer of the third century B.C., spoke of points and lines, he was speaking of idealized entities, points that have no dimension and lines that have no width. All points and lines that exist in the real world—in, say, physics or engineering—do have dimension and thus are only imperfect imitations of the pure constructs that geometers ponder. Only in this idealized world do the angles of every triangle always sum to precisely 180 degrees.

Numbers, too, can have this transcendent quality. Take the prime numbers, integers like 2, 3, 5, 7, 11, 13, and 17, which are evenly divisible only by themselves and the number 1. We happen to have ten fingers, and our number system is conveniently based on ten digits. But the same primes, with all the same properties, exist in any number system. If we had twenty-six fingers and constructed our number system accordingly, there would still be primes. The universality of primes is the key to Carl Sagan's novel *Contact*, in which extraterrestrials, with God only knows how many fingers, signal earthlings by emitting radio signals at prime-number frequencies. But little green men need not be invoked in order to conceive of a culture that doesn't use base 10. We have had plenty here on Earth. Computers use a binary system, and the Babylonians had a base-60 system, vestiges of which are evident in the way we measure time (sixty seconds in a minute, sixty minutes in an hour). Cumbersome as this sexagesimal system was, it too contained the primes.

Prime numbers are like atoms. They are the building blocks of all integers. Every integer is either itself a prime or the unique product of primes. For example, 11 is a prime; 12 is the product of the primes 2, 2, and 3; 13 is a prime; 14 is the product of the primes 2 and 7; 15 is the product of the primes 3 and 5, and so on. Some 2,300 years ago, in proposition 20 of Book IX of his *Elements*, Euclid gave a proof, "straight from the Book," that the supply of primes is inexhaustible. As of this writing, the largest known prime is a 65,050-digit number formed by raising 2 to the 216,091st power and subtracting 1. But Euclid's work shows that there are infinitely many others. Only in mathematics, of all the sciences, do the ancients occasionally have the final word.

Prime numbers have always had an almost mystical appeal. "I even know of a mathematician who slept with his wife only on prime-numbered days," Graham says. "It was pretty good early in the month—two, three, five, seven—but got tough toward the end, when the primes are thinner, nineteen, twenty-three, then a big gap till twenty-nine." Prime numbers are appealing because, in spite of their apparent simplicity, their properties are extremely elusive. All sorts of basic questions about them remain unanswered, even though they have been scrutinized by generations of the sharpest mathematical minds. In 1742, for example, Christian Goldbach conjectured that every even number greater than 2 is the sum of two primes: $4 = 2 + 2, 6 = 3 + 3, 8 = 5 + 3, 10 = 5 + 5, 12 = 7 + 5, 14 = 7 + 7$, and so on. With the aid of computers, twentieth-century mathematicians have decomposed all even numbers up to 100 million into the sum of two primes, but they have not been able to prove that Goldbach's simple conjecture is universally true. Similarly, computer searches have revealed numerous "twin primes," pairs of consecutive odd numbers both of which are prime: 3 and 5; 5 and 7; 11 and 13; 71 and 73; 1,000,000,000,061 and 1,000,000,000,063. Number theorists believe that the supply of twin primes is inexhaustible, like the supply of primes themselves, but no one has been able to prove this. On an even deeper level, no one has found an easy way of telling in advance how far one prime number will be from the next one.

The prime numbers are Erdös's intimate friends. He understands them better than anyone else does. "When I was ten," he says, "my father told me about Euclid's proof, and I was hooked." Seven years later, as a college freshman, he caused a stir in Hungarian mathematics circles with a simple proof that a prime can always be found between any integer (greater than 1) and its double. This result had already been proved in about 1850 by one of the fathers of Russian mathematics, Pafnuty Lvovitch Chebyshev. But Chebyshev's proof was too heavy-handed to be in the Book. He had used a steam shovel to transplant a rosebush, whereas Erdös managed with a silver spoon. News of Erdös's youthful triumph was spread by the ditty "Chebyshev said it, and I say it again/There is always a prime between n and $2n$."

In 1939 Erdös attended a lecture at Princeton by Marc Kac, a Polish émigré mathematical physicist who would contribute to the American development of radar during the Second World War. "He half-dozed through most of my lecture," Kac wrote in his autobiography. "The subject matter was too far removed from his interests. Toward the end I described briefly my difficulties with the number of prime divisors. At the mention of number theory Erdös perked up and asked me to explain once again what the difficulty was. Within the next few minutes, even before the lecture was over, he interrupted to announce that he had the solution!"

In 1949 Erdös had his greatest victory over the prime numbers, although the victory is one he doesn't like to talk about, because it was marred by controversy. Although mathematicians have no effective way of telling exactly where prime numbers lie, they have known since 1896 a formula that describes the statistical distribution of primes, how on average the primes thin out the further out you go. Like Chebyshev's proof, the 1896 proof of what's called the Prime Number Theorem depended on heavy machinery, and the brightest mathematical minds were convinced that the theorem couldn't be proved with anything less. Erdös and Atle Selberg, a colleague who was not yet well known, stunned the mathematics world with an "elementary" proof. According to Erdös's friends, the two agreed that they'd publish back-to-back papers in a leading journal delineating their respective contributions to the proof. Erdös then sent out postcards to mathematicians informing them that he and Selberg had conquered the Prime Number Theorem. Selberg apparently ran into a mathematician he didn't know who had received a postcard, and the mathematician immediately said, "Have you heard? Erdös and What's His Name have an elementary proof of the Prime Number Theorem." Reportedly, Selberg was so injured that he raced ahead and published without Erdös, and thus got the lion's share of credit for the proof. In 1950 Selberg alone was awarded the Fields medal, the closest equivalent in mathematics to a Nobel Prize, in large part for his work on the Prime Number Theorem.

Priority fights are not uncommon in mathematics. Unlike other scientists, mathematicians leave no trail of laboratory results to substantiate who did what. Indeed, Erdös has been spending much time these days mediating a priority fight among three of his closest collaborators. "When I was a graduate student," Joel Spencer says, "I thought only third-rate mathematicians would have these fights. But it's actually first-rate mathematicians. They're the ones who are passionate about mathematics." If they can't fathom what's in the SF's Book, they don't want anyone else to. The late R. L. Moore, a strong Texas mathematician, put it bluntly: "I'd rather a theorem not be thought of than I not be the one who thinks of it."

In February, Erdös and 320 of his colleagues gathered at Florida Atlantic University, in Boca Raton, for the largest conference ever in combinatorics, a burgeoning branch of mathematics that encompasses problems involving objects that must be counted and classified. (Combinatorics was officially launched in 1736 in the East Prussian city of Königsberg, now the Soviet town of Kaliningrad, when Leonhard Euler, a twenty-nine-year-old mathematical phenom, proved that one couldn't take a round-trip stroll across all of the city's seven bridges without crossing at least one bridge more than once, and then generalized his argument to apply to any odd number of bridges.) At Boca Raton one of the combinatorialists gave a formal talk in which he presented a result but refused to share the proof. The proof apparently introduced a powerful technique that he wanted to keep secret until he had squeezed it dry of whatever other results it might yield.

Erdös doesn't like to think about such competitiveness. For him mathematics is a glorious combination of science and art. On the one hand, it is the science of certainty, because its conclusions are logically unassailable. Unlike biologists, chemists, or even physicists, Erdös, Graham, and their fellow mathematicians *prove* things. Their conclusions follow syllogistically from premises, in the same way that the conclusion "Ronald Reagan is mortal" follows from the premises "All Presidents are mortal" and "Ronald Reagan is a President." On the other hand, mathematics has an aesthetic side. A conjecture can be "obvious" or "unexpected." A result can be "trivial" or "beautiful." A proof can be "messy," "surprising," or, as Erdös would say, "straight from the Book."

What is more, a proof should ideally provide insight into why a particular result is true. Consider one of the most famous results in modern mathematics, the four-color-map theorem, which states that no more than four colors are needed to paint any conceivable flat map of real or imaginary countries in such a way that no two bordering countries have the same color. From the middle of the nineteenth century most mathematicians believed that this seductively simple theorem was true, but for 124 years a parade of distinguished mathematicians and dedicated amateurs searched in vain for a proof (or, conceivably, a counterexample). In 1976 Kenneth Appel and Wolfgang Haken, of the University of Illinois, finally conquered this mathematical Mount Everest. I was an undergraduate at Harvard at the time, and when word of the proof reached

Cambridge, my instructor in calculus cut short his lecture and served champagne. Some days later we learned to our dismay that Appel and Haken's proof had made unprecedented use of high-speed computers: more than 1,000 hours logged among three machines. What Appel and Haken had done was to demonstrate that all possible maps are variations of more than 1,500 fundamental cases, each of which the computer was then able to paint using at most four colors. The proof was simply too long to be checked by hand, and some mathematicians feared that the computer might have slipped up and made a subtle error. Today, more than a decade later, validity of the proof is generally acknowledged, but many still regard the proof as unsatisfactory. "I'm not an expert on the four-color problem," Erdös says, "but I assume the proof is true. However, it's not beautiful. I'd prefer to see a proof that gives insight into why four colors are sufficient."

Beauty and *insight*—these are words that Erdös and his colleagues use freely but have difficulty explaining. "It's like asking why Beethoven's Ninth Symphony is beautiful," Erdös says. "If you don't see why, someone can't tell you. I *know* numbers are beautiful. If they aren't beautiful, nothing is."

Pythagoras of Samos evidently felt the same way. In the sixth century B.C. he made a kind of religion out of numbers, believing that they were not merely instruments of enumeration but sacred, perfect, friendly, lucky, or evil. Pythagoras saw perfection in any integer that equaled the sum of all the other integers that divided evenly into it. The first perfect number is 6. It's evenly divisible by 1, 2, and 3, and it's also the sum of 1, 2, and 3. The second perfect number is 28. Its divisors are 1, 2, 4, 7, and 14, and they add up to 28. During the Middle Ages religious scholars asserted that the perfection of 6 and 28 was part of the fabric of the universe: God created the world in six days and the moon orbits the earth every 28 days. Saint Augustine believed that the properties of the numbers themselves, not any connection to the empirical world, made them perfect: "Six is a number perfect in itself, and not because God created all things in six days; rather than the inverse is true; God created all things in six days because this number is perfect. And it would remain perfect even if the work of the six days did not exist."

The ancient Greeks knew of only two perfect numbers besides 6 and 28: 496 and 8,128. Since the four perfect numbers they knew were all even, they wondered whether an odd perfect number existed. Today Erdös and his colleagues know thirty perfect numbers, the largest having 130,100 digits, and all thirty are even. But they cannot rule out the possibility that the thirty-first perfect number will be odd. Whether an odd perfect number exists is among the oldest unsolved problems in mathematics. Equally daunting is the unsolved problem of how many perfect numbers there are.

Pythagoras considered the numbers 220 and 284 to be "friendly." His concept of a friendly number was based on the idea that a human friend is a kind of alter ego. Pythagoras wrote, "[A friend] is the other I, such as are 220 and 284." These numbers have a special mathematical property: each is equal to the sum of the other's divisors. That is, the divisors of 220 are 1, 2, 4, 5, 10, 11, 20, 22, 44, 55, and 110, and they sum to 284; the divisors of 284 are 1, 2, 4, 71, and 142, and they sum to 220. Like perfect numbers, friendly numbers appear in the Bible. In Genesis 32:14, Jacob gives Esau 220 goats ("two hundred she-goats and twenty he-goats") as a gesture of friendship.

A second pair of friendly numbers (17,296 and 18,416) was not discovered until 1636, by Pierre de Fermat. By the middle of the nineteenth century many able mathematicians had searched for pairs of friendly numbers, and some sixty had been found. But not until 1866 was the second *smallest* pair, 1,184 and 1,210, discovered, by a sixteen-year-old Italian. By now hundreds of friendly numbers have been discovered, but, as with perfect numbers and twin primes, even today no one knows whether their supply is inexhaustible. Erdös thinks it is, and he wrote one of the earliest papers in the literature on the distribution of friendly numbers. Why it should be so much easier to prove that the number of primes is infinite is one of the great unanswered meta-questions of mathematics.

Perfect numbers and friendly numbers are among the areas of mathematics in which child prodigies tend to show their stuff. Like chess and music, such areas do not require much technical expertise. No child prodigies exist among historians or legal scholars, because years are needed to master those disciplines. A child can learn the rules of chess in a few minutes, and native ability takes over from there. So it is with areas of mathematics like these, which are aspects of elementary number theory, or the study of the integers, and combinatorics. You can easily explain prime numbers, perfect numbers, and friendly numbers to a child, and he can start playing around with them and exploring their properties. Many areas of mathematics, however, require technical expertise, which is acquired over years of assimilating definitions and previous results. By the time mathematical prodigies mature and enter college, they usually have the patience to master these more technical areas—and often go on to make great discoveries in them. Erdös is an exception. He has stuck chiefly to areas of mathematics in which prodigies excel.

This is not to say that his mathematical interests are narrow. On the contrary, he has opened up whole new areas of mathematics. But, like number theory, these areas typically require a minimum of technical knowledge.

These are areas that the next generation of prodigies will find captivating.

Erdös's forte is coming up with short, clever solutions. He solves problems not by grinding out pages of equations but by constructing succinct, insightful arguments. He is a mathematical wit, and his shrewdness often extends to problems outside his areas of specialty. "In 1976 we were having coffee in the mathematics lounge at Texas A & M," recalls George Purdy, a geometer who has worked with Erdös since 1967. "There was a problem on the blackboard in functional analysis, a field Erdös knew nothing about. I happened to know that two analysts had just come up with a thirty-page solution to the problem and were very proud of it. Erdös looked up at the board and said, 'What's that? Is it a problem?' I said yes, and he went up to the board and squinted at the tersely written statement. He asked a few questions about what the symbols represented, and then he effortlessly wrote down a two-line solution. If that's not magic, what is?"

Erdös is the consummate problem solver. Most elderly mathematicians, if they're still going strong, are theory builders. They have stopped solving problems and are setting a general agenda for mathematical research, pointing to new or neglected areas that younger talent should pursue. Not Erdös. As long as problems remain to be solved, he'll be slugging it out in the trenches.

One of the areas in which Erdös has pioneered is a philosophically appealing aspect of combinatorics called Ramsey theory. It is the area in which Graham's record-setting number comes into play. The idea underlying Ramsey theory is that complete disorder is an impossibility. The appearance of disorder is really a matter of scale. Any mathematical "object" can be found if sought in a large enough universe. "In the TV series *Cosmos*, Carl Sagan appealed to Ramsey theory without knowing that's what he was doing," Graham says. "Sagan said people often look up and see, say, eight stars that are almost in a straight line. Since the stars are lined up, the temptation is to think they were artificially put there, as beacons for an interstellar trade route, perhaps. Well, Sagan said, if you look at a large enough group of stars, you can see almost anything you want. That's Ramsey theory in action."

In Sagan's example the mathematician would want to know the smallest group of arbitrarily positioned stars that will always contain eight that are lined up. In general, the Ramsey theorist seeks the smallest "universe" that's guaranteed to contain a certain object. Suppose the object is not eight stars in a row but two people of the same sex. In this case the Ramsey theorist wants to know the smallest number of people that will always include two people of the same sex. Obviously, the answer is three.

Ramsey theory takes its name from Frank Plumpton Ramsey, a brilliant student of Bertrand Russell, G. E. Moore, Ludwig Wittgenstein, and John Maynard Keynes, who might well have surpassed his teachers had he not died of jaundice in 1930, at the age of twenty-six. While his brother Michael pursued the transcendent reality that theology offers (he became the Archbishop of Canterbury), Frank Ramsey, a spirited atheist, pursued the transcendent reality that mathematics offers. He also studied philosophy and economics, writing two papers on taxation and savings that were heralded by Keynes and are still widely cited in the economics literature. But it is eight pages of mathematics that have made him eponymous — eight pages that Erdös seized on and developed into a full-fledged branch of mathematics. Like all the problems Erdös works on, Ramsey problems can be simply stated, although the solutions are often hard to come by.

The classic Ramsey problem involves guests at a party.

What is the minimum number of guests that need to be invited so that either at least three guests will know each other or at least three won't? Mathematicians, as is their trademark, are careful to articulate their assumptions. Here they assume that the relation of knowing someone is symmetric: if Sally knows Billy, Billy knows Sally.

With this assumption in mind, consider a party of six. Call one of the guests David. Now, since David knows or doesn't know each of the other five, he will either know at least three of them or not know at least three. Assume the former (the argument works the same way if we assume the latter). Now consider what relationships David's three acquaintances might have among themselves. If any two of the three are acquaintances, they and David will constitute three who know each other—and we have our quorum. That leaves only the possibility that David's three aquaintances are all strangers to one another—but that achieves the quorum too, for they constitute three guests who do not know each other. To understand why a party of five is not enough to guarantee either three people all of whom know each other or three people none of whom do, ponder the case of Michael, who knows two and only two people, each of whom knows a different one of the two people Michael doesn't know.

Q.E.D., or *quod erat demonstrandum*, as Erdös would say. We have just written out a mathematical proof— perhaps not one from the Book, but a proof nonetheless. And the proof provides *insight* into why a party of six must include at least three mutual acquaintances or three mutual strangers. Another way to prove this is by brute force, listing all conceivable combinations of acquaintanceship among six people—32,768 such possibilities exist—and checking to see that each combination includes the desired relationship. This brute-force proof, however, would not provide insight.

Suppose we want not a threesome but a foursome who

either all know each other or are strangers. How large must the party be? Erdös and Graham and their fellow Ramsey theorists can prove that eighteen guests are necessary. But raise the ante again, to a fivesome, and no one knows how many guests are required. The answer is known to lie between forty-two and fifty-five. That much has been known for two decades, and Graham suspects that the precise number won't be found for at least a hundred years. The case of a sixsome is even more daunting, with the answer known to lie between 102 and 169. The ranges grow wider still for higher numbers.

Erdös likes to tell the story of an evil spirit that can ask you anything it wants. If you answer incorrectly, it will destroy humanity. "Suppose," Erdös says, "it decides to ask you the Ramsey party problem for the case of a fivesome. Your best tactic, I think, is to get all the computers in the world to drop what they're doing and work on the problem, the brute-force approach of trying all the specific cases"—of which there are more than 10 to the 200th power (the number 1 followed by 200 zeroes). "But if the spirit asks about a sixsome, your best survival strategy would be to attack the spirit before it attacks you. There are too many cases even for computers."

Graham's record-setting number comes up in a similar problem. Take any number of people and list every possible committee that could be formed from them, including committees of one and a committee of the whole. The "object" Graham wants to find is four committees that can be split into two groups of two committees each in such a way that each person belongs to the same number of committees in each group. How many people are required to guarantee the presence of four such committees? Graham suspects that the answer is six, but all that he or anyone else has been able to prove is that four such committees will always exist if the number of people is equal to his record-setting number. This astonishing gap between what is suspected, based on observations of specific cases, and what is known shows how hard Ramsey theory is.

Graham, whose license plate reads RAMSEY, thinks that centuries may pass before much of Erdös's and his work in Ramsey theory has applications in physics, engineering, or elsewhere in the real world, including his place of employment, AT&T. "The applications aren't the point," Graham says. "I look at mathematics pretty globally. It represents the ultimate structure and order. And I associate doing mathematics with control. Jugglers like to be able to control a situation. There's a well-known saying in juggling: 'The trouble is that the balls go where you throw them.' It's just you. It's not the phases of the moon, or someone else's fault. It's like chess. It's all out in the open. Mathematics is really there, for you to discover. The Prime Number Theorem was the same theorem before people were here, and it will be the same theorem after we're all gone. It's the Prime Number Theorem."

"In a way," Erdös says, "mathematics is the only infinite human activity. It is conceivable that humanity could eventually learn everything in physics or biology. But humanity certainly won't ever be able to find out everything in mathematics, because the subject is infinite. Numbers themselves are infinite. That's why mathematics is really my only interest." One can reconstruct chapters of the SF's Book, but only the SF has it from beginning to end.

"The trouble with the integers is that we have examined only the small ones," says Graham. "Maybe all the exciting stuff happens at really big numbers, ones we can't get our hands on or even begin to think about in any very definite way. So maybe all the action is really inaccessible and we're just fiddling around. Our brains have evolved to get us out of the rain, find where the berries are, and keep us from getting killed. Our brains did not evolve to help us grasp really large numbers or to look at things in a hundred thousand dimensions. I've had this image of a creature, in another galaxy perhaps, a child creature, and he's playing a game with his friends. For a moment he's distracted. He just thinks about numbers, primes, a simple proof of the twin-prime conjecture, and much more. Then he loses interest and returns to his game."

We earthlings, where are we in our understanding of numbers? Each result—say, Erdös's proof that a prime can always be found between an integer and its double— although touted in the mathematics journals, is only an imperceptible advance toward some kind of cosmic understanding of the integers. "It will be millions of years before we'll have any understanding," Erdös says, "and even then it won't be a complete understanding, because we're up against the infinite."

It is late January in San Antonio, and Mayor Henry Cisneros, a rising star in Democratic politics, has proclaimed Math Day, in honor of the 2,575 mathematicians who have descended on the city for the annual conferences of the American Mathematical Society and the Mathematical Association of America. Cisneros's gesture has not advanced his cause with the conferees I am with, who wonder whether he has ever met a mathematician, let alone heard of Paul Erdös. The schedules include meetings to discuss whether mathematicians should accept Star Wars money and whether the National Security Agency, whose code-cracking wing is the largest employer of mathematicians in the United States, qualifies for corporate membership in the AMS. But except for a few zealots, most of the mathematicians have come to San Antonio not to discuss ethics and politics but to do mathematics. At physics conferences or psychoanalytic meetings, the participants do not perform experiments on subatomic particles or practice psychotherapy—they just talk about it. At mathematics conferences the attendees actually do mathematics, on blackboards, napkins, place-mats, and toilet-stall walls, and in their minds.

Erdös rarely attends the scheduled talks at these meetings, preferring to work simultaneously with several mathematicians in a hotel room. Today Erdös has taken over someone else's room at the Marriott and is working on six problems with six different mathematicians, who are sprawled across two double beds and the floor. "What about 647? Is it a prime?" asks a man who looks like a plump Moses. "I can no longer do them in my head." A woman in a multicolored dress comes to his rescue by pulling out a 276-page printout of all the primes up to two million—148,933 of them, ranging from 2 to 1,999,993. Sure enough, 647 is on the list.

Erdös doesn't seem to be paying attention. He is slumped over in a chair, his head in his hands, like an invalid in a nursing home. But every few minutes he perks up and suggests a line of attack to one of his colleagues, who then scrambles to implement the master's suggestion. The others wait patiently for Erdös to have a flash of insight about their problem. Sometimes when Erdös raises his head, he fools them, and they lean forward like the people seeking hot tips in an E. F. Hutton commercial. Instead of sharing a mathematical inspiration, he utters an aphoristic statement having to do with death—"Soon I will be cured of the incurable disease of life" or "This meeting, like life, will soon come to an end, but the meeting was much more pleasant"—and then bows his head again. No one picks up on these comments, and the cycle of mathematical insights and reflections on death continues all morning.

"In ten years," says the man who looks like Moses, "I want you to talk to the SF on my behalf."

"What do you want from the SF?" Erdös says.

"I want to see the Book."

"No one ever sees the Book. At most, you get glimpses."

Moses turns on the TV. "Television," Erdös says, "is something the Russians invented to destroy American education." The news comes on, and Ronald Reagan fills the screen. "Eisenhower was an enthusiastic but not very good golfer," Erdös says. "Someone said at the time that it was okay to elect a golfer, but why not a good golfer? I say, it's okay to elect an actor, but why not a good actor, like Chaplin?" Reagan dissolves, and the newscast switches to a story about AIDS. "Both bosses and slaves tell me people are less promiscuous," Erdös says, "but I wouldn't know." When the conversation strays from mathematics and death, it's a sure sign that Erdös is bored and ready to find new mathematical soul mates.

Two hours and five milligrams of Benzedrine later, Erdös is on a flight to Newark. From there he'll be going in quick succession to Memphis, Boca Raton, San Juan, Gainesville, Haifa, Tel Aviv, Montreal, Boston, Madison, DeKalb, Chicago, Champaign, Philadelphia, and Graham's house. His schedule has a small problem, however: two mathematicians in different states want him to open his brain to them at the same time. "You've heard about my mother's theorem?" Erdös says. "My mother said, 'Even you, Paul, can be in only one place at one time.' Maybe soon I will be relieved of this disadvantage. Maybe, once I've left, I'll be able to be in many places at the same time. Maybe then I'll be able to collaborate with Archimedes and Euclid."

5

SHANNON BROWNLEE

Cancer's Bad Seeds

U.S. News & World Report,
December 11, 1989

*Like many of the new generation of science writers,
Shannon Brownlee was trained in science, with a master's
degree in marine biology. Like many great science stories,
"Cancer's Bad Seeds" came from a combination of serendipity and ability. It was only the third science article
Brownlee had attempted for U.S. News & World Report. "I
didn't feel I knew what made a news story, but I knew what
made a story," she says. "At that time oncogenes were everywhere you looked, but there had been little to put the research into perspective." The subject might have been
impossible had she not stumbled across Harvard researchers
Michael Bishop and Harold Varmus on their way to winning a Nobel Prize, a tribute to her science acumen that
gave her the news peg she needed.*

*"Still I was in terra incognita," she admits. "Scientists
were drawing pictures to explain the stuff to me." To write
the lead she recalled the advice of Lin Rosellini, the feature
writer for U.S. News. "Cram all of your best stuff into the
first few paragraphs. The great stuff will rise to the top from
your reporting and the crucial connections will follow."*

A University of Santa Cruz–trained science writer, Brown-

lee landed a researcher position at Discover in 1982. "There were so many people I learned from there—like Natalie Angier and Dennis Overbye. But it was the editor Leon Jaroff who taught me that science was a great, great thing to write about."

Brownlee went on to Sports Illustrated and then U.S. News & World Report, where she is now a senior editor. Recently she finished a year as a Knight-Ridder Science Fellow at Stanford University, where she began studying fiction. "Because I started as a scientist, I'm constantly trying to learn how to write. My models are the great murder writer Edna Buchanan, and Louise Erdrich and Paul Bowles. The others were Natalie and Dennis: I literally pulled apart their stories to see how they ticked."

"Cancer's Bad Seeds" won the 1990 General Motors Cancer Research Award and a $10,000 grant, and the recognition launched Brownlee in a second career as crusader for more science criticism from journalists. She rues the new sophistication of scientists in dealing with the press. "Now the focus is on biotechnology and biotech companies, and when there's big money at stake the scientists have just shut up when talking to the press. It's making my job a lot harder."

T WO YEARS AGO, DOCTORS CARING FOR AN 18-month-old girl faced a difficult decision. The toddler was in the early stages of neuroblastoma, a rare childhood cancer of nerve cells, and had undergone surgery to remove her tumor, a procedure that cures the disease at this stage in 90 percent of cases. But a new, highly experimental test developed by Robert Seeger of Children's Hospital of Los Angeles and Garrett Brodeur of Washington University in St. Louis revealed something worrisome—multiple copies

of a mutated gene in the girl's tumor cells. Despite successful surgery and what would normally be an excellent prognosis, the researchers recommended more-radical, and painful, treatment.

The patient underwent chemotherapy, whole-body radiation and a bone-marrow transplant. In her marrow, Seeger found tiny new tumors, evidence that their unorthodox treatment had been correct. Alive and well today, the girl probably would have died without it.

Seeger and Brodeur based their decision on a snippet of DNA that, just a short time ago, would have had no predictive value. But in the past decade, cancer research has shifted dramatically to focus on the genes that underlie the cellular abnormalities of cancer. The disfigured fragment of DNA that alerted the researchers is just one of the many tumor-causing genes whose role in cancer is now understood. Called oncogenes, from the Greek *onkos*, for mass, these genes come in two forms. When whole and healthy, they govern the orderly growth and reproduction of cells. But when mutated—perhaps by carcinogens in cigarette smoke or a chance mishap during cell division— oncogenes wreak terrible mischief, creating proteins that cause cells to proliferate out of control.

So important are oncogenes to the understanding of human cancer that this year's Nobel Prize in medicine was awarded to J. Michael Bishop and Harold Varmus, researchers at the University of California in San Francisco, for making the first solid connection between cancer and these genes 14 years ago. Since then, more than 50 oncogenes have been extracted from a variety of animals, and it is now believed that oncogenes must work in teams to transform cells.

Researchers have just begun the painstaking experiments necessary to trace the biochemical pathways leading from mutated genes to tumors, but already they are sounding atypically sanguine: "Cancer is no longer a mysterious, fully inexplicable process," says Robert Weinberg, a molecular biologist at the Whitehead Institute for Biomedical Research in Cambridge, Mass. "We are in the process of understanding almost all of it in the next decade, and when I say understanding, I mean understanding its causal forces." Indeed, researchers have not only learned to use oncogenes to make prognoses in four types of cancer, they have also worked out for the first time the structure of the protein made by an oncogene and, just this year, have found a drug that may block the protein's action.

GENETIC CORRUPTION

Oncogenes lead double lives, serving crucial roles in normal cell activity until they turn deadly—a phenomenon that scientists have been observing since Bishop and Varmus first plucked an oncogene from chicken cells in 1975. They discovered that a section of genetic material that made a virus capable of causing tumors in chickens was almost identical to a scrap of DNA belonging to a chicken's healthy cells, confirming a controversial theory that cancer-causing genes were mutated versions of perfectly normal ones. They subsequently found similar lengths of DNA in a zoo full of species, from fish to fowl to people, and concluded that in its uncorrupted form, this oncogene must be vital to the workings of cells.

The implication of this discovery was enormous, for it meant that we carry the seeds of cancer in our own genetic code. Indeed, researchers soon realized that the oncogenes do not actually need a virus to incite cancer. Like a thief who uses his victim's own gun, the virus simply pilfered a section of DNA from a cell, mangling it in the process and rendering it deadly. But the genes, they discovered, could also be mangled within the cell.

Not until 1982 did these findings appear to have any significance to human cancer, however. That year, Weinberg's lab isolated the cancer-causing gene from human-bladder cancer and showed it was the same as an oncogene teased from a rat-tumor virus. This hank of DNA, known as *ras*, would turn out to be a kingpin oncogene, one that would be found in half a dozen types of human tumor.

Most oncogenes are only bit players in the tragedy of human cancer. But a select handful are found again and again in a variety of human tumors, and researchers surmised early on that in their intact form, these key segments of genetic material must play central roles in regulating cell growth and division. Conversely, they reasoned, an oncogene in its perverted form sends cells multiplying out of control. But they did not know why.

As it happens, it takes surprisingly little to pervert some genes. *Ras*, for example, differs from its healthy cousin by a single change in its sequence of base pairs, the molecules forming the "letters" of the DNA code. A healthy *ras* gene makes a protein involved in signaling the cell to multiply by cell division—during rapid fetal growth, for instance. When enough new cells have been made, division stops. But the mutated *ras* protein screams at the cell like some Biblical command to be fruitful and multiply. The obedient progeny become a tumor.

Fortunately, it takes more than one type of oncogene to propel a cell down the path to malignancy, and the emerging view of cancer is of a chorus of oncogenes working in concert. Researchers have evidence that at least two oncogenes, and often as many as five or six, are mutated in tumors. Advanced colon cancers, for example, generally have at least five mutated oncogenes, or "hits," and almost invariably *ras* is among them.

It now appears that recessive oncogenes—genes that

can do damage only when both copies have been mutated—are also necessary for cancer's ravages. The first of these recessive oncogenes, also known as tumor suppressor genes, was cloned by Weinberg's lab and Dr. Thaddeus Dryja in 1986. It is responsible for a rare and grisly childhood cancer called retinoblastoma, which produces glittering tumors on the retina and afflicts about 1 in 20,000 children a year. Eventually, the child is blinded or even killed if the eye is not removed.

Unlike most oncogenes, the one that causes retinoblastoma, called *rb*, causes cancer not by triggering uncontrollable cell division, but by failing to turn it off. A child inherits two copies of the *rb* gene, one from each parent. A healthy *rb* gene keeps cell growth in check, and when only one copy of *rb* is bad, the good copy can still maintain sovereignty over cells of the retina. But when both copies are defective or missing, tumors grow without restraint. Scientists have fished *rb* from a number of other human cancers, including colon, breast and lung cancer, which together account for two thirds of cancer deaths.

Despite the rapid progress in the field, identifying oncogenes is only the first step in preventing or curing cancer. Researchers are now launching experiments to probe the intricate biochemical reactions that cause cells to proliferate in the early stages of cancer. It appears that the loss of good copies of *rb*, or any of the six additional recessive oncogenes discovered thus far, leaves a cell with fewer of the proteins that restrict growth, thus clearing the way for oncogenes like *ras* to goad the cell into dividing madly. And recessive oncogenes, says John Minna, of the National Cancer Institute in Bethesda, Md., are turning out to be at least as important as the oncogenes that promote cell growth.

In cancer's final stages, other oncogenes may be responsible for the disease's spreading. Individual cells break away from the primary tumor, floating through the blood and lymph fluid to alight in other parts of the body and sprout new tumors. To do so, the cells must penetrate other tissues, a diabolical capacity that William Hayward of Sloan-Kettering Institute for Cancer Research in New York speculates is made possible by an oncogene. Such findings will ultimately lead to more effective treatments. Just this year, researchers at the University of California at Berkeley reported that a drug developed to combat cholesterol can interfere with the mutated *ras* protein in a lab.

KEYS TO PROGNOSIS

Even before new treatments are found, doctors will use oncogenes to help predict which patients need additional treatment after surgery. Based on an analysis of more than 800 neuroblastoma tumors, Seeger believes that multiple copies of the oncogene *n-myc* are probably the best sign of a patient's prognosis. Similarly, Minna has found that lung-cancer patients with the worst outcome have multiple copies—as many as 50 per tumor cell—of *c-myc*, an oncogene in the same family, and earlier this year researchers reported that other oncogenes can accurately predict the course of breast and colon cancer.

Many questions remain concerning how genes are mutated in the first place, but increasingly researchers believe that both heredity and carcinogens are to blame. Radiation, chemicals, even sunlight can damage genes, and people are born with varying degrees of susceptibility to carcinogens' corrupting influence.

Now, evidence is mounting that people inherit defective oncogenes. Working alone in cells, one or even two inherited defective oncogenes are insufficient to trigger cancer. But if carcinogens mutate other genes in a cell, the inherited and environmentally damaged genes together can unleash cancer. A new test identifies fetuses at risk from *rb*, and other tests will identify those people who are most susceptible to other types of cancer, a prospect that raises both ethical questions—the use of genetic prognosticators by insurance companies, for instance—and the opportunity to halt tumors before they appear. As Nobel laureate Bishop has said, we now know that the seeds of our own destruction lie in our genes. So, too, will the seeds of our salvation as we learn more about the genetics of the disease.

6

GARY TAUBES

———————

The Wager

From *Bad Science:*
The Short Life and Weird Times of Cold Fusion, Random House,
1993

Like Shannon Brownlee, Gary Taubes is a writer trained in science, in his case with a bachelor's degree from Harvard in applied physics and a master's in engineering from Stanford University. Even more than Brownlee, though, he disdains much of what he sees in science writing today. "The tendency is to put scientists on pedestals all the time," he says. "It's wimpy journalism." As an object of criticism he holds up the Tuesday New York Times *Science section in particular. "You need some skepticism, some distance, because a great deal of science out there is bad science."*

Bad Science: The Short Life and Weird Times of Cold Fusion *reads like a morality play and made-for-TV script wrapped together. In it two maverick chemists seemingly defy the laws of physics by unleashing a limitless energy supply using high school lab equipment at the University of Utah. They make headlines and nearly net a multimillion-dollar government grant, and only the painstaking process of science itself—using high school lab rules of control experiments and communicating the lack of results by E-mail across the world—caught the fraud. The press certainly did not get it, at least at first. Taubes's work offers a powerful* cautionary tale for anyone who claims to make, or report, a breakthrough that breaks all known physical laws.

It also shows the powerful attraction of the rebel image, even in science. Researchers in the dominant field of recent science, physics, had looked down on the search for cold fusion—nuclear fusion without superheated temperatures as occur inside the sun. So when chemists Stanley Pons and Martin Fleischmann were questioned about their claims, their reply was that the big institutions and press from the East Coast were jealously trying to undermine their efforts.

In this selection, the cast includes Pons and Fleischmann; Chase Peterson, University of Utah Vice-President for Health Sciences; and Steven Jones, a rival at Brigham Young University.

Born in 1957, Taubes came to science journalism in the post-Watergate flood of would-be investigative reporters. Sparked by reading The Great Gatsby as a college freshman, he finally dropped science as a career and earned a second master's degree from the Columbia University School of Journalism. "But I didn't have any clips," he recalls. "The only person who would give me a job was a friend in Dallas." He came back to New York for a starting position at Discover in 1980, joining the now familiar world of creative science journalism that magazine spearheaded.

Taubes's introduction to the flaws of science started with his first book, Nobel Dreams (1986), for which he lived six months with high-energy researchers at the particle accelerator called CERN in Switzerland. His riveting, and critical, account of CERN's Nobel Prize–winning director Carl Rubbia led to a threatened lawsuit. "But many other scientists told me privately that it was about time he had been exposed," Taubes points out. That experience—of living with a top research team as it works—is crucial to any science writer and yet shared by only a few, like Overbye and Angier. "You get to see how often scientists break their own rules," says Taubes.

Taubes approaches writing as a good researcher ap-
proaches science, triple-checking claims, listening to an in-
ner voice that lets him know if something sounds wrong. A
huge fan of the controversial science writer John Crewd-
son, Taubes cites as his models the familiar names of James
Watson and Tracy Kidder. He also points to less well known
books, like Cliff Stoll's The Cuckoo's Egg *and Emilio*
Segre's A Mind Always in Motion, *as works he admires.*

And he has a secret: he learned his dramatic sense of
story—of the combination of carnival and tragedy in daily
American life—from an unusual source. "I put myself
through graduate school by stringing for the National En-
quirer," *he says. "But you won't mention that, will you?"*

IF COLD FUSION HAD A PATRON SAINT, THAT DUBI-
ous honor would probably go to Blaise Pascal, the re-
nowned seventeenth-century physicist, mathematician,
and philosopher. Pascal renounced a life of science for
one of faith, which many of the proponents of cold fusion
seem to have done, and he wrote down the terms of the
wager that, for him, made this choice inevitable. Pascal argued that to bet on the existence of God and to be wrong
is to lose little or nothing. To wager correctly that there is
a God is to be rewarded with an "infinity of infinitely
happy life." "Let us assess the two cases," he wrote: "if you
win you win everything, if you lose you lose nothing. Do
not hesitate then; wager that he does exist."

Throughout the cold fusion episode, the proponents of
cold fusion would subscribe to the logic of Pascal's wager.
To bet that cold fusion existed and to win was to be rewarded with a payoff that, while not literally infinite, certainly seemed like it at times. To bet wrongly cost
relatively nothing: a few million dollars, a few months of

work, or a reputation would always seem inconsequential in comparison to the potential reward.[1]

One year later, for instance, Chase Peterson insisted that he had never believed that cold fusion necessarily was real, but that what was important was that it could have been real. Here was Pascal's wager. Peterson said, "You get burned if cold fusion doesn't work, but you sure get burned if you don't do anything about it and it does work. So you've just got to be smart."

After March 23, the conventional wisdom was that somehow the lawyers had forced the press conference on Pons and Fleischmann. Nobody knew exactly which lawyers, maybe the patent lawyers, but that was not the point. What was certain was that the two chemists would not willingly have initiated such a piece of shameless grandstanding, and the administration of a respectable university surely could not have been responsible for it. So lawyers were the natural scapegoats. But in the final analysis they were only accountable for one third of the responsibility.

When Peterson realized that the equation he had worked out with BYU was not a workable one and that cold fusion, with its prodigious potential, could not be left in the hands of the principle investigators alone, he repeated the procedure he had employed with the artificial heart six and a half years earlier.

At that time, Peterson had gathered all the key players: the surgeon, Bill DeVries, and his assistant; the regular and intensive-care nurses; the research team; the lawyers;

1. Pascal's wager could also be interpreted as what Robert Park of the American Physical Society later called derisively the Pennsylvania Lottery principle, which is to say, "If the pot is big enough, we shouldn't pay too much attention to the odds." Again, one wagers an inconsequential amount for an enormous payoff. Now, however, the payoff is acknowledged to be less than infinite, and the probability of winning was effectively zero. With this revised set of odds, the decision to abstain from playing no longer seems to invoke the renunciation of reason.

the hospital security people; the public relations staff; and the hospital administrators who would finance the procedure. Then he said, "I'm not in charge of this, but I'm going to moderate. You describe to me what you think your role will be if we ever choose a patient for the artificial heart." They went around the room, and everyone spoke honestly and directly. Once they had worked out all the complications to everyone's satisfaction—and once they had located a viable patient, the redoubtable Barney Clark—they went for it.

With cold fusion, Peterson had a considerably smaller team to assemble. He brought in the lawyers: Peter Dehlinger from Palo Alto and two whom Pons had requested personally, C. Gary Triggs and Gary Sawyer, another North Carolina patent expert who had worked with both Pons and Triggs in the past. From the university were Jim Brophy, the vice president for research; Norm Brown, head of the Office of Technology Transfer; and, of course, Pons and Fleischmann.

This meeting convened in Peterson's office on March 16, and the lawyers began with their agenda. As Peterson recalled, "They began to say, 'This is crazy. This has got to be identified now as the Pons-Fleischmann phenomenon. It's got to be so identified. And the patent primacy rests partly on lab books and all the rest just on being ahead of the game.' "

Pons and Fleischmann demonstrated to the lawyers that they could document their provenance, which was consideration number one. They discussed dates of invention and decided, on whatever evidence, which nobody would later admit to actually having seen, that they had priority.

Peterson then shifted the discussion to the issue of economic development. He was out to assure that any economic benefits accrued by the technology of cold fusion would go to the state and the university. He had already arranged with Pons and Fleischmann that royalties would be split, one third to the two chemists, one third to the university, and one third, up to a preset limit, to the chemistry department. Now he wanted to assure that there would be royalties, that if cold fusion blossomed into a viable energy source, it would happen in Utah and not Silicon Valley or Japan.

Pons and Fleischmann now explained the status of the BYU cold fusion research. Upon reading their proposal, Steve Jones had obviously made a major shift in the emphasis of his research. They believed that his electrolysis experiments from 1986 were just one of many approaches he had tried, and that they hadn't panned out. They considered meaningless Jones's notarized lab book page—the one on which he had set down his ideas of cold fusion. They were idle scribblings. Yes, Jones had mentioned palladium, but not in any specific context, and he had never gotten around to using palladium electrodes, or at least not until after reading their proposal, which coincided with his return to the electrolysis experiments.

The two chemists said they believed that Ryszard Gajewski was responsible for initiating the dispute, and thus their present troubles. The way they had come to see it, Gajewski had been funding Jones to the tune of a few million dollars over six years and had nothing to show for it. Suddenly they appeared with a startling idea of great promise, one that would certainly justify substantial federal funding if it panned out. And, equally suddenly, Gajewski began to stall. Their funding seemed to be contingent on a collaboration with Jones. They believed that Gajewski was trying to validate somehow all that muon-catalyzed fusion money by linking it to their cold fusion. They had used their connections at the Department of Energy to check Jones's funding history, and what they had found was all muon-catalyzed fusion. They had looked up his various publications and found only that one insignificant paper on piezonuclear fusion.

Pons and Fleischmann's most important conclusion was that, like Peterson, they could not trust Jones's "naïveté." ("Naïveté," Peterson later remarked, "is one way of saying it. There are other ways of saying it.")

Peterson's congregation then decided that they owed Jones and BYU nothing. They believed that they had developed their technology independent of Jones, and they could let history, the peer review process, or the patent board determine whether Jones had taken anything from them.

Norm Brown described it as a case of apples and oranges. "We could let Jones do his thing," Brown said, "and we would do ours, as long as we did ours first. Then Jones could say, 'Yeah, me too.' Or he could say, 'Well, I found out this other interesting thing,' which is what he ended up doing. It could hurt us, on the other hand, if we say, 'Yes, Jones invented the same thing,' which is what is implied by having back-to-back publications. So we ended up thinking that we would be legitimizing Jones, building a mountain out of a molehill, if we did that."

Peterson apparently did suggest momentarily that he call Jeffrey Holland at BYU just to inform him that they were not going to abide by their agreement, but he was quickly convinced that that was not a wise idea. If he gave Holland five days' notice, or even two days', BYU might go public immediately. That was a risk they wouldn't take, so there would be no communication with BYU.

As long as the Utah patents were on file—Dehlinger had filed one on March 13 and would have a second filed by the twenty-first—they would retain domestic rights to cold fusion even if Jones announced first.

In the United States, patent rights go to the first to invent, which is to say the person who can establish the earliest date for a working prototype of the device in question. In the event of a public disclosure, anyone believing he or she has a claim to the patent has one year from that moment to file. In all foreign nations, however, with the exception of Australia and Canada, the patent goes to the first to file. Once the invention is disclosed publicly, no patents will be awarded. Thus, any hold on the foreign rights would be lost the instant Jones made his disclosure.

Public disclosure has a relatively wide definition: writing up the invention in a company newsletter, for instance; discussing the technology with anyone not party to a secrecy agreement; or releasing any information that would allow an expert to reproduce the invention might constitute public disclosure.

The abstract that Jones had submitted to the American Physical Society, even with two meager sentences on cold fusion, might constitute a public disclosure once it appeared in print. It was scheduled for the first week of April. That became the deadline for whatever had to be done, which gave the U roughly three weeks. The option of having Pons unveil cold fusion at the American Chemical Society meeting in the second week of April was no longer viable. Jones's APS abstract would appear a week before the meeting.

Peterson, Pons, and Fleischmann had bandied about the idea of throwing a press conference since the BYU summit meeting. The two chemists had already discussed the situation with Roger Parsons and Ron Fawcett, the editors of the *Journal of Electroanalytical Chemistry*, and had received their assurance that a press conference would not jeopardize the publication of their paper. (In fact, *JEAC*'s decision to publish was somehow treated as justification for the announcement. That the paper would not be peer-reviewed, but rather accepted on the strength of Parsons's judgment alone, was considered a trivial technicality.)[2]

Initially it was Peterson who suggested the public announcement, but the three lawyers apparently embraced its wisdom. Dehlinger later supposed that the decision might have gone the same way even if everyone but Peterson had been against a press conference. But such was not the case. "The fact is," Dehlinger said, "the three lawyers were arguing that there is no second place in this kind of business. Either you're there first or no one remembers you. Gary Triggs was particularly adamant because he is such a fanatic believer in Stan that he was the most upset at the idea of sharing this with Steve Jones."

Dehlinger concluded, "We all, I think, supported and were trying to overcome the resistance of Stan and Martin."

Pons seemed most concerned with the logistics problem at hand. How would they write the *Nature* paper, finish the *JEAC* paper, prepare a press release, and complete the necessary research, all in one week? But he agreed to go along with a public announcement. He trusted Triggs, perhaps even as much as he trusted Fleischmann. As Dehlinger recalled it, "Gary Triggs never doubted the science. And with that position he also never doubted that this was one of the great scientific breakthroughs of the twentieth century, and his friend Pons was going to get credit only if he was bold, and he was certainly pushing Pons to be as bold as possible." Norm Brown later observed that the relationship between Pons and Triggs transcended that of lawyer and client. "Stan relied on Triggs a lot," Brown said. "Pons looks to him for advice, and so,

---

2. Another justification for the announcement, according to Norm Brown, was that DOE was ready to fund the work. This was perceived as "a form of scientific endorsement." Of course, DOE had decided to support cold fusion on the strength of Steve Jones's begrudging recommendation and ambiguous confirmation.

de facto, if Pons wasn't satisfied, the university had a problem, and if Triggs wasn't satisfied, Pons wasn't satisfied."

Dehlinger's recollection of the meeting also had Fleischmann "almost in tears" as the consensus finally emerged that they would call a press conference. This contradicts Peterson, who later said he would never have gone on with the announcement had Fleischmann been so noticeably against it. Maybe so.

Either way, Fleischmann certainly was the most prescient about the ugliness of the deluge that would follow a news conference. And afterward it was Fleischmann who would lay the entire responsibility for the decision and the subsequent circus on the U administration. "That was the decision of the university," he said. "You can read into that anything you want." Nonetheless, at that point, Pons and Fleischmann still could have put a stop to the affair. They did not.

The administrators and lawyers had only to worry about whether Pons and Fleischmann were correct in their interpretation of their experiment. Peterson later said that he believed in cold fusion, to the extent that he did, because Pons and Fleischmann were "very competent electrochemists. They say that they've got something that cannot be explained by a chemical reaction. Well, these guys ought to know what a chemical reaction is." He also believed because Jim Brophy believed it unconditionally, and Brophy had been trained as a physicist. And Peterson was impressed with Fleischmann's brilliance, as was everyone else. Although Fleischmann was not a physicist, he appeared to have a deep understanding of the field.

It was the account of the explosion, however, the famous meltdown, more than anything that convinced the lawyers and administrators. All the other evidence of nuclear fusion—heat, neutrons, gamma rays, and tritium—paled next to the tangibility of the explosion. "Frankly," said Dehlinger, the biophysicist turned patent attorney, "if there was one thing that made me feel good and think that there is something there, it was the explosion. Yes, it can be chemical, but that didn't seem likely. Something pretty significant in terms of heat generation must have been happening. It was the anchor which many of us were using. Whenever you're doing science, lots of things can go wrong and get in the way of reproducibility. We took comfort in the few events which seemed spectacular."

In a sense, Peterson and his congregation ultimately believed in cold fusion because it was too big to question. It was Pascal's wager. "If there is any merit to this," Peterson said later, "can we afford to let it go the way of classical, normative science, that is, a very dignified, reserved announcement, a very slow and methodical process of development and substantiation?" The answer was no.

One final consideration still might have prevented a press conference, however. Brown suggested that before going public they give serious thought to the political implications of their announcement. Pons and Fleischmann, after all, were claiming that it would be possible to build nuclear weapons with the technology. Brown observed that should this be the case, as with Pandora, there'd be no going back once they opened the box. "What if this gives Qaddafi the ability to make a nuclear bomb for fifty dollars?" asked Brown. "Is this something that we really want to do without thinking about it ahead of time?"

This was somehow too profound to contemplate in the short time they had, so it was ignored. Brown recalled that Peterson and the others gave it a few seconds' thought and in effect said, "Okay, now we've thought about it, let's throw a press conference."

As the meeting concluded, Pam Fogle, the university's news director, was called in to discuss how to handle the press. She was informed that her office could interview

Pons and Fleischmann the following day, which was Friday the seventeenth; then she would have the weekend to write a press release. It would have to be ready by Monday so that the scientists, lawyers, and administrators could review the draft. Be careful, Fogle was told, that no drafts of the press release fall "into the wrong hands." It sounded like a spy novel.

Fogle said the determination was made then to schedule the public announcement tentatively for March 23, one week later. Once they had committed themselves, secrecy became a greater concern than the validity of the science. Peterson, for instance, chose not to consult any of the physicists on campus. He feared they might leak news of the "F-word" to the outside world, or even leak word of the press conference to Jones. He also believed his chemistry department was the "more prestigious department." Thus, employing logic that seems dangerously specious, Peterson concluded that his prestigious chemists did not need assistance from physicists to solve a physics problem.

Peterson did seek advice from Hans Bethe, one of the legendary figures in nuclear physics. Bethe, who was eighty-two years old, still taught quantum physics at Cornell. Physicists liked to say that taking quantum mechanics from Bethe was like taking Russian literature from Tolstoy. (Peterson and Bethe were distantly related through their children's marriages. Bethe's daughter-in-law had a brother who was married to Peterson's daughter.) Peterson phoned Bethe and told him that Pons and Fleischmann had observed electrochemically induced cold fusion.

Bethe replied that this sounded very unlikely.

Then Peterson said that physicists at Brigham Young University were also claiming cold fusion and were going to publish a paper. He didn't want his university left out.

"Let BYU publish alone," Bethe said. "Let them make fools of themselves."

Peterson ignored the advice, apparently because it was not what he wanted to hear. And Bethe wasn't swayed by the persuasiveness of Pascal's wager. Indeed, as far as the wager went, to sit quietly and let Jones and BYU publicly announce the discovery of cold fusion was, in effect, to bet that cold fusion did not exist. Bethe, with his deep understanding of canonical nuclear physics, might be able to do that. Peterson could not.[3]

Peterson spent March 20 in Washington on business unrelated to cold fusion. He flew back to Utah the next day. On the flight were two Utah physicists, Pierre Sokolsky and Michael Salamon, who had been visiting their benefactors at the Department of Energy. Half of the remaining passengers, or so it seemed, were adolescent girls returning from a Washington field trip. Sokolsky and Salamon escaped their chatter by hiding in the galley.

Peterson also fled to the galley. After some brief small talk, Peterson told the two physicists that he'd been doing some reading, and he'd like to know what they could tell him about muon-catalyzed physics. Salamon and Sokolsky were astonished. Muon-catalyzed fusion was esoteric even within the refined field of nuclear physics. It was certainly not a subject that they would have expected to pique the interest of a man of Chase Peterson's medical and administrative background. In fact, the two physicists had never given it much thought themselves, although as physicists they knew of it and could explain it, which they did.

3. Six months later, Carlton Detar, a Utah physicist, observed that the only two scientists to whom Peterson went for advice were Bethe and Jim Brophy. "What I say to that," Detar said, "is if you want good advice, you should talk to someone who is both an expert and has access to the information. What Peterson did was pick one of each." This was unfair only in that Bethe happened to be dead right anyway.

For the better part of an hour, Peterson interrogated the two on various fusion mechanisms, using correctly all the technical jargon. Later Salamon and Sokolsky recalled that Peterson never explained the motivation for his curiosity. Nonetheless, their opinion of Peterson, which had not been high, skyrocketed.

On March 21, Dave Williams at Harwell faxed a succinct message to Martin Fleischmann in Utah:

5 days now & no neutrons. Any suggestions?

Fleischmann called Williams and told him they could not sit on cold fusion much longer. Now, however, Fleischmann was optimistic. He said he was confident that he had counted neutrons, having detected apparently three times as many coming from the vicinity of the fusion cells as from the background. Although this was not the billionfold or trillionfold increase predicted by nuclear physics, it sounded convincing to Williams. (But Williams later admitted, "I don't know anything about neutron counting.")

Fleischmann also said that they had been detecting gamma rays from a cell with an eight-millimeter palladium electrode but that these rays had vanished. They did, however, seem to be registering a very definite gamma ray signal from a cell with a four-millimeter electrode. "And so he concluded," Williams recalled, "that the eight-millimeter rod had died. Therefore there was a possibility that the experiment could die, or maybe not even work. So he knew at that time that the thing was irreproducible."

The effect may simply have required a fine tuning of the cells that was hit-or-miss. Some cells worked and some didn't. Williams had his five-day-old cells removed from the neutron counter at Harwell and three new cells inserted.

That same day, Pons telephoned Steve Jones, wanting to know if he still planned to publish his paper.[4] Jones said it was almost written, and they were committed because of the APS meeting. The two then agreed that they would rendezvous to send off the papers at the Federal Express office at the Salt Lake City Airport, at 2:00 P.M. on March 24. Fleischmann was returning to England that day, and it would also be the day after the Utah press conference.

Jones noted in his lab book that when he asked Pons if the Utah cold fusion paper might be submitted early, "e.g. by Fleischman [sic], he said no." So Jones was suspicious. He simply had not asked the right question.

On the morning of March 22, Pam Fogle began alerting the local and national press to the coming news conference. Once she called Jerry Bishop of The Wall Street Journal, the story began to leak, as the administration had feared. Bishop was a ponytailed Texan whose working wardrobe ran to cowboy boots and blue jeans and who did not look like a reporter for the country's preeminent conservative business paper. But he had been a science reporter for three decades. When Fogle told him that Utah had sustained a nuclear fusion reaction at room temperature for one hundred days, Bishop refused to believe her.

After talking to Fogle, Bishop went to lunch with a freelance science writer who was connected with the Council for the Advancement of Science Writing. Bishop described the call, and the friend reminded him of a recent meeting at which a physicist from Utah had discussed

4. The source is Paul Palmer.

some kind of strange fusion. Bishop went back to his office, checked through his files, and found a copy of a Steve Jones paper on muon-catalyzed fusion. Bishop called BYU, managed to reach Paul Palmer, and asked what the story was with the University of Utah announcement. "All we can say is our results don't confirm theirs," Palmer told him.

From that moment, Bishop knew he had a story. His story in the *Journal* the next morning reported that a new fusion breakthrough would be unveiled and speculated that it would show "that hydrogen atoms can be forced to fuse together inside of a solid material." Bishop reviewed Jones's previous work in muon-catalyzed fusion and noted that both the University of Utah and BYU had simultaneously submitted papers to *Nature*.*

As it turned out, the *Financial Times* of London beat Bishop to the story. It seems Fleischmann had gone to an old friend at Southampton, Richard Cookson, a retired chemistry professor, to get advice on giving the story to the British press. Cookson put Fleischmann in touch with his son Clive, who was a reporter at the *Financial Times*.

Young Cookson had explained to Fleischmann that the *Financial Times* would not be published on March 24 because it was Good Friday. If Fleischmann wanted the British press to get the story before the long weekend, he would have to let them publish it on Thursday, the day of the press conference. Fleischmann apparently talked it over with Pons and maybe Brophy, then gave his permission and the necessary information.

Harwell physicist Ron Bullough suggested that Fleischmann's act was motivated by national concern. "Since he's a true Brit," said Bullough, "he felt he had to do that. I think he was using Cookson to warn the establishment

---

*Actually, that had not yet happened and was looking less and less likely.

and the government that all hell was about to break loose."[5]

With Cookson and Bishop working the story on Wednesday morning, the news immediately got back to BYU. Like all rumors, the story appears to have evolved spontaneously as it spread. Bishop apparently tracked Jones back to Gajewski, whom he called to find out what he knew about the Utah press conference. That prompted Gajewski to call Jones and tell him that "all hell has broken loose" at the Department of Energy.

As Gajewski heard it, apparently misunderstanding Bishop, the University of Utah had a press release that claimed heat production by cold fusion, while simultaneously claiming that a reviewer of the proposal confirmed the result. Jones, of course, was outraged. "Baloney!" he scrawled in his lab book:

And why should they announce our unpublished results to the press? Press release also flies in face of our agreements not to speak of results publicly until papers back-to-back were in (Friday 3/24/89).

Before the day was out, Jones also received calls from the *Financial Times*, to confirm that he had confirmed Utah, and from a broker in Boston, who apparently

5. On Wednesday afternoon Pam Fogle also called Ed Yeates, who reported on science for the CBS affiliate in Salt Lake City. Fogle said there was a major press conference the next day, and if ever Yeates should go to a press conference this was it. She told Yeates that it would involve a new, revolutionary kind of fusion, but that was all she would say. Yeates immediately began calling physicists he knew at Los Alamos. Two were already familiar with the story, which indicates how fast the word was leaking. Yeates told one "that there was a major news conference that was going to drop a bombshell." This physicist then called around until he could give Yeates all the pertinent details. Then Yeates called Fogle and asked for permission to break the embargo. After all, he said, "the word is out; you can't keep a lid on this." Fogle gave Yeates her sanction, and he ran the story Wednesday night on the local news. So Yeates was first.

wanted to know if they really used palladium, in which case should he buy futures?

As the reports of BYU's confirmation escalated, Grant Mason, dean of the College of Physical and Mathematical Sciences at BYU, left a message for Paul Richards, the university's public communications director:

> Apparently the U of U has released a story to the press indicating that BYU backs up or supports some research they are doing on cold fusion. [Mason] is concerned that this could be quite sensational since we do not in fact support their conclusions. We need to know if the press release went out and exactly what it said, and he also wants to prepare a statement as a disclaimer.

Richards called Ray Haeckel, his opposite number at the University of Utah, and Haeckel read him a copy of the press release, which made no mention of any confirmation whatsoever. "I can't imagine how you have this," Haeckel said, "because we haven't even sent it out yet. We're not going to send it out until tonight."

Richards reported back to Mason, who promptly phoned Jim Brophy. Brophy also insisted that Utah hadn't issued any press release, which was still true. They had been working on a draft, Brophy said, and they had been very careful not to mention BYU at all.

"But people are quoting us," Mason said. "They've got something."

"If you find out where it came from," said Brophy, "let me know. Because I don't know where."

Mason then warned Brophy that should Utah hold a press conference, the BYU administration would consider it "a stab in the back."

The phone calls continued through the afternoon.

Steve Jones called Joe Ballif with the news that Pons and Fleischmann might be holding a press conference. Ballif refused to believe it: a Utah press conference constituted betrayal of a magnitude he simply could not accept. He had Chase Peterson pulled out of a meeting to take his call. He said that he'd heard a rumor of a press conference, which must not be true. And Peterson replied, "We have talked about that, yes. We intended to make some kind of announcement." Peterson went on to say that he'd never been satisfied with the outcome of the meeting in Provo. He said he'd call Ballif back, which he never did.

The announcement was made the following day in the main foyer of the Henry B. Eyring Chemistry Building on the Utah campus. The available seating space was quickly taken by press, administrators, students, and curious scientists.

Marvin Hawkins attended the press conference with his wife, his father, and his in-laws, and managed to find seats three rows back. Fleischmann had warned him that their lives would never be the same after they went public and that the activity unleashed would be astounding. Hawkins thought he was prepared for the worst. He would say later that he knew that something ugly was going to happen. Still, he added, "in my wildest imaginations, I never expected what happened."

7

JOHN SEABROOK

E-Mail from Bill

The New Yorker,
January 10, 1994

Virtually every major general interest and science magazine has run a recent feature article on E-mail and its information networks. People either love it or hate it, but they're all talking about a technology many scientists have been addicted to for years. About the same time E-mail took hold of the popular imagination, New Yorker writer John Seabrook was making a breakthrough in his distinctive style of science writing—a kind of rumination out loud with all the formality, daring, and tentative testing of ideas that occurs in an E-mail correspondence. In "E-Mail from Bill" Seabrook not only chronicles the Henry Ford of our time, Bill Gates, but also makes a pitch to become one of the first literary stylists of the new underground technology.

Seabrook's previous science feature for The New Yorker *chronicled another cutting edge industry—biotechnology. In charting the development of a new supermarket tomato, Seabrook uncovered a key to his style when he penciled in a paragraph after the article was in galley stage. In it he spoke of his upbringing in the tomato farm town of Salem, New Jersey, and of the pervasive influence of tomatoes on economic life there. "It's important in science writing to re-*

create the reasons for your interest and the process of your learning," says Seabrook. "It surprised me that those parts attracted the most comment from scientists and readers."

A staff writer at The New Yorker for the past two years, Seabrook is one of the few science writers today who puts himself into his stories. It's a dangerous device. "You're walking a fine line," Seabrook says of a practice inherited from the new journalism, which often descends into an "I discover molecules" mode of writing when applied by lesser talents. "I like taking that risk," he says.

Born in 1959, Seabrook received a B.A. in English at Princeton, where he studied under John McPhee, who modeled the "extraordinary work ethic involved in literary science writing." After getting a master's in literature at Oxford University, where he wrote his thesis on T. S. Eliot, Seabrook came to write for Manhattan, Inc. in the mid-1980s and freelanced for The New Yorker before being hired there. "I learned how to write from doing the old Talk of the Town pieces, when you had nine thousand words and a subject and had to achieve some sort of closure."

"E-Mail from Bill" is composed of a number of such subsections—each profiling another element in the complex personality and world of Bill Gates. Citing an interview technique he learned from the filmmaker Errol Morris (The Thin Blue Line and A Brief History of Time), Seabrook tends to tell his subjects what he's thinking about and then let them do all the talking. That method was particularly effective in "E-Mail from Bill," which resulted in a flood of E-mail for its author and a whole new experience, being "flamed"—receiving hate mail via the new communications technology.

AT THE MOMENT, THE BEST WAY TO COMMUNI-cate with another person on the information highway is to exchange electronic mail: to write a message on a computer and send it through the telephone lines into someone else's computer. In the future, people will send each other sound and pictures as well as text, and do it in real time, and improved technology will make it possible to have rich, human electronic exchanges, but at present E-mail is the closest thing we have to that. Even now, E-mail allows you to meet and communicate with people in a way that would be impossible on the phone, through the regular mail, or face to face, as I discovered while I was working on this story. Sitting at my computer one day, I realized that I could try to communicate with Bill Gates, the chairman and co-founder of the software giant Microsoft, on the information highway. At least, I could send E-mail to his electronic address, which is widely available, not tell anyone at Microsoft I was doing it, and see what happened. I wrote:

> Dear Bill,
> I am the guy who is writing the article about you for The New Yorker. It occurs to me that we ought to be able to do some of the work through e-mail. Which raises this fascinating question—What kind of understanding of another person can e-mail give you? . . .
> You could begin by telling me what you think is unique about e-mail as a form of communication.
>
> John

I hit "return," and the computer said, "mail sent." I walked out to the kitchen to get a drink of water and played with the cat for a while, then came back and sat at my computer. Thinking that I was probably wasting money, I nevertheless logged on again and entered my password. "You have mail," the computer said.

I typed "get mail," and the computer got the following:

From: Bill Gates <billg@microsoft.com>
Ok, let me know if you get this email.

According to my computer, eighteen minutes had passed between the time I E-mailed Bill and he E-mailed me back. His message said:

> E-mail is a unique communication vehicle for a lot of reasons. However email is not a substitute for direct interaction. . . .
>
> There are people who I have corresponded with on email for months before actually meeting them—people at work and otherwise. If someone isn't saying something of interest its easier to not respond to their mail than it is not to answer the phone. In fact I give out my home phone number to almost no one but my email address is known very broadly. I am the only person who reads my email so no one has to worry about embarrassing themselves or going around people when they send a message. Our email is completely secure. . . .
>
> Email helps out with other types of communication. It allows you to exchange a lot of information in advance of a meeting and make the meeting far far more valuable. . . .
>
> Email is not a good way to get mad at someone since you can't interact. You can send friendly messages very easily since those are harder to misinterpret.

We began to E-mail each other three or four times a week. I would have a question about something and say to myself, "I'm going to E-mail Bill about that," and I'd write him a message and get a one- or two-page message back within twenty-four hours, sometimes much sooner. At the beginning of our electronic relationship, I would wake up in the middle of the night and lie in bed wondering if I had E-mail from Bill. Generally, he seemed to write messages at night, sleep (maybe), then send them the next morning. We were intimate in a curious way, in the sense of being wired into each other's minds, but our contact was elaborately stylized, like ballroom dancing.

In some ways, my E-mail relationship with Bill was like an ongoing, monthlong conversation, except that there was a pause after each response to think; it was like football players huddling up after each play. There was no beginning or end to Gates' messages—no time wasted on stuff like "Dear" and "Yours"—and I quickly corrected this etiquette breach in my own messages. Nor were there any fifth-grade-composition-book standards like "It may have come to your attention that" and "Looking forward to hearing from you." Social niceties are not what Bill Gates is about. Good spelling is not what Bill Gates is about, either. He never signed his messages to me, but sometimes he put an "&" at the end, which, I learned, means "Write back" in E-mail language. After a while, he stopped putting the "&," but I wrote back anyway. He never addressed me by name. Instead of a letterhead, there was this:

Sender: billg@microsoft.com
Received: from netmail.microsoft.com by dub-img-2.compuserve.com (5.67/5.930129sam) id AA03768; Wed, 6 Oct 93 14:00:51-0400
Received: by netmail.microsoft.com (5.65/25—eef) id AA27745; Fri, 8 Oct 93 10:56:01-0700
Message-Id:
<9310081756.AA27745@netmail.microsoft.com>
X-Msmail-Message-Id: 15305A55
X-Msmail-Conversation-Id: 15305A55
From: Bill Gates <billg@microsoft.com>
To: 73124.1524@CompuServe.COM

For years after the telephone was invented in 1876, people thought it was a device that would transmit news, drama, and music: the idea that the telephone was a way to talk to other people took about twenty years to sink in here, and about thirty years in Europe. Similarly, today one hears about shopping, banking, and renting movies on the information highway. These are all possible ways of making money, of course, but the point of the information highway, it seems to me, is that it offers a new way of talking to other people. The trouble people have understanding this simple point is the same trouble people in the nineteenth century had understanding the telephone.

Bill Gates, aged thirty-eight, is one of the richest men in the country—the richest in 1992, and the second richest, after the investor Warren Buffett, in 1993, with a fortune of six billion one hundred and sixty million dollars, according to *Forbes*. Last March, when he announced his engagement to Melinda French, a twenty-nine-year-old manager at Microsoft, the news made the front page of the *Wall Street Journal*. Gates controls the computer industry to an extent matched by no other person in any other major industry. The Justice Department is currently trying to determine whether his control constitutes a monopoly. Microsoft now supplies eighty per cent of all the personal-computer operating-system software in the world—that is, the layer of software that translates your commands so that the computer can act on them—and fifty per cent of all the application software, which is the tools, like Microsoft Word (writing) and Excel (accounting), that run on top of the operating system. Microsoft uses its leverage in the operating-system market as a competitive advantage in the applications market—a practice that is not nice but is not necessarily illegal. "You could say, as I have said to Bill, that having achieved this much power you should turn your attention to being magnanimous," a rival software executive told me. "But Bill believes that now is not the time for statesmanship. Now is the time to conquer new foes, plunder new lands. He doesn't like being compared to John D. Rockefeller—he goes, 'Hey, I'm not a grasping monopolist, am I?'—but he doesn't know how to behave any other way. To hold war councils and to design strategies with the explicit aim of crushing an opponent—this is very American. You know, Mother Teresa is not going to build the broadband network of the future."

Recently, the wife of a software developer was listening to her husband describe for me what it was like to be in the same industry as Bill Gates: he was saying, in a pained but stoical way, that maybe Gates didn't have to be quite so competitive now that he had achieved great power, and that it might be better for the computer industry as a whole if he behaved in a more benevolent way, when his wife interrupted and said to me, "No. You don't understand. We talk about Bill Gates every night at home. We think about Bill Gates all the time. It's like Bill Gates lives with us." This enveloping sense of Bill Gates is hard for someone outside the computer industry to fathom. To people who are unfamiliar with computers, Gates is just a nerd, and if you try to get them to square the negative connotation of the word "nerd" with Gates' incredible success, and with the fact that, far from being on the margin of society, Gates is now in a position to determine what society is like, they're likely to say, "Well, I guess it really is the revenge of the nerds." Actually, Gates probably represents the end of the word "nerd" as we know it.

But all Gates' influence and success are small potatoes compared with the influence he could have and with the opportunity that now lies before him. The computer, which in twenty-five years has evolved from a room-size mainframe into a laptop device, appears to be turning into a new kind of machine. The new machine will be a communications device that connects people to the information highway. It will penetrate far beyond the fifteen per cent of American households that now own a computer, and it will control, or absorb, other communications machines now in people's homes—the phone, the fax, the television. It will sit in the living room, not in the study. The problem of getting people to feel comfortable with such a powerful machine will be partly solved by putting it inside one of the most unobtrusive objects in the house—the set-top converter, which is the featureless black box on top of a cable-connected TV set (the one the cat likes to sit on if the VCR is occupied).

Gates would like to have his software inside that box. Microsoft's ambition is to supply the standard operating-system software for the information-highway machine, just as it now supplies the standard operating-system software, called Windows, for the personal computer. Microsoft has two billion dollars in cash, and no debt, and is spending a hundred million dollars a year developing software for the new machine, which is a lot more than anyone else is spending. The plan is first to supply the software that allows people to rent videos over the TV and makes home shopping more attractive, and then to use money from the video-rental and home-shopping businesses to pay for the development of the rest of the software. Therefore, Gates is now meeting with people like Mike Ovitz and Barry Diller to discuss better ways of delivering their products into people's homes. "I actually requested a meeting with him," Ovitz told me last October. "I flew up to Seattle and we had dinner together and spent three or four hours just talking about the future."

"Could you say specifically what you talked about?"

"It was just very deep stuff about the future."

"Well, for example, did you talk about information-highway software?"

"It goes much deeper than that."

At Microsoft's main office, in Redmond, a suburb of Seattle, I saw a demo of an early version of the company's operating software for the information-highway machine, in which the user points at the TV screen with a remote control, clicks onto icons, and selects from menus. I heard a lot about "intelligent agents," which will at first be animated characters that occasionally appear in the corner of your TV screen and inform you, for example, that President Aristide is on "Meet the Press," because they know you're interested in Haitian politics, but will eventually be out there on the information highway, filtering the torrent of information roaring along it, picking out books or articles or movies for you, or receiving messages from individuals. As the agents become steadily more intelligent, they will begin to replace more and more of the functions of human intelligent agents—stockbrokers, postal workers, travel agents, librarians, editors, reporters. While I was at Microsoft, I sometimes felt like prey.

Gates' greatest disadvantage in this new market is that Microsoft doesn't own any wires into people's homes, nor does it have the computers installed to handle all the switching and billing that two-way communication requires. To solve this problem, Microsoft needs to make an alliance with a cable company or a telephone company, or both. Microsoft has an alliance with Intel Corporation, the world's leading manufacturer of microprocessors, and General Instrument, a maker of set-top converters, but it is not a very powerful alliance compared with Bell Atlantic's alliance with Tele-Communications, Inc., the largest cable company in the United States, or with U S West's alliance with Time Warner, the second-largest cable company. Gates is currently negotiating an alliance involving Time Warner and Tele-Communications, Inc.—a kind of granddaddy of all alliances, which would have the power to set the standard for the information-highway machine.

A major issue in the negotiations will be the extent to which Microsoft would own the software in the machine. Gates would like to retain the rights to the software; Gerald Levin, the C.E.O. of Time Warner, and John Malone, the C.E.O. of T.C.I., will not want to give Gates those rights.

If Gates does succeed in providing the operating system for the new machine, he will have tremendous influence over the way people communicate with one another: he, more than anyone else, will determine what it is like to use the information highway. His great advantage is that Microsoft knows how to make software. Another advantage Bill Gates has is that he already lives on the information highway.

New employees at Microsoft are likely to encounter Bill Gates electronically long before they meet him in person. Some get to thinking of him by his E-mail handle, which is "billg," rather than by his real name. You'll be chatting with a Microsoft employee in the employee's office, the computer will make a little belch or squeak, indicating an incoming piece of electronic mail, and it'll be E-mail from Bill. It is not unusual to hear a young employee say, "Hey, that's a good idea, I'm going to E-mail Bill about that." While I was attending a lunchtime cookout at Microsoft headquarters one day, I heard several people start conversations by asking about E-mail from Bill: "Did you get mail from Bill today?" "Did you see Bill's mail?" Bill and Melinda were in Africa at the time, touring the valley where the oldest human skeleton, Lucy, was discovered, but I had the sense that he was present, in the network, flying around the Microsoft campus and popping into people's computers.

The Microsoft campus looks like a college campus:

there are playing fields, and employees in T-shirts and jeans who aren't much older than college students. Nowhere on earth do more millionaires and billionaires go to work every day than do so here—about twenty-two hundred of the fifteen thousand employees own at least a million dollars' worth of Microsoft stock—but the campus is in no respect worldly. Workers spend much of their day staring into large computer monitors and occasionally exploding into a rapid fingering of keys. Empty soda cans and cardboard latte cups collect on their desks. Designing software—or "writing code," as people in the trade say—is a sort of intellectual handiwork. Operating systems, the most monumental of all software constructions, are like medieval cathedrals: thousands of laborers toil for years on small parts of them, each one working by hand, fashioning zeroes and ones into patterns that control switches inside microprocessors, which constitute the brains of a computer. The platonic nature of software—it is invisible, weightless, and odorless; it doesn't exist in the physical world—determines much of the culture that surrounds it. At Microsoft, workers often describe each other as "smart" or "supersmart" or "one of the smartest people you'll meet around here," and it is almost an article of faith that Bill Gates, who co-founded the company with Paul Allen, a friend from his high-school days, in 1975, when he was nineteen years old, is the smartest person of all. "Bill is just smarter than everyone else," Mike Maples, an executive vice-president of Microsoft, says. "There are probably more smart people per square foot right here than anywhere else in the world, but Bill is just smarter."

Gates' office is exactly twice as large as the offices of junior employees, and his carpeting is a little richer than the carpeting in other offices; otherwise, there is nothing fancy about the place. A large monitor sits on his desk, and on the wall behind the desk are pictures from important moments in Gates' career, many of which coincide with important moments in the history of the personal computer. There are also pictures of Gates' two sisters, and of his mother and father. (No picture of Melinda French is visible, partly because Gates wants to keep her job as normal as he can.) As in all the Microsoft offices, one rarely hears the sound of a ringing phone. The employees send a total of two hundred million E-mail messages to each other every month. (Over at McCaw Cellular Communications, another prominent high-tech company, whose headquarters is a few miles from Microsoft's, phones ring all the time, and everyone wears a beeper.) Gates spends at least two hours a day at his desk staring into his monitor, reading and writing E-mail. E-mail allows Gates to run the company in his head, in a sense. While he is working, he rocks. Whether he is in business meetings, on airplanes, or listening to a speech, his upper body rocks down to an almost forty-five-degree angle, rocks back up, rocks down again. His elbows are often folded together, resting in his crotch. He rocks at different levels of intensity according to his mood. Sometimes people who are in the meetings begin to rock with him. "I think it's just excess energy," Gates said to me about his rocking. "I should stop, but I haven't yet. They claim I started at an extremely young age. I had a rocking horse and they used to put me to sleep on my rocking horse, and I think that addicted me."

Gates does not have the physical charisma of, say, Steve Jobs, the co-founder of Apple Computer. Like Lenin, Gates leads by sheer force of intellect. He looks like a teen-ager, but not because he actually looks younger than thirty-eight. In some ways, he looks older—a very old little boy. It is the oddly undeveloped quality in his pale, freckled face that makes him seem boyish. His hair is brown and is almost always uncombed. He has heavy lips, which contort into odd shapes when he talks. His characteristic pose when he is standing is pelvis pushed forward slightly, one arm wrapped around his body, the other arm occasionally going up into the air as he talks—kind of flying up, almost spastically, with the palm outstretched, then settling again somewhere on his chest. His voice is toneless, with a somewhat weary note of enthusiasm permanently etched into it, and his vocabulary is bland: "stuff" is "cool," "neat," "crummy," "super," "supercool."

When Gates was in his twenties, his mother color-coordinated his clothes—he had green days, beige days, blue days—and then the job was taken over by girlfriends, and now it will presumably fall to his wife, but so far no one has really handled the task successfully. "A lot of his friends have said, 'Bill, come on, let's go on a shopping spree, we'll buy you some clothes,' but it never works," Ann Winblad, who is now a highly respected venture capitalist in Silicon Valley, and was the woman in Bill's life for five years, told me. "Bill just doesn't think about clothes. And his hygiene is not good. And his glasses—how can he see out of them? But Bill's attitude is: I'm in this pure mind state, and clothes and hygiene are last on the list." Esther Dyson, who edits a computer-industry newletter called *Release 1.0.*, says, "I'm told that within Microsoft certain people are allowed to take Bill's glasses off and wipe them, but I've never done it. You know, it's like—'Don't try this at home.'"

Gates is famously confrontational. If he strongly disagrees with what you're saying, he is in the habit of blurting out, "That's the stupidest fucking thing I've ever heard!" People tell stories of Gates spraying saliva into the face of some hapless employee as he yells, "This stuff isn't hard! I could do this stuff in a weekend!" What you're supposed to do in a situation like this, as in encounters with grizzly bears, is stand your ground: if you flee, the bear will think you're game and will pursue you, and you can't outrun a bear. I had a chance to try this approach one day in Gates' office, when I made a remark to him about Microsoft's antitrust problems, and he got mad at me. I had mentioned the theory that Anne Bingaman, who is the head of the Antitrust Division of the Department of Justice, would not have taken the highly unusual and public action of requesting the Microsoft file from the Federal Trade Commission, which had pursued a three-year investigation of Microsoft, if she had not felt she could make a good case against the company. (In the end, the F.T.C. did not file any charges.) All the soft planes in Gates' face contorted into an expression of pure sarcasm. "I think you're a little *confused*," he said. "You're saying that before they read even a single piece of paper they judge what kind of case they have?" He choked slightly on his disgust for my stupidity. "I think you're confused," he said again. "The Justice Department *chose* to get the information to *decide* what to do. Saying they have a pretty good case before they've read anything—is that how these things work?" Going by the book, I answered that someone at the F.T.C. could have *told* someone in the Justice Department that the case against Microsoft was strong. This seemed to make the situation worse. "Look," Gates said. "The Department of Justice is looking at these files. You know? It's *justice?* You're supposed to have *facts* before you decide things?" I felt a trickle of sweat run down my back.

All the executives directly under Gates are male, and almost all are in their mid-thirties. Nathan Mhyrvold, thirty-four, who as a graduate student at Cambridge University interpreted for Stephen Hawking, is in charge of new technology. Steve Ballmer, thirty-seven, who is Gates' best friend, runs the numbers side of the business. He and Gates met during freshman year at Harvard, when they lived down the hall from each other. Cramming together for an advanced-economics exam was a determining event in their relationship. Ballmer acted this scene out for me, pacing around the room, waving his arms, the shirttail of his oxford shirt poking out of his khakis, as he cried, " 'Yes! We're golden! We're going to pass! No! Shit! We're screwed! We're going to fail! No! Yes! We're golden! We're screwed!' We'd get real up or real down, and it's still that way. We love to get up and down."

Ballmer is the reason Gates always flies coach when he is travelling on business. "If you're going to work for this company," Ballmer told me, "you're going to rent a certain kind of car and stay in a certain kind of hotel and fly coach, because that's business, and anything else is just aggrandizement." Gates once chartered a plane because he had to get somewhere in a hurry, but Ballmer gave him so much grief that Gates is still explaining why he did it. Experienced fliers into and out of Seattle know to scan the cabin for a man with a blanket over his head—that's Bill Gates, taking a nap.

Because Bill Gates was my first E-mail relationship, I wasn't always sure how to comport myself electronically, and occasionally I solicited advice from experienced E-mailers. Once, while I was questioning a media analyst named Mark Stahlman about a point of E-mail etiquette, he said to me, "Well, hey, you're not a digital guy!" This line often popped into my head when I was E-mailing Bill. Was I behaving like a digital guy? Is digital guyhood what nerds will molt into when the information highway reaches everyone's door? One evening, I was at home listening to some music, doing this geeky dance I do and, as usual, wondering whether the Wall Street types across the street were watching me, when I suddenly thought, Would Bill Gates care about those guys? I took this as a sign I was becoming a digital guy. Around the same time, I read an essay in *Wired* magazine by Paul Saffo, who is a director of the Institute for the Future, a think tank in Menlo Park, which argued that the information highway is going to cause a flowering of personal expression not seen in our society since the sixties, and that when this happens (maybe in five years) people whom we now think of as computer nerds will have the same hipness that in retrospect we now assign to beatniks.

I wrote Gates a message with the title "How does the future make you feel?" (Putting a title on messages is one of the different things about E-mail communication. It is a little like writing a publicity release for what you have to say. However, it does focus the message.)

> How does the rapid change in the power of microprocessors make you feel? The certainty that microprocessors will grow twice as fast every eighteen months and that nothing in Nature, no fire or earthquake or tidal wave, is powerful enough to stop this from happening. Are you thrilled by this? Do you think that this power is God, as you understand God? Is it possible this power could be bad?

Gates wrote back:

> Feelings are pretty personal. I love coming up with new ideas or seeing in advance what is going to count and then making it happen. I love working with smart people. . . . Our business is very very competitive — one or two false moves and you can fall behind in a way that would wipe you out. Market share does not give you the right to relax. IBM is the best example of this. This is very scary but also makes it very interesting.
>
> The digital revolution is all about facilitation — creating tools to make things easy. When I was a kid

I was a lot more curious than I am today—perhaps I have lost less curiosity than the average adult but if I had had the information tools we are building today I would know a lot more and not have given up learning some things.

These tools will be really cool. Say today you want to meet someone with similar interests to talk or take a trip together or whatever? Its hard and somewhat random. Say you want to make sure you pick a good doctor or read a good book? We can make all of these things work so well—its empowering stuff.

Enough for now.

I wrote a message titled "TV as the Opium of the People":

Some people are afraid of interactive TV. TV is a drug, goes the argument, and the technology that Microsoft and others are supplying is going to make the drug stronger. People will be inside more than ever, cut off from their neighbors, watching interactive monster truck contests. Or porno. They will pile up large cable and credit card charges. A "T.S. Eliot wasteland . . . a nation of housebound zombies," as Michael Eisner put it recently in a speech. Do you think this could happen? What difference does it make if you invest smart boxes to deliver dumb programming?

Gates wrote:

Interactive TV is probably a really bad name for the in-home device connected to the information highway.

Lets say I am sitting at home wondering about some new drug that was prescribed to me. Or wanting to ask a question to my children's teacher. Or curious about my social security status. Or wondering about crime in my neighborhood. Or wanting to exchange information with other people thinking about visiting Tanzania. Or wondering if the new lawn mower I want to buy works well and if it's a good price. Or I want to ask people who read a book what they thought of it before I take my time reading it. In all of these cases being able to reach out and communicate by using a messaging or bulletin board type system lets me do something I could never do before. Assume that the infrastructure and device to do this is easy to use and it was funded by the cable or phone company primarily because I like to watch movies and video-conference with my relatives.

All of the above is about how adults will use the system. Kids will use it in ways we can't even imagine.

The opportunity for people to reach out and share is amazing. This doesn't mean you will spend more time inside! It means you will use your time more effectively and get to do the things you like more than in the past as well as doing new things. If you like to get outside you will find out a lot more about the places that are not crowded and find good companions to go with.

The bottom line is that 2 way communication is a very different beast than 1 way communication. In some ways a phone that has an unbelievable directory, lets you talk or send messages to lots of people, and works with text and pictures is a better analogy than TV. The phone did change the world by making it a smaller place. This will be even more dramatic. There will be some secondary effects that people will worry about but they won't be the same as TV. We are involved in creating a new media but it is not up to us to be the censors or referees of this media—it is up to public policy to make those decisions.

Because TV had very few channels the value of TV time was very high so only things of VERY broad interest could be aired on those few channels. The information highway will be the opposite of this—more like the library of congress but with an easy way to find things.

I sometimes felt that this correspondence was a game I was playing with Gates through the computer, or maybe a game I was playing against a computer. What is the right move? What question will get me past the dragon and into the wizard's star chamber, where the rich information is stored? I had no idea where Gates was when he wrote to me, except that once he told me he was on a "think week" at his family's summer place on Hood Canal. I could not tell whether he was impatient or bored with my questions and was merely answering them because it served his interest. Because we couldn't talk at the same time, there was little chance for the conversation to move spontaneously. On the other hand, his answers meant more, in a certain way, being written, than answers I would have received on the phone. I worried that he might think I was being "random" (a big putdown at Microsoft) because I jumped from topic to topic. I sometimes wondered if I was actually communicating with Bill Gates. How hard would it be for an assistant to write these messages? Or for an intelligent agent to do it?

I wrote a message titled "What motivates you?":

> You love to compete, right? Is that where your energy comes from—love of the game? I wonder how it feels to win on your level. How much do you fear losing? How about immortality—being remembered for a thousand years after you're dead—does that excite you? How strong is your desire to improve people's lives (by providing them with better tools for thinking and communicating)? Some driven people are trying to heal a wound or to recover a loss. Is that the case with you?

Gates wrote back:

Its easy to understand why I think I have the best job around because of day to day enjoyment rather than some grand long term deep psychological explanation. It's a lot of fun to work with very smart people in a competitive environment. . . . We get to hire the best people coming out of school and give them challenging jobs. We get to try and figure out how to sell software in every part of the world. Sometimes our ideas work very well and sometimes they work very poorly. As long as we stay in the feedback loop and keep trying its a lot of fun.

It is pretty cool that the products we work on empower individuals and make their jobs more interesting. It helps a lot in inventing new software ideas that I will be one of the users of the software so I can model what's important. . . .

Just thinking of things as winning is a terrible approach. Success comes from focusing in on what you really like and are good at—not challenging every random thing. My original vision of a personal computer on every desk and every home will take more than 15 years to achieve so there will have been more than 30 years since I first got excited about that goal. My work is not like sports where you actually win a game and its over after a short period of time.

Besides a lot of luck, a high energy level and perhaps some IQ I think having an ability to deal with things at a very detailed level and a very broad level and synthesize between them is probably the thing that helps me the most. This allows someone to take deep technical understanding and figure out a business strategy that fits together with it.

It's ridiculous to consider how things will be remembered after you are dead. The pioneers of personal computers including Jobs, Kapor, Lampson, Roberts, Kaye, are all great people but I don't think any of us will merit an entry in a history book.

I don't remember being wounded or losing something big so I don't think that is driving me. I have
wonderful parents and great siblings. I live in the same
neighborhood I grew up in (although I will be moving
across the lake when my new house is done). I can't remember any major disappointments. I did figure out at
one point that if I pursued pure mathematics it would
be hard to make a major contribution and there were
a few girls who turned me down when I asked them
out.

At the end of one message, I wrote:

This reporting via e-mail is really fascinating and I
think you are going to come across in an attractive way,
in case you weren't sure of that.

Gates wrote:

I comb my hair everytime before I send email hoping to appear attractive. I try and use punctuation in a
friendly way also. I send :) and never :(.

I wrote a message asking Gates whether it was possible
that the alliance with Time Warner and T.C.I. was on
shaky ground because Gerald Levin and John Malone
were afraid that Gates was too smart for them.
Gates wrote:

Your mail is the first time I have ever heard anyone
suggest that John Malone and Jerry Levin deserve sympathy. They are both great people. They are both
smarter about deal making than I will ever be. John
and Jerry and I share a vision of what the Information
Highway can become. It's an incredible opportunity for
all 3 companies and we have been spending time dis-

cussing how we might help each other. We don't have anything concrete at this stage although we have developed a high level of trust for each other.

I sent a message asking how much of his money Gates was planning on giving away:

Will there one day be a Gates Foundation, the way we have Rockefeller, Ford, Carnegie Foundations? When? How acutely do you feel a sense of social responsibility? What kinds of philanthropy would you like your money to perform? How do you feel about leaving a lot of money to your kids?

Gates replied:

I think that giving money away takes a lot of effort. Not as much effort as making it but still a lot to do it properly. Therefore when I am old and have time I will put some effort into that. Assuming I still have a lot of money by the time I retire which is certainly no certain thing I will give away well over 90% of it since I don't believe in kids having too much money. I am like my friend Warren Buffett in this respect. I have already done some giving like to UW for a biotechnology department [Gates gave the University of Washington twelve million dollars] and some to Stanford for a computer science building [six million] and some to United Way which I really believe in. I do believe in funding great research so some of my philanthropy will relate to that. Some to human service activities. Some to education. Some to population control efforts if it looks like donations can really help there.

I wrote mail about "The Great Gatsby," which is one of Gates' favorite books. ("The Catcher in the Rye" and "A Separate Peace" are other favorites.) Gates dressed as

Gatsby for his thirtieth birthday, and again for an engagement party that friends and colleagues in Silicon Valley
threw for him and Melinda in September. (Melinda
dressed as Daisy Buchanan.)

Gates wrote:

> Gatsby had a dream and he pursued it not even re-
> ally thinking he might fail or worse that what he
> dreamed of wasn't real. The green light is a symbol of
> his optimism—he had come so far he could hardly fail
> to grasp it. At the end Fitz is reinforcing what a roman-
> tic figure Gatsby is. Its also sort of about America but
> I think of it more in terms of the people.

Once, when I was composing E-mail to Gates on an
airplane, I felt physically closer to him than when I was
composing from home. Perhaps I was thinking of all the
thousands of people who have encountered this remarkable person on airplanes, restlessly wandering the aisles
with his shoes off, or sitting in a seat staring into the
screen of his laptop computer, rocking, writing E-mail
that will be fired into the network when the plane lands
and send hundreds of people at Microsoft scurrying into
action.

Many executives in the telegraph industry, which had
enjoyed control of the communications field since about
1840, believed that the telephone did not present a threat
to their business, because no one would want a communications machine that did not leave a written record of the
conversation, as telegrams did. When William Orton, the
president of Western Union, which was the Microsoft of
its day, was offered the opportunity to buy Alexander Graham Bell's patent on the telephone for a hundred thousand dollars, he is said to have replied, "What use could
this company make of an electric toy?" This remark seems
less dim to me now.

*   *   *

Technological change is not democratic, but if we did have a choice would we vote for a man who sometimes behaves like a ten-year-old boy to be the principal architect of the way we communicate with each other in the future? Or is it Gates' gift that he isn't socialized in a way you'd expect a corporate executive to be? When I was ten, I would sit around with my friends watching it snow, and someone would say, "I wonder what the deepest snowfall ever was," or something like that, and someone else would say, "*Yeah*, it would be *cool* to know that." It seemed that there should be this giant, all-knowing brain, which could answer that kind of question. One of the lessons you learn in becoming an adult is that it doesn't always pay to be curious. Some people learn to avoid curiosity altogether. Gates appears to have completely failed to absorb this lesson. My impression is that he still has the fantasy of the giant, all-knowing brain, and that this is what the information highway means to him. It's a place where curiosity is rewarded.

Not long ago, Paul Saffo, of the Institute for the Future, said to me, "Bill Gates is an introvert. He is not the kind of person you want building the social network of the future." Ann Winblad, Gates' former girlfriend, told me, "People who know Bill know that you have to bring him into a group—say, 'Hey, Bill, tell us the story of such-and-such'—because he doesn't have the social skills to do it on his own. But that doesn't mean he isn't social. Bill is an open, emotional guy—very. He's actually more open with his feelings than most men I know. He is not afraid to express fear, or sadness, but hardly anyone sees that. You can't show that when you're in Bill's position, when everyone is watching your tiniest gesture. It's not good leadership to show weakness." An executive with a leading competitor of Microsoft's says of Gates, "Hey—I think the guy is truly dangerous. Bill is the most surprisingly conscience-free individual I've ever met, and that amount of power in the hands of a guy without a conscience is dangerous. Big Brother did not happen in 1984, but it could happen in 2004. Ask yourself, 'If there was to be a technology-oriented dictator by the year 2004, who would he be? Bill Gates?"

Gates argues that Microsoft has to behave aggressively because of a principle called Moore's Law, which is named after Gordon Moore, one of the founders of the Intel Corporation. Moore's Law is the reason the computer industry is fundamentally different from any other industry in history. It states that microprocessors get twice as powerful, or twice as cheap, every eighteen months. This means that in twenty years what now takes a year of computing will take fifteen minutes. We have no idea what we are going to do with this power, but it will exist whether we want it to or not. No natural calamity or political upheaval short of world-wide anarchy is powerful enough to stop it. Nathan Mhyrvold, of Microsoft, said to me, "Nature has already signed off on this stuff." Moore's Law is the primary reason that all the companies that dominated the computer industry in the nineteen-seventies are now struggling or gone, and the reason that Microsoft, for all its power, could disappear in a decade.

Scott McNealy, the head of Sun Microsystems, which is a leading manufacturer of computer workstations, told me, "I like Bill. Bill is a smart guy. But I think the problem is that Microsoft has caught the bunny. You know, when you go to the dog track they have that mechanical bunny that makes the dogs run? Well, sometimes a dog is so fast he catches the bunny and then the other dogs don't run anymore. That's the situation in the software business today: Bill has caught the bunny. I admire Bill for catching the bunny, but now we can't have a race. He ought to be loosed from the bunny, to give the other dogs a chance." When I ran this statement by Gates, he smiled and said, "What can I say? I want more bunnies."

The argument that Microsoft is shaping up to be the Standard Oil of the Information Age and that the government ought to loose Bill from the bunny before this happens is now being heard within the Department of Justice. As the head of the Department's Antitrust Division, Anne Bingaman is an anti-monopolist, the sort of person who was common around the Justice Department in the nineteen-thirties and forties, and was thoroughly weeded out in the eighties, a period during which the laws on what constitutes a monopoly were relaxed, making it harder for people like Bingaman to operate. Now Bingaman is expected to regain some of the ground lost by the anti-monopolists, and she seems to be using Microsoft as her vehicle. There is substantial political pressure not to prosecute Microsoft. Microsoft is the principal reason that the United States is by far the world leader in software production, an industry that has an unimaginable potential for growth. Also, the government's huge antitrust case against I.B.M., which was filed in 1969 and ended with the government's giving up on it in 1982, distracted and weakened that organization, and helped companies like Microsoft to get the better of it. Some people argue that the computer industry actually wants and needs a monopolistic presence like Microsoft, because such a presence can work to create a standard computer language that other companies can design products for and that the public can use in common. That is the role I.B.M. played, and now that I.B.M. has been dethroned, thanks partly to Microsoft, people expect Microsoft to perform it.

*　　*　　*

One big difference between Gates and other early software entrepreneurs is that, whereas the others were bright kids from middle-class homes who achieved success beyond their expectations, Gates was born to rule. His childhood was emphatically not the stuff of Horatio Alger novels. His father, Bill Gates, Jr., is a well-known corporate lawyer in Seattle and a former president of the Washington State Bar Association, and his mother, Mary Gates, is a former regent at the University of Washington and was on the national board of the United Way and of U S West. Washington State governors and senators were guests at the house when Bill was a boy. At dinner, the parents would lead the children—Bill and his sisters, Kristi and Libby—in discussions of current affairs. The family also played a lot of games and horsed around together. "I really like Bill's family, but it would be nice if you could talk to them once in a while when they weren't in a human pyramid," Ida Cole, a former Microsoft executive, has said. Water-skiing was and remains a passion of Gates': several Seattleites have described for me the experience of coming across the Evergreen Bridge early on a Sunday morning in the summer and seeing Gates' big powerboat on Lake Washington, with Gates' white, toneless body water-skiing behind it and throwing up a big coxcomb of spray. Young Bill was obsessive about improving aspects of himself he didn't like. "He was always upset about his little toe curling in, so he'd work on it. He'd spend time holding it out so he'd have a straight toe," his sister Kristi told Stephen Manes and Paul Andrews, the co-authors of "Gates," a recently published biography. Gates used to try to impress his sisters by jumping out of a trash can, and he still occasionally jumps over his office chair from a standstill. Sometimes, on his way to a business meeting, he suddenly jumps up and tries to touch as high as he can on a wall, or to touch higher than the spot he touched last time, but he says, in "Gates," "I don't jump spontaneously the way I used to, in the early years of the company ... or even in a meeting.... Now the jumping is not that common." However, he has planned a full-size trampoline for a house he is building. In Japan, a comic book about the adventures of a boy modelled on Bill Gates is called "Young Jump."

Gates attended Lakeside School, one of the best private schools in the Seattle area, and there he met Paul Allen, who was three years older. The two began spending a lot of time in the school's computer room. In 1971, when Gates was sixteen, he wrote a program that made it easier for cities to collect traffic statistics. That same year, he and Allen started a company called Traf-o-Data. In the Lakeside yearbook for 1973, Gates' senior year, there is a picture of Gates in the computer room with a stocking cap pulled over his head and lying on a table, over the caption "Who is this man?"

Joseph Weizenbaum, a computer scientist at M.I.T., perhaps overstating the case a little for effect, wrote, in "Computer Power and Human Reason," this early portrait of computer hackers: "Bright young men of disheveled appearance, often with sunken glowing eyes, [who] can be seen sitting at computer consoles ... on which their attention seems to be as riveted as a gambler's on the rolling dice.... They work until they nearly drop, twenty, thirty hours at a time. Their food, if they arrange it, is brought to them: coffee, Cokes, sandwiches.... Their rumpled clothes, their unwashed and unshaven faces, and their uncombed hair all testify that they are oblivious to their bodies and to the world in which they move." This description matches Gates' outward appearance, but Gates was different from most hackers in one important respect: Hackers were interested in computers as a hobby, mostly just for fun, whereas Gates always saw computers as a way of making money.

Gates and Allen sometimes talked about how cool it

would be to design the software for the first personal computer, which appeared to be on the horizon, but this was not a serious career goal of Bill's. His father wanted him to become a lawyer. "When I was in college, it was really hard to pick a career, because everything seemed so attractive, and when you had to pick a specific one you had to say no to all the others," Gates told me. "I'd think, Well, if I went to that law firm some partner might not like me, and they might assign me to these crummy cases, and I'd think, Well, *God*, that could be really *crummy*." The question was settled in dramatic fashion in December, 1974, when Allen, who was working in Boston, passed a newsstand in Harvard Square and saw on the cover of *Popular Electronics* a computer called the Altair 8800. The Altair 8800 was the first computer that ordinary electronics hobbyists could afford to buy and that people with reasonable technical knowledge could assemble in their homes. Basically, it was the first personal computer. Allen bought the magazine, rushed over to Gates' dorm, and showed it to him. "Look!" Allen said. "It's going to happen! I told you this was going to happen! And we're going to miss it!"

They called Ed Roberts, the man who created the Altair, and told him that they had written a version of a programming language called BASIC for his computer. That wasn't true. It was an early use of a now common strategy in the computer industry, and at Microsoft in particular: announcing products that don't exist (known in the industry as "vaporware") in order to discourage possible competitors. After talking to Roberts, Bill and Paul went on an eight-week code-writing binge, with Gates writing most of the code, often falling asleep at the keyboard, dreaming in code, waking up, and immediately starting to write code again, with no real transition between dreaming and waking—just code. ("It was the coolest program I ever wrote," Gates later said.) At the end of the eight weeks, Allen flew out to Albuquerque, met with Roberts, loaded the software into the Altair, and typed "PRINT 2 + 2." The Altair spat out "4." The program worked.

By the end of 1975, Gates and Allen had founded a company, Micro-soft, to sell their BASIC. (The hyphen was dropped a few years later.) Now came what is perhaps the pivotal moment in the early history of the software industry. Computer hobbyists who had bought the Altair were dismayed to find that it didn't come with the software to operate it, and were even more dismayed when they learned that they had to buy the software for four hundred and fifty dollars from Micro-soft. At that time, no one thought of software as something you paid for. Software was just rolls of paper tape with the little holes punched in it. A hacker would write a cool piece of software for fun, copy it, and give it away to his friends. Altair owners began to do the same thing with Micro-soft's BASIC. Then, in February of 1976, Gates published "An Open Letter to Hobbyists" in the Altair newsletter, and the letter now stands as a sort of Magna Carta of the software industry—the underpinning of the intellectual-property structure. It stated, "As the majority of hobbyists must be aware, most of you steal your software," and went on to argue that software was just as much a commodity as hardware, because it represented someone's intellectual work, and that the creators of the software should be compensated just as creators of hardware were.

Gates shuttled between Harvard and Albuquerque until the start of his senior year, when he dropped out for good. The business expanded, and he and Allen relocated it to Seattle in 1978. In 1980, I.B.M. approached Gates to write an operating system for the personal computer it was designing, the I.B.M. PC. Gates flew down to Florida to meet the I.B.M. executives working on the project, realized on the way that he had forgotten to bring a tie, and drove around looking for a place to buy one. The I.B.M. executives, who had never laid eyes on Gates, were stunned to see that their prospective partner looked exactly like one of the hackers they were beginning to read about in the press. They told Gates they needed an operating system in three months—an impossibly short time—and Gates accepted the job. Upon returning to Seattle, he bought an operating system called QDOS, which was short for Quick and Dirty Operating System, from another software developer, Seattle Computer, for around seventy-five thousand dollars, renamed it MS-DOS, and, in a three-month code-writing marathon, converted it to I.B.M.'s specifications.

Software is sometimes said to be to the age of information as oil was to the age of the machine. Software is what makes information systems operate. Software is like a natural resource, except that its source is not in the earth but in the human mind: people carry pools of software in their heads. Its lack of physical existence makes its importance easy to underestimate. I.B.M., which was one of the great business organizations in history, and which was perfectly placed to own the personal-computer business, disastrously failed to appreciate the importance of the software Gates designed for it. Because I.B.M. thought that the money was going to be in the hardware, in the computers themselves, it allowed Gates to retain the rights to MS-DOS. During the nineteen-eighties, the PC was cloned by other American manufacturers and by the Japanese, who could make and sell the machines more cheaply than I.B.M. could, but no one knew how to clone MS-DOS, and Bill Gates collected a fee for every PC and every PC clone sold in the world.

Two books about the fall of I.B.M. and Gates' role in it have recently appeared—"Big Blues," by Paul Carroll, and "Computer Wars," by Charles H. Ferguson and Charles R. Morris—and an occasional chill runs up the spine of anyone reading them at the ease with which Gates eviscerated men much older and more experienced than he was. "I kept wanting to say to Cannavino, 'We need a shorthand because these meetings are taking too long,'" Gates says in "Big Blues." James Cannavino was an I.B.M. executive with whom Gates negotiated about operating systems. Cannavino would begin meetings by making small talk about, say, his new car, in a misguided effort to establish some sort of personal rapport with Gates. Also, like many other American corporate executives of his generation, Cannavino would spend a lot of time talking about his company's values. This would drive Gates mad. "Every time you say 'thirteen,' I'll know that what that means is that all you want to do is what the customer wants," Gates says he imagined himself saying to Cannavino. "And for every one of these other gibberish slogans, we can also get little numbers. There are a lot of small integers available. We'll just tighten these meetings up. You know, Cannavino, if you want to talk about how you're going to save the U.S. educational system, okay, we've heard that story. That's a good fifteen-minute one. That can be number eleven." However, Gates managed to swallow these thoughts and let Cannavino talk. "I'm really very good at this stuff," he says. "I know how to be somebody's son. You know, 'Yes, Dad.'"

A prominent software executive told me, "I.B.M. thought they had Gates by the balls. He's just a hacker, they thought. A harmless nerd. What they actually had by the balls was an organism which has been bred for the accumulation of great power and maximum profit, the child of a lawyer, who knew the language of contracts, and who just ripped those I.B.M. guys apart." Another leading executive in the software industry said, "Think of I.B.M. and Microsoft as being a chess game, where Microsoft plays black. So they're at a disadvantage. So they have to set up a trap. Microsoft becomes the only supplier of a commodity that I.B.M. could not produce itself. Having done that, it proceeds to market that asset to weaken its partner's position. It's brilliant!"

Now, thirteen years after that contract, Microsoft is by far the largest software company in the world. It has a market capitalization of twenty-three billion dollars—more than General Motors, Xerox, or I.B.M. To what extent Gates is mainly a product of I.B.M.'s blunder, and therefore a kind of historical accident, and to what extent he is the first person to imagine software as a shrink-wrapped commodity, and is therefore a visionary, is a good question to ask if you are seated next to a computer-industry executive at a dinner party. Although Microsoft continues to manufacture MS-DOS, it has severed most of its ties with I.B.M. The break came over the operating system Windows, which Gates introduced in 1985. (Paul Allen, who had a scary encounter with Hodgkin's disease in 1983, retired, cashed in some of his Microsoft stock, bought the Portland Trail Blazers basketball team, and built a house with a basketball court on the property, where the team could practice. He also provided the funds for a Jimi Hendrix museum in Seattle. Lately, Allen, whose Microsoft stock is now worth $2.9 billion, has been in the news for buying nearly twenty-five per cent of America Online, an information service, and, most recently, for buying eighty per cent of TicketMaster.)

Windows is a graphical user interface, or GUI (computer people pronounce it "gooey"). Instead of operating the computer with keyboard commands, as you do in DOS, in Windows you use a pointing device—a mouse—to access little folders and documents on your electronic desktop. Xerox developed the desktop metaphor in the late seventies, and in the early eighties Apple Computer commercialized it. Gates saw that Apple's GUI was an easier system to use than DOS, and borrowed it. When

Windows first appeared, it was widely viewed as a kludge (an inelegant construction): it was buggy (it had glitches) and was a memory hog (it used up a lot of RAM), and it was generally less elegant than Apple's GUI. But Gates stayed with Windows and kept improving it. Also, whereas Apple chose to keep its software proprietary—it could run only on machines that Apple made—Gates licensed Windows to any computer manufacturer that wanted it, just as he had done with DOS. When Apple realized its mistake—its strategy limited Apple's share of the operating-system market to the number of computers Apple could sell—it sued Microsoft for copyright infringement, but a federal court ruled that "the look and feel" of the desktop metaphor was not covered under Apple's copyright.

It is often said by Gates' detractors that he has never invented anything, and this is true in a sense, but you could say the same thing about Henry Ford. When the Model T appeared, in 1908, it was by no means the best car on the road, but it worked well enough, and it was affordable and easy to produce, and Ford stayed with it. Even today, most users still find Apple's operating system more intuitive than Windows, but, because the market for Windows is so much larger, other software manufacturers are more inclined to make applications for Windows than for Apple's operating system. If there is to be a standard computer language—which from the point of view of the public is greatly desirable—it now appears that Windows will be the one. But Gates has to worry that someone will do to Microsoft what Microsoft did to Apple. Apple is designing a new operating system with I.B.M.; it's code-named Pink, and is expected to appear sometime in 1995.

After a month of E-mail between Gates and me, my hour in his physical presence arrived. As we shook hands, he said, "Hello, I'm Bill Gates," and emitted a low, vaguely embarrassed chuckle. Is this the sound one E-mailer makes to another when they finally meet in real space? I was aware of a feeling of being discovered. In the front part of Gates' office, we sat down at right angles to each other. Gates had on normal-looking clothes—a green shirt with purple stripes, brown pants, black loafers. He rocked throughout our time together. He did not look at me very often but either looked down as he was talking or lifted his eyes above my head to look out the window in the direction of the campus. The angle of the light caused the purple stripes in his shirt to reflect in his glasses, which, in turn, threw an indigo tinge into the dark circles around his eyes.

The emotional boundaries of our encounter seemed to have been much expanded by the E-mail that preceded it: Gates would be angry one minute, almost goofily happy the next. I wondered if he was consciously using our present form of communication to express feelings that E-mail cannot convey. Maybe this is the way lots of people will communicate in the future: meet on the information highway, exchange messages, get to know the lining of each other's mind, then meet face to face. In each other's physical presence, they will be able to eliminate a lot of the polite formalities that clutter people's encounters now, and say what they really mean. If this happens, it will be a good thing about the information highway: electronic communication won't reduce face-to-face communication; instead, it will focus it.

I had been told not to ask Gates about his marriage, because he didn't want to talk about it, but I was emboldened by the familiarity that E-mail had established between us and asked anyway. Gates was silent, rocking gently (I interpreted that as a good sign) and staring down at his shoes. "Well, it's a pretty conventional marriage," he said after a while. "I'm male, and I'm marrying a female.

And there's just two of us. And we plan to have rings on our fingers. And there'll be a minister. Or, actually, a priest, I think. Since I'm marrying a Catholic." He giggled. "Pretty standard stuff. In most dimensions, including this one, I'm just like everybody else. I found a girl and fell in love with her. I'm kind of old." As he talked, he began to make a peculiar *ahhh* sound—a sort of rapturous vocalized pause, with a little shyness in it, as if he were confiding in me.

"Some of your competitors are hoping that marriage is going to make you spend less time in the office," I said.

"Yeah, I think . . . ahhh . . . that's a pretty strange thing. Being married I don't think is that big a change. It did take up a lot of energy and time being single. I think in a way it's more complicated than being married. I mean, marriage has its own complexities, but they're different . . . ahhh . . . and I don't think timewise they're much different. And I've been going out with this person off and on for a number of years, so it's not like the day I get married it will be, like, whoa, wait a minute, she uses curlers to curl her hair, my God!"

Gates and his bride are constructing a thirty-five-million-dollar house on the eastern slope of Lake Washington, just outside Seattle—a series of five pavilions connected by underground passageways, with display screens scattered throughout the rooms and linked to a central data base containing hundreds of thousands of famous works of art in digital form. Gates does not own the art; he owns the right to reproduce the art digitally, and he and his assistants continue to throw museum officials around the world into confusion by offering to buy the digital rights to works in their collections.

"Do you worry that your wealth is going to corrupt you?"

"Absolutely." Gates sat upright and raised his arms in

the air. "Absolutely. Hey. Being in the spotlight is a corrupting thing. Being successful is a corrupting thing. Having lots of money is a corrupting thing. These are very
dangerous things, to be guarded against carefully. And I
think that's very, very hard to do."

"How do you do it?"

"I'm very close to my family. And that's important to
me. It's a very centering thing. I live in the same neighborhood I grew up in. One of my sisters lives there. We get
together as a family a lot. The woman I'm marrying wants
when we have kids to have a normal environment for
them. So we'll mutually brainstorm about how to do the
best we can at that." Gates thought for a while, then said,
"I am a person who is very conscious of, like, why don't I
have a TV in my house? I think TV is great. When I'm in
a hotel room, I sit there and try all these new channels
and see what's going on. I probably stay up too late watching stuff. TV is neat. I don't have a TV at home, because
I would probably watch it, and I prefer to spend that time
thinking—or, mostly, reading. So I'm pretty conscious
about not letting myself get used to certain things."

"So do you consider yourself a puritanical person?"

"Oh, no no no. I'm not a puritan," Gates said. "Hey, if
I was a puritan—" He grinned, apparently mentally flipping through a sequence of unpuritanical acts he had
committed. "O.K., it's a little bit like this. I go to a baseball game, and I'm having a good time, watching the
game, but then I feel myself getting drawn in. I start wondering, Who are these guys? Who are the good ones? How
much are they paid? How are the other teams compared
to this one? How have the rules changed? How do these
guys compare to the guys twenty years ago? It just gets so
interesting. I know if I let myself go to ten games I'd be
addicted, and I'd want to go more. And there's only so
much time in the day. And, frankly, it's easy for me to

get interested in anything. I think, Gosh, am I going to get good at tennis? Well, we got these kayaks recently. I think, you know, Are we going to get into that? I was just in Africa. I think, Should I do my next two or three trips there—there's just so much there—but I'd sort of like to go to China, and actually I think I'll end up doing that for my next big trip, in two or three years. So there's all these choices, but time is this very scarce resource."

As we were saying goodbye, Gates said, "Well, you're welcome to keep sending me mail."

I walked out to my car, drove off the Microsoft campus, and headed back over the Evergreen Bridge to Seattle. When I got to my hotel, I logged on and saw I had E-mail from Bill. It had been written about two hours after I left his office. There was no reference to our having just met. He was responding to mail I had sent him several days earlier, asking what he thought of Henry Ford:

> Ford is not that admirable—he did great things but he was very very narrow minded and was willing to use brute force power too much. His relationship with his family is tragic. His model of the world was plain wrong in a lot of ways. He decided he knew everything he needed to fairly early in his life.

8

DEBORAH BLUM

The Monkey Wars

Sacramento *Bee*,
November 24, 1991

Deborah Blum is one of the new generation of science writers trained specifically in science writing, in her case at the University of Wisconsin. Science, too, is in her background. "My dad is a university entomologist," she explains, "so we had to take every science and math course when I was growing up." After starting as a reporter for the Fresno Bee, she transferred to the Sacramento Bee, where in 1991 she conceived and began to pursue her Pulitzer and American Association for the Advancement of Science– Westinghouse Writing prize-winning series called "The Monkey Wars."

The series, now published as a book, is a triumph of one writer's determination. Blum began by looking into an outbreak of the deadly Ebola virus among research primates. Tracing the California labs that use monkeys in their research, and for what purpose, Blum spent months requesting public records before she got answers. Then she hit a deeper problem: Scientists would not talk, out of fear of animal rights activists, some of whom were issuing phone threats and burning university researchers in effigy. To scientists, billions of dollars and the lives of potential benefi-

ciaries of therapies resulting from primate research were at stake.

Blum employed numerous tactics to overcome both the scientists' fear and activists' suspicion. She developed a network of allies who vouched for her in the two opposing communities. She sent out writing samples first and arranged a meeting with researchers at which she laid her cards on the table. "I warned scientists who spoke enthusiastically about the benefits of a pro-research series that they wouldn't like everything I wrote." She made her coffee addiction into a running joke as animal rights demonstrators picketed outside. She recalls, "One longtime caretaker told me it was the first interview he had given in twenty-four years."

She won over the animal rights proponents, too, with her "no surprises" approach. One longtime activist, Shirley McGreal, eventually allowed Blum to look over her years of notes, unattended. The result of such access is a drama that reveals brilliance and flaws on both sides, pointing to the need for primate research and public vigil.

In the end Blum's battle to overcome the scientists' fear, the activists' emotion, and the violence both on the operating table and outside the lab became part of the story. To capture its full impact, she insisted to her editor that she wanted to use a novelistic style. "Some science stories force you to that," she says. "It makes it vivid and exciting."

The following is the lead article of a series that ran from November 24 to November 27, 1991. The effect was immediate. Some scientists were appalled at her popularization. Others invited her to speak at their meetings, where she received both criticism and praise. Perhaps the biggest praise was the fact that many researchers took up her cue to become outspoken and open participants in the public debate, meeting legislators and appearing on TV and radio talk shows.

The toll for scientists, too, was heavy. In the narrative

lead and closing, Blum used Allen Merritt, a University of California pediatrics researcher trying to develop better lung-protecting surfactants for newborns. Over his department chair's objections, Merritt allowed Blum and her photographer nearly full access to his lab. As soon as the article ran, an anonymous male caller began phoning him and threatening him and his family. After three calls the harassment stopped, but the researcher invested in a new state-of-the-art burglar alarm system and sent his children away from home for a while. Though he was glad he did the interviews, he has not spoken to Blum since her story ran.

O<small>N THE DAYS WHEN HE'S SCHEDULED TO KILL,</small> Allen Merritt summons up his ghosts.

They come to him from the shadows of a 20-year-old memory. Eleven human babies, from his first year out of medical school. All born prematurely. All lost within one week when their lungs failed.

"We were virtually helpless," said Merritt, now head of the neonatal intensive care unit at the University of California–Davis Medical Center.

"There's nothing worse than being a new physician and standing there watching babies die. It's a strong motivator to make things different."

On this cool morning, he needs that memory. The experiment he's doing is deceptively simple: a test of a new chemical to help premature babies breathe. But it's no clinical arrangement of glass tubes. He's trying the drug on two tiny rhesus monkeys, each weighing barely one-third of a pound. At the end of the experiment, he plans to cut their lungs apart, to see how it worked.

Even his ghosts don't make that easy. Nestled in a towel on a surgical table, eyes shut, hands curled, the monkeys look unnervingly human. "The link between people and monkeys is very close," Merritt said. "Much closer than some people would like to think. There's a real sense of sadness, that we can only get the information we need if we kill them."

Once, there was no such need to justify. Once, American researchers could go through 200,000 monkeys a year, without question. Now, the numbers are less—perhaps 20,000 monkeys will die every year, out of an estimated 40,000 used in experiments. But the pressures are greater.

These days, it seems that if researchers plan one little study—slicing the toes off squirrel monkeys, siphoning blood from rhesus macaques, hiding baby monkeys from their mothers—they face not just questions, but picket signs, lawsuits and death threats phoned in at night.

The middle ground in the war over research with monkeys and apes has become so narrow as to be nearly invisible. And even that is eroding.

Intelligent, agile, fast, but not fast enough, these non-human primates are rapidly being driven from the planet, lost to heavy trapping and vanishing rain forests. Of 63 primate species in Asia—where most research monkeys come from—only one is not listed as vulnerable.

Primate researchers believe they are making the hard choice, using non-human primates for medical research because they must, because no other animal so closely mirrors the human body and brain. During the 1950s, American scientists did kill hundreds of thousands of monkeys for polio research, using the animals' organs to grow virus, dissecting their brains to track the spread of the infection. But out of those experiments came a polio vaccine. Using monkeys, scientists have created vaccines for measles, learned to fight leprosy, developed anti-rejection drugs that make organ transplants possible.

Outside the well-guarded laboratory wall, that choice

can seem less obvious. Animal rights advocates draw a dark description of research. They point out that AIDS researchers have used endangered chimpanzees, without, so far, managing to help people dying of the disease. Further, conservationists fear that the research is introducing dangerous infection into the country's chimpanzee breeding program, badly needed to help counter the loss of wild animals.

"They're guzzling up money and animals, and for what?" asked Shirley McGreal, head of the non-profit International Primate Protection League. "Why not use those resources in helping sick people, why infect healthy animals?"

Her argument is that of animal advocates across the country—that scientists are sacrificing our genetic next-of-kin for their own curiosity, dubious medical gains and countless tax dollars.

No one is sure exactly how much money scientists spend experimenting on monkeys, although the National Institutes of Health alone allocates almost $40 million annually to its primate research programs, including one in Davis. Overall, more than half of NIH's research grants— approaching $5 billion—involve at least some animal research.

Rats and mice are the most abundant, some 15 million are used in experiments every year. But primates are the most expensive; monkeys cost a basic $1,000, chimpanzees start at $50,000.

For people such as McGreal, these are animals in a very wrong place. McGreal's long-term goal for monkeys is simple: out of the laboratory, back into what remains of the rain forests.

"I used to think that we could persuade those people to understand what we do," said Frederick King, director of the Yerkes Regional Primate Research Center in Atlanta.

"But it's impossible. And that's why I no longer describe this as a battle. I describe it as a war."

The rift is so sharp that it is beginning to reshape science itself.

"Science has organized," marveled Alex Pacheco, founder of the country's most powerful animal rights group, People for Ethical Treatment of Animals. "Researchers are out-lobbying us and outspending us. They've become so aggressive that it puts new pressure on us. We're going to have to fight tougher too."

In the past year, researchers have made it clear just how much they dislike the role of victim. If Pacheco wants to call scientists "sadistic bastards"—which he does frequently—then Fred King is more than ready to counter with his description of PETA: "Fanatic, fringe, one of the most despicable organizations in the country."

But beyond name-calling, the research community is realizing its political power. Its lobbyists are pushing for laws that would heavily penalize protesters who interfere with research projects. And this year, to the fury of animal rights groups, primate researchers were able to win a special exemption from the public records laws, shielding their plans for captive monkey care.

For researchers, the attention focused on them is an almost dizzying turnabout. Not so long ago, they could have hung their monkey care plans as banners across streets and no one would have read them.

"When I first started, 20 years ago, monkeys were $25 each," said Roy Henrickson, chief of lab animal care at the University of California, Berkeley. "You'd use one once and you'd throw it away. I'd talk to lab vets who were under pressure about dogs and I'd say, I'm sure glad I'm in non-human primates. Nobody cares about them."

He can date the change precisely, back to 1981, the year Pacheco went undercover in the laboratory of Edward

Taub. Taub was a specialist in nerve damage, working in Silver Springs, Md. To explore the effects of ruined nerves, he took 17 rhesus monkeys and sliced apart nerves close to the spinal column, crippling their limbs. Then he studied the way they coped with the damage.

Pacheco left the laboratory with an enduring mistrust of scientists and an armload of inflammatory photographs: monkeys wrenched into vices, packed into filthy cages. Monkeys who, with no feeling in their hands, had gnawed their fingers to the bone. Some of the wounds were oozing with infection, darkening with gangrene.

Many believe those battered monkeys were the fuse, lighting the current, combative cycle of animal rights. In the fury over the Silver Springs monkeys, Pacheco was able to build People for Ethical Treatment of Animals into a national force, and across the country, the movement gained power. Today, membership in animal advocacy groups tops 12 million; the 30 largest organizations report a combined annual income approaching $70 million.

And primate researchers have suddenly found themselves under scrutiny of the most hostile kind.

There are experiments, such as Allen Merritt's work to salvage premature infants, that the critics will sometimes reluctantly accept. The compound that Merritt is testing on young monkeys is a kind of lubricant for the lungs, a slippery ooze that coats the tissues within, allowing them to flex as air comes in and out.

Without the ooze—called surfactant—the tissues don't stretch. They rip. The problem for premature babies is that the body doesn't develop surfactant until late in fetal development, some 35 weeks into a pregnancy. Although artificial surfactants are now available, Merritt doesn't believe they're good enough. Two-thirds of the tiniest premature babies, weighing less than a pound at birth, still die as their lungs shred. He's trying to improve the medicine.

"There could be a scientific defense for doing that, even though it's extremely cruel," said Elliot Katz, head of In Defense of Animals, a national animal rights group, headquartered in San Rafael.

But Katz finds most of the work indefensible. He can rapidly cite examples of a different sort: a U.S. Air Force experiment, which involved draining 40 percent of the blood from rhesus macaques and then spinning them on a centrifuge, to simulate injured astronauts; a New York University study of addiction in which monkeys were strapped into metal boxes and forced to inhale concentrated cocaine fumes.

Last year, animal advocates rallied against a proposed study at the Seattle center, a plan to take 13 baby rhesus macaques from their mothers and try to drive them crazy through isolation, keeping them caged away from their mothers and without company. The scientists acknowledged that they might drive the monkeys to self-mutilation; rhesus macaques do badly in isolation, rocking, pulling out their hair, sometimes tearing their skin open.

This year, protesters have been holding candlelight vigils outside the home of a researcher at a Maryland military facility, the Uniformed Services University of the Health Sciences. That project involves cutting the toes from kittens and young squirrel monkeys and then, after they've wobbled into adjustment, killing them to look at their brains.

In both cases, there are scientific explanations. The Washington scientists wanted to analyze the chemistry of a troubled brain, saying that it could benefit people with mental illness. The Maryland researchers are brain-mapping, drafting a careful picture of how the mind reorganizes itself to cope with crippling injury.

But these are not—and may never be—explanations

acceptable to those crusading for animal rights. "This is just an example of someone doing something horrible to animals because he can get paid for it," said Laurie Raymond, of Seattle's Progressive Animal Welfare Society, which campaigned against the baby monkey experiment and takes credit for the fact that it failed to get federal funding.

Researchers are tired of telling the public about their work, documenting it in public records—and having that very openness used against them. The Washington protesters learned about the baby monkey experiment through a meeting of the university's animal care committee—which is public. The Maryland work came to light through a listing of military funded research—which is public.

When the U.S. Department of Agriculture, which inspects research facilities annually, complained about the housekeeping at the Tulane Regional Primate Research Center in Louisiana, the director wrote the agency a furious letter. Didn't administrators realize that the report was public—and made scientists look bad?

"The point I am making is that USDA, without intending to do so, is playing into the hands of the animal rights/anti-vivisectionists whose stated goal is to abolish animal research," wrote center head Peter Gerone, arguing that the complaints could have been handled privately. "If you are trying to placate the animal rights activists by nitpicking inspections . . . you will only serve to do us irreparable harm."

When Arnold Arluke, a sociologist at Boston's Northeastern University, spent six years studying lab workers and drafted a report saying that some actually felt guilty about killing animals, he found himself suddenly under pressure. "I was told putting that information out would be like giving ammunition to the enemy," he said.

He titled his first talk "Guilt Among Animal Research-

ers." The manager of the laboratory where he spoke
changed "guilt" to stress. When he published that in a
journal, the editors thought that stress was too controversial. They changed the title to "Uneasiness Among Lab
Workers." When he gave another talk at a pharmaceutical
company, he was told uneasiness was too strong. They
changed the title to "How to Deal with Your Feelings."
Arluke figures his next talk will be untitled.

"People in animal research don't even want to tell others what they do," he said. "One woman I talked to was
standing in line at a grocery store, and when she told the
person next to her what she did, the woman started yelling
at her: 'You should be ashamed of yourself.'"

And when new lab animal care rules were published
this year, it was clear that researchers were no longer willing to freely hand over every record of operation.

The new regulations resulted from congressional
changes in 1985 to the Animal Welfare Act. They included
a special provision for the care of laboratory primates; legislators wanted scientists to recognize that these were so-
ciable, intelligent animals.

The provision—perhaps the most controversial in the
entire act—was called "psychological well-being of primates." When the USDA began drafting rules, in response to
the new law, it received a record 35,000 letters of comment. And 14,000 consisted of a written shouting match
over how to make primates happy. It took six years before
the agency could come up with rules that the research
community could accept.

Originally, the USDA proposed firm standards: Laboratories would have to give monkeys bigger cages, let them
share space, provide them with puzzles and toys from a
list.

Researchers argued that was unreasonable: Every monkey species was different, the rigid standards might satisfy

one animal and make another miserable. Now, each institution is asked to do what it thinks best for its monkeys; USDA inspectors will be free to study, criticize and ask for changes in those plans.

But animal rights groups will not. Research lobbyists persuaded the USDA to bypass the federal Freedom of Information Act; the president of the American Society of Primatologists told the agency that making the plans public would be like giving a road map to terrorists. Under the new rules, the plans will be kept at the individual institutions rather than filed with the federal government, as has been standard practice. That makes them institutional property—exempted from any requests for federal records.

Tom Wolfle, director of the Institute for Laboratory Animal Resources in Washington, D.C., the federal government's chief advisory division on animal issues, said the research community simply needed some clear space. "The idea was to prevent unreasonable criticism by uninformed people," he said.

Advocacy groups have sued the government over the new rules, saying they unlawfully shut the public out of research that it pays for. "In the end, they just handed everything back to the researchers and said, here, it's all yours," said Christine Stevens, an executive with the nonprofit Animal Welfare Institute.

Stevens, daughter of a Michigan physiology researcher, finds this the ultimate contradiction, as well as "foolish and short-sighted." She thinks that science, of all professions, should be one of open ideas.

On this point, she has some unlikely allies. Frederick King, of Yerkes, no friend to the animal rights movement, is also unhappy with the research community's tendency to withdraw. "I don't know about the law," he said. "But our plans for taking care of our primates will be open.

"We are using taxpayers' money. In my judgment, we

have an obligation to tell the public what we're about. And the fact that we haven't done that, I think, is one of the greatest mistakes over the last half-century, hell, the last century, that scientists have made."

Against that conflict, Allen Merritt's decision to make public an experiment in which he kills monkeys was not an easy one. His wife worried that anti-research fanatics would stalk their home. His supervisors worried that animal lovers would be alienated; one administrator even called the Davis primate center, suggesting that Merritt's work should not be publicly linked to the medical school's pediatrics department.

But Merritt, like King, believes that his profession will only lose if it remains hidden from the public. "People need to understand what we're doing. If I were to take a new drug first to a nursery, and unforeseen complications occurred, and a baby died—who would accept that?"

So, on a breezy morning, he opens the way to the final test of lung-lubricating surfactants that he will do this year, a 24-hour-countdown for two baby monkeys. Those hours are critical to whether these drugs work. If human premature babies last from their first morning to the next one, their survival odds soar.

The tiny monkeys—one male, one female—taken by C-section, are hurried into an intensive care unit, dried and warmed with a blow drier, put onto folded towels, hooked up to ventilators, heart monitors, intravenous drip lines. During the experiment, they will never be conscious, never open their eyes.

"OK, let's treat," Merritt says. His technician gently lifts the tube from the ventilator, which carries oxygen into the monkey's lungs. A white mist of surfactant fills the tube, spraying into the lungs. And then, through the night, the medical team watches and waits.

The next morning, they decide to kill the female early.

An intravenous line going into her leg is starting to cause bleeding problems. The monkey is twitching a little in her unconsciousness, as if in pain. Merritt sees no point in dragging her through the experiment's official end.

But the male keeps breathing. As the sun brightens to midday, the scientists inject a lethal dose of anesthesia. Still, the monkey's chest keeps moving, up and down, up and down with the push of the ventilator. But, behind him, the heart monitor shows only a straight green line.

For a few seconds, before they shut the machines down and begin the lung dissection, Allen Merritt stands quietly by the small dead monkey, marshaling the ghosts of the babies he couldn't save, a long time ago.

9

JAMES GLEICK

In Search of Genius

From *Genius: The Life and Science of Richard Feynman,*
Pantheon, 1992

A New York Times *reporter and editor, James Gleick first broke new ground in science writing in 1986 with his best-selling book,* Chaos: Making a New Science, *which pulled together developments in fields from mathematics to meteorology. That book affected numerous other academic disciplines, as well as business and technology. Few science writers have ever had such an impact on contemporary thought outside of science, but in that case perhaps only a science writer could have synthesized from so many different fields the simultaneous advances in a then unrecognized field. The source of inspiration was quite ordinary. Gleick became interested in chaos theory because it tried to explain so many everyday processes in our world—predicting weather or the population crashes of wild animals, uncovering economic trends and ominous patterns in the pulses of a human heart.*

Born in 1954, Gleick liked science and mathematics as a child but never took up the subjects in his undergraduate studies at Harvard. Today he hesitates to categorize himself as a science writer. He sees the field as simply a specialized domain of journalism and chastens those who might con-

fuse it with educating: science writing is the "act of telling people what's news, what's happening, what the trends are both short-term and long-term."

Gleick came to science because he followed his interests, he has said, one of which led him to the biography of Nobel Prize–winning physicist Richard Feynman. Gleick notes, "There are few figures so influential in science and yet so unknown to a wider public." This excerpt from Genius: The Life and Science of Richard Feynman *focuses on the elusive task of defining genius. An unorthodox and brilliant researcher with an equally boisterous personality, Richard Feynman was universally considered a genius by those who knew him. Yet he appears far more approachable on a personal level than, say, a Newton or Einstein. Part of the reason is our proximity to his lifetime and part the iconoclastic nature of his style. Part, too, is Gleick's fluid study, which leads to a larger contemplation of intellect itself.*

IN THE SPRING OF 1955 THE MAN MOST PLAINLY and universally identified with the word *genius* died at Princeton Hospital. Most of his body was cremated, the ashes scattered, but not the brain. The hospital's pathologist, Dr. Thomas S. Harvey, removed his last remnant to a jar of formaldehyde.

Harvey weighed it. A mediocre two and two-thirds pounds. One more negative datum to sabotage the notion that the brain's size might account for the difference between ordinary and extraordinary mental ability—a notion that various nineteenth-century researchers had labored futilely to establish (claiming along the way to have demonstrated the superiority of men over women, white men over black men, and Germans over Frenchmen). The brain of the great mathematician Carl Friedrich Gauss had been turned over to such scientists. It disappointed them. Now, with Einstein's cerebrum on their hands, researchers proposed more subtle ways of searching for the secret of genius: measuring the density of surrounding blood vessels, the percentage of glial cells, the degree of neuronal branching. Decades passed. Microscope sections and photographic slides of Einstein's brain circulated among a tight circle of anatomically minded psychologists, called neuropsychologists, unable to let go of the idea that a detectable sign of the qualities that made Einstein famous might remain somewhere in these fragmentary trophies. By the 1980s this most famous of brains had been whittled down to small gray shreds preserved in the office of a pathologist retired to Wichita, Kansas—a sodden testament to the elusiveness of the quality called genius.

Eventually the findings were inconclusive, though that did not make them unpublishable. (One researcher counted a large excess of branching cells in the parietal sector called Brodmann area 39.) Those searching for genius's corporeal basis had little enough material from which to work. "Is there a neurological substrate for talent?" asked the editors of one neuropsychology volume. "Of course, as neuropsychologists we hypothesize that there must be such a substrate and would hardly think to relegate talent somehow to 'mind.' What evidence currently exists would be the results of the work on Einstein's brain . . ."—the brain that created the post-Newtonian universe, that released the pins binding us to absolute space and time, that visualized (in its parietal lobe?) a plastic fourth dimension, that banished the ether, that refused to believe God played dice, that piloted such a kindly, forgetful form about the shaded streets of Princeton. There was only one Einstein. For schoolchildren and neuropsychologists alike, he stood as an icon of intellectual power. He seemed—but was this true?—to have possessed a rare and distinct quality, genius as an essence, not a mere statistical extremum on a supposed bell-curve of intelligence. This was the conundrum of genius. Was genius truly special? Or was it a matter of degree—a miler breaking 3:50 rather than 4:10? (A shifting bell-curve, too: yesterday's record-setter, today's also-ran.) Meanwhile, no one had thought to dissect the brains of Neils Bohr, Paul A. M. Dirac, Enrico Fermi; Sigmund Freud, Pablo Picasso, Virginia Woolf; Jascha Heifetz, Isadora Duncan, Babe Ruth; or any of the other exceptional, creative, intuitive souls to whom the word was so often and so lubriciously applied.

What a strange and bewildering literature grew up around the term *genius*—defining it, analyzing it, categorizing it, rationalizing and reifying it. Commentators have contrasted it with such qualities as (mere) talent, intellect, imagination, originality, industriousness, sweep of mind and elegance of style; or have shown how genius is composed of these in various combinations. Psychologists and philosophers, musicologists and art critics, historians of science and scientists themselves have all stepped into this quagmire, a capacious one. Their several centuries of labor have produced no consensus on any of the necessary questions. Is there such a quality? If so, where does it come from? (A glial surplus in Brodmann area 39? A doting, faintly unsuccessful father who channels his intellectual ambition into his son? A frightful early encounter with the unknown, such as the death of a sibling?) When otherwise sober scientists speak of the genius as magician, wizard, or superhuman, are they merely indulging in a flight of literary fancy? When people speak of the borderline between genius and madness, why is it so evident what they mean? And a question that has barely been asked (the where-are-the-400-hitters question): Why, as the pool of available humans has risen from one hundred million to one billion to five billion, has the production of

geniuses—Shakespeares, Newtons, Mozarts, Einsteins—
seemingly choked off to nothing, genius itself coming to
seem like the property of the past?

"Enlightened, penetrating, and capacious minds," as
William Duff chose to put it two hundred years ago,
speaking of such exemplars as Homer, Quintilian, and
Michelangelo in one of a string of influential essays by
mid-eighteenth-century Englishmen that gave birth to the
modern meaning of the word *genius*. Earlier, it had meant
spirit, the magical spirit of a jinni or more often the spirit
of a nation. Duff and his contemporaries wished to identify genius with the godlike power of invention, of creation, of making what never was before, and to do so they
had to create a psychology of imagination: imagination
with a "RAMBLING and VOLATILE POWER"; imagination
"perpetually attempting to soar" and "apt to deviate into
the mazes of error."

> Imagination is that faculty whereby the mind not only
> reflects on its own operations, but which assembles the
> various ideas conveyed to the understanding by the ca-
> nal of sensation, and treasured up in the repository of
> the memory, compounding or disjoining them at plea-
> sure; and which, by its plastic power of inventing new
> associations of ideas, and of combining them with infi-
> nite variety, is enabled to present a creation of its own,
> and to exhibit scenes and objects which never existed
> in nature.

These were qualities that remained two centuries later
at the center of cognitive scientists' efforts to understand
creativity: the mind's capacity for self-reflection, self-
reference, self-comprehension; the dynamical and fluid
creation of concepts and associations. The early essayists
on genius, writing with a proper earnestness, attempting to

reduce and regularize a phenomenon with (they admitted) an odor of the inexplicable, nevertheless saw that genius allowed a certain recklessness, even a lack of craftsmanship. Genius seemed natural, unlearned, uncultivated. Shakespeare was—"in point of genius," Alexander Gerard wrote in 1774—Milton's superior, despite a "defective" handling of poetic details. The torrent of analyses and polemics on genius that appeared in those years introduced a rhetoric of ranking and comparing that became a standard method of the literature. Homer versus Virgil, Milton versus Virgil, Shakespeare versus Milton. The results—a sort of tennis ladder for the genius league—did not always wear well with the passage of time. Newton versus Bacon? In Gerard's view Newton's discoveries amounted to a filling in of a framework developed with more profound originality by Bacon—"who, without any assistance, sketched out the whole design." Still, there were those bits of Newtonian mathematics to consider. On reflection Gerard chose to leave for posterity "a question of very difficult solution, which of the two had the greatest genius."

He and his contemporary essayists had a purpose. By understanding genius, rationalizing it, celebrating it, and teasing out its mechanisms, perhaps they could make the process of discovery and invention less accidental. In later times that motivation has not disappeared. More overtly than ever, the nature of genius—genius as the engine of scientific discovery—has become an issue bound up with the economic fortunes of nations. Amid the vast modern network of universities, corporate laboratories, and national science foundations has arisen an awareness that the best financed and best organized of research enterprises have not learned to engender, perhaps not even to recognize, world-turning originality.

Genius, Gerard summed up in 1774, "is confessed to be

a subject of capital importance, without the knowledge of which a regular method of invention cannot be established, and useful discoveries must continue to be made, as they have generally been made hitherto, merely by chance." Hitherto, as well. In our time he continues to be echoed by historians of science frustrated by the sheer ineffability of it all. But they keep trying to replace awe with understanding. J. D. Bernal said in 1939:

> It is one of the hopes of the science of science that, by careful analysis of past discovery, we shall find a way of separating the effects of good organization from those of pure luck, and enabling us to operate on calculated risks rather than blind chance.

Yet how could anyone rationalize a quality as fleeting and accident-prone as a genius's inspiration: Archimedes and his bath, Newton and his apple? People love stories about geniuses as alien heroes, possessing a quality beyond human understanding, and scientists may be the world's happiest consumers of such stories. A modern example:

A physicist studying quantum field theory with Murray Gell-Mann at the California Institute of Technology in the 1950s, before standard texts have become available, discovers unpublished lecture notes by Richard Feynman, circulating samizdat style. He asks Gell-Mann about them. Gell-Mann says no, Dick's methods are not the same as the methods used here. The student asks, well, what are Feynman's methods? Gell-Mann leans coyly against the blackboard and says, Dick's method is this. You write down the problem. You think very hard. (He shuts his eyes and presses his knuckles parodically to his forehead.) Then you write down the answer.

The same story appeared over and over again. It was an old genre. From an 1851 tract titled *Genius and Industry*:

(A professor from the University of Cambridge calls upon a genius of mathematics working in Manchester as a lowly clerk.) ". . . from Geometry to Logarithms, and to the Differential and Integral Calculus; and thence again to questions the most foreign and profound: at last, a question was proposed to the poor clerk—a question which weeks had been required to solve. Upon a simple slip of paper it was answered immediately. 'But how,' said the Professor, 'do you work this? show me the rule! . . . The answer is correct but you have reached it by a different way.'

" 'I have worked it,' said the clerk, 'from a rule in my own mind. I cannot show you the law—I never saw it myself; the law is in my mind.'

" 'Ah!' said the Professor, 'If you talk of a law within your mind, I have done; I cannot follow you there.' "

Magicians again. As Mark Kac said: ". . . The working of their minds is for all intents and purposes incomprehensible. Even after we understand what they have done, the process by which they have done it is completely dark." The notion places a few individuals at the margin of their community—the impractical margin, since the stock in trade of the scientist is the method that *can* be transferred from one practitioner to the next.

If the most distinguished physicists and mathematicians believe in the genius as magician, it is partly for psychological protection. A merely excellent scientist could suffer an unpleasant shock when he discussed his work with Feynman. It happened again and again: physicists would wait for an opportunity to get Feynman's judgment of a result on which they had staked weeks or months of their career. Typically Feynman would refuse to allow them to give a full explanation. He said it spoiled his fun. He would let them describe just the outline of the problem before he would jump up and say, *Oh, I know that . . .* and scrawl on the blackboard not his visitor's results, A, but a harder, more general theorem, X. So A (about to be mailed, perhaps, to the *Physical Review*) was merely a special case. This could cause pain. Sometimes it was not clear whether Feynman's lightning answers came from instantaneous calculation or from a storehouse of previously worked-out—and unpublished—knowledge. The astrophysicist Willy Fowler proposed at a Caltech seminar in the 1960s that quasars—mysterious blazing radiation sources lately discovered in the distant sky—were supermassive stars, and Feynman immediately rose, astonishingly, to say that such objects would be gravitationally unstable. Furthermore, he said that the instability followed from general relativity. The claim required a calculation of the subtle countervailing effects of stellar forces and relativistic gravity. Fowler thought he was talking through his hat. A colleague later discovered that Feynman had done a hundred pages of work on the problem years before. The Chicago astrophysicist Subrahmanyan Chandrasekhar independently produced Feynman's result—it was part of the work for which he won a Nobel Prize twenty years later. Feynman himself never bothered to publish. Someone with a new idea always risked finding, as one colleague said, "that Feynman had signed the guest book and already left."

A great physicist who accumulated knowledge without taking the trouble to publish could be a genuine danger to his colleagues. At best it was unnerving to learn that one's potentially career-advancing discovery had been, to Feynman, below the threshold of publishability. At worst it undermined one's confidence in the landscape of the known and not known. There was an uneasy subtext to the genus of story prompted by this habit. It was said of Lars Onsager, for example, that a visitor would ask him about a new result; sitting in his office chair he would say, *I believe that is correct*; then he would bend forward diffidently to open a file drawer, glance sidelong at a long-buried page of notes, and say, *Yes, I thought so; that is correct.* This was not always precisely what the visitor had hoped to hear.

A person with a mysterious storehouse of unwritten knowledge was a wizard. So was a person with the power to tease from nature its hidden secrets—a scientist, that is. The modern scientist's view of his quest harkened back to something ancient and cabalistic: laws, rules, symmetries hidden just beneath the visible surface. Sometimes this view of the search for knowledge became overwhelming, even oppressive. John Maynard Keynes, facing a small audience in a darkened room at Cambridge a few years before his death, spoke of Newton as "this strange spirit, who was tempted by the Devil to believe . . . that he could reach *all* the secrets of God and Nature by the pure power of mind—Copernicus and Faustus in one."

> Why do I call him a magician? Because he looked on the whole universe and all that is in it *as a riddle*, as a secret which could be read by applying pure thought to certain evidence, certain mystic clues which God had laid about the world to allow a sort of philosopher's treasure hunt to this esoteric brotherhood. . . . He *did* read the riddle of the heavens. And he believed that by the same powers of his introspective imagination he would read the riddle of the Godhead, the riddle of past and future events divinely foreordained, the riddle of the elements and their constitution. . . .

In his audience, intently absorbing these words, aware of the cold and the gloom and the seeming exhaustion of the speaker, was the young Freeman Dyson. Dyson came to accept much of Keynes's view of genius, winnowing away the seeming mysticism. He made the case for magicians in the calmest, most rational way. No "magical mumbo-jumbo," he wrote. "I am suggesting that anyone who is transcendentally great as a scientist is likely also to have personal qualities that ordinary people would consider in some sense superhuman." The greatest scientists are deliverers and destroyers, he said. Those are myths, of course, but myths are part of the reality of the scientific enterprise.

When Keynes, in that Cambridge gloom, described Newton as a wizard, he was actually pressing back to a moderate view of genius—for after the eighteenth century's sober tracts had come a wild turning. Where the first writers on genius had noticed in Homer and Shakespeare a forgivable disregard for the niceties of prosody, the romantics of the late nineteenth century saw powerful, liberating heroes, throwing off shackles, defying God and convention. They also saw a bent of mind that could turn fully pathological. Genius was linked with insanity—*was* insanity. That feeling of divine inspiration, the breath of revelation seemingly from without, actually came from within, where melancholy and madness twisted the brain. The roots of this idea were old. "Oh! how near are genius and madness!" Denis Dideot had written. ". . . Men imprison them and chain them, or raise statues to them." It was a side effect of the change in focus from God-centeredness to human-centeredness. The very notion of revelation, in the absence of a Revealer, became disturbing, particularly to those who experienced it: ". . . something profoundly convulsive and disturbing suddenly becomes visible and audible with indescribable definiteness and exactness," Friedrich Nietzsche wrote. "One hears—one does not seek; one takes—one does not ask who gives: a thought flashes out like lightning. . . ." Genius now suggested Charles Pierre Baudelaire or Ludwig van Beethoven, flying off the tracks of normality. *Crooked roads*, William Blake had said: "Improvement makes strait roads; but the crooked roads without Improvement are roads of Genius."

An 1891 treatise on genius by Cesare Lombroso listed some associated symptoms. *Degeneration. Rickets. Pallor. Emaciation. Lefthandedness.* A sense of the mind as a cauldron in tumult was emerging in European culture, along with an often contradictory hodgepodge of psychic terminology, all awaiting the genius of Freud to provide a structure and a coherent jargon. In the meantime: *Misoneism. Vagabondage. Unconsciousness.* More presumed clues to genius. *Hyperesthesia. Amnesia. Originality. Fondness for special words.* "Between the physiology of the man of genius, therefore, and the pathology of the insane," Lombroso concluded, "there are many points of coincidence. . . ." The genius, disturbed as he is, makes errors and wrong turns that the ordinary person avoids. Still, these madmen, "despising and overcoming obstacles which would have dismayed the cool and deliberate mind—hasten by whole centuries the unfolding of truth."

The notion never vanished; in fact it softened into a cliché. Geniuses display an undeniable obsessiveness resembling, at times, monomania. Geniuses of certain kinds—mathematicians, chess players, computer programmers—seem, if not mad, at least lacking in the social skills most easily identified with sanity. Nevertheless, the lunatic-genius-wizard did not play as well in America, notwithstanding the relatively unbuttoned examples of writers like Whitman and Melville. There was a reason. American genius as the nineteenth century neared its end was not busy making culture, playing with words, creating music and art, or otherwise impressing the academy. It was busy sending its output to the patent office. Alexander Graham Bell was a genius. Eli Whitney and Samuel Morse were geniuses. Let European romantics celebrate the genius as erotic hero (Don Juan) or the genius as martyr (Werther). Let them bend their definitions to accommodate the genius composers who succeeded Mozart, with their increasingly direct pipelines to the emotions. In America what newspapers already called the machine age was under way. The consummate genius, the genius who defined the word for the next generation, was Thomas Alva Edison.

By his own description he was no wizard, this Wizard of Menlo Park. Anyone who knew anything about Edison knew that his genius was ninety-nine percent perspiration. The stories that defined his style were not about inspiration in the mode of the Newtonian apple. They spoke of exhaustive, laborious trial and error: every conceivable lamp filament, from human hair to bamboo fiber. "I speak without exaggeration," Edison declared (certainly exaggerating), "when I say that I have constructed three thousand different theories in connection with the electric light, each one of them reasonable and apparently likely to be true." He added that he had methodically disproved 2,998 of them by experiment. He claimed to have carried out fifty thousand individual experiments on a particular type of battery. He had a classic American education: three months in a Michigan public school. The essential creativity that led him to the phonograph, the electric light, and more than a thousand other patented inventions was deliberately played down by those who built and those who absorbed his legend. Perhaps understandably so—for after centuries in which a rationalizing science had systematically drained magic from the world, the machine-shop inventions of Edison and other heroes were now loosing a magic with a frightening, transforming power. This magic buried itself in the walls of houses or beamed itself invisibly through the air.

"Mr. Edison is not a wizard," reported a 1917 biography.

Like all people who have prodigiously assisted civilization, his processes are clear, logical and normal.

Wizardry is the expression of superhuman gifts and,
as such, is an impossible thing. . . .

And yet, Mr. Edison can bid the voices of the dead
to speak, and command men in their tombs to pass before our eyes.

"Edison was not a wizard," announced a 1933 magazine
article. "If he had what seems suspiciously like a magic
touch, it was because he was markedly in harmony with
his environment. . . ." And there the explication of Edison-
ian genius came more or less to an end. All that remained
was to ask—but few did—one of those impossible late-
night *what if* questions: What if Edison had never lived?
What if this self-schooled, indefatigable mind with its
knack for conceiving images of new devices, methods,
processes had not been there when the flood began to
break? The question answers itself, for it was a flood that
Edison rode. Electricity had burst upon a world nearing
the limits of merely mechanical ingenuity. The ability to
understand and control currents of electrons had suddenly made possible a vast taxonomy of new machines—
telegraphs, dynamos, lights, telephones, motors, heaters,
devices to sew, grind, saw, toast, iron, and suck up dirt, all
waiting at the misty edge of potentiality. No sooner had
Hans Christian Oersted noticed, in 1820, that a current
could move a compass needle than inventors—not just
Samuel Morse but André-Marie Ampère and a half-dozen
others—conceived of telegraphy. Even more people invented generators, and by the time enough pieces of technology had accumulated to make television possible, no
one inventor could plausibly serve as its Edison.

The demystification of genius in the age of inventors
shaped the scientific culture—with its plainspoken positiv-

ism, its experiment-oriented technical schools—that nurtured Feynman and his contemporaries in the twenties and thirties, even as the pendulum swung again toward the more mysterious, more intuitive, and conspicuously less practical image of Einstein. Edison may have changed the world, after all, but Einstein seemed to have reinvented it whole, by means of a single, incomprehensible act of visualization. He saw how the universe must be and announced that it was so. Not since Newton . . .

By then the profession of science was expanding rapidly, counting not hundreds but tens of thousands of practitioners. Clearly most of their work, most of science, was ordinary—as Freeman Dyson put it, a business of "honest craftsmen," "solid work," "collaborative efforts where to be reliable is more important than to be original." In modern times it became almost impossible to talk about the processes of scientific change without echoing Thomas S. Kuhn, whose *Structure of Scientific Revolutions* so thoroughly changed the discourse of historians of science. Kuhn distinguished between normal science—problem solving, the fleshing out of existing frameworks, the unsurprising craft that occupies virtually all working researchers—and revolutions, the vertiginous intellectual upheavals through which knowledge lurches genuinely forward. Nothing in Kuhn's scheme required individual genius to turn the crank of revolutions. Still, it was Einstein's relativity, Heisenberg's uncertainty, Wegener's continental drift. The new mythology of revolutions dovetailed neatly with the older mythology of genius—minds breaking with the standard methods and seeing the world new. Dyson's kind of genius destroyed and delivered. Schwinger's quantum electrodynamics and Feynman's may have been mathematically the same, but one was conservative and the other revolutionary. One extended an existing line of thought. The other broke with the past decisively enough to mystify its intended audience. One represented an ending: a mathematical style doomed to grow fatally overcomplex. The other, for those willing to follow Feynman into a new style of visualization, served as a beginning. Feynman's style was risky, even megalomaniacal. Reflecting later on what had happened, Dyson saw his own goals, like Schwinger's, as conservative ("I accepted the orthodox view . . . I was looking for a neat set of equations . . .") and Feynman's as visionary: "He was searching for general principles that would be flexible enough so that he could adapt them to anything in the universe."

Other ways of seeking the source of scientific creativity had appeared. It seemed a long way from such an inspirational, how-to view of discovery to the view of neuropsychologists looking for a *substrate*, refusing to speak merely about "mind." Why had *mind* become such a contemptible word to neuropsychologists? Because they saw the term as a soft escape route, a deus ex machina for a scientist short on explanations. Feynman himself learned about neurons; he taught himself some brain anatomy when trying to understand color vision; but usually he considered *mind* to be the level worth studying. Mind must be a sort of dynamical pattern, not so much founded in a neurological substrate as floating above it, independent of it. "So what is this mind of ours?" he remarked. "What are these atoms with consciousness?"

> Last week's potatoes! They can now *remember* what was going on in my mind a year ago—a mind which has long ago been replaced. . . . The atoms come into my brain, dance a dance, and then go out—there are always new atoms, but always doing the same dance, remembering what the dance was yesterday.

Genius was not a word in his customary vocabulary. Like many physicists he was wary of the term. Among scientists it became a kind of style violation, a faux pas suggesting greenhorn credulity, to use the word *genius* about a living colleague. Popular usage had cheapened the word. Almost anyone could be a genius for the duration of a magazine article. Briefly Stephen Hawking, a British cosmologist esteemed but not revered by his peers, developed a reputation among some nonscientists as Einstein's heir to the mantle. For Hawking, who suffered from a progressively degenerative muscular disease, the image of genius was heightened by the drama of a formidable intelligence fighting to express itself within a withering body. Still, in terms of raw brilliance and hard accomplishment, a few score of his professional colleagues felt that he was no more a genius than they.

In part, scientists avoided the word because they did not believe in the concept. In part, the same scientists avoided it because they believed all too well, like Jews afraid to speak the name of Yahweh. It was generally safe to say only that Einstein had been a genius; after Einstein, perhaps Bohr, who had served as a guiding father figure during the formative era of quantum mechanics; after Bohr perhaps Dirac, perhaps Fermi, perhaps Bethe ... All these seemed to deserve the term. Yet Bethe, with no obvious embarrassment or false modesty, would quote Mark Kac's faintly oxymoronic assessment that Bethe's genius was "ordinary," by contrast to Feynman's: "An ordinary genius is a fellow that you and I would be just as good as, if we were only many times better." *You and I would be just as good* ... Much of what passes for genius is mere excellence, the difference a matter of degree. A colleague of Fermi's said: "Knowing what Fermi could do did not make me humble. You just realize that some people are smarter than you are, that's all. You can't run as fast as some people or do mathematics as fast as Fermi."

In the domains of criticism that fell under the spell of

structuralism and then deconstructionism, even this unmagical view of genius became suspect. Literary and music theory, and the history of science as well, lost interest not only in the old-fashioned sports-fan approach — Homer versus Virgil — but also in the very idea of genius itself as a quality in the possession of certain historical figures. Perhaps genius was an artifact of a culture's psychology, a symptom of a particular form of hero worship. Reputations of greatness come and go, after all, propped up by the sociopolitical needs of an empowered sector of the community and then slapped away by a restructuring of the historical context. The music of Mozart strikes certain ears as evidence of genius, but it was not always so — critics of another time considered it prissy and bewigged — nor will it always be. In the modern style, to ask about his genius is to ask the wrong question. Even to ask why he was "better" than, say, Antonio Salieri would be the crudest of gaffes. A modern music theorist might, in his secret heart, carry an undeconstructed torch for Mozart, might feel the old damnably ineffable rapture; still he understands that *genius* is a relic of outmoded romanticism. Mozart's listeners are as inextricable a part of the magic as the observer is a part of the quantum-mechanical equation. Their interests and desires help from the context without which the music is no more than an abstract sequence of notes — or so the argument goes. Mozart's genius, if it existed at all, was not a substance, not even a quality of mind, but a byplay, a give and take within a cultural context.

How strange, then, that cooly rational scientists should be the last serious scholars to believe not just in genius but in geniuses; to maintain a mental pantheon of heroes; and to bow, with Mark Kac and Freeman Dyson, before the magicians.

*　　*　　*

"Genius is the fire that lights itself," someone had said. Originality; imagination; the self-driving ability to set one's mind free from the worn channels of tradition. Those who tried to take Feynman's measure always came back to originality. "He was the most original mind of his generation," declared Dyson. The generation coming up behind him, with the advantage of hindsight, still found nothing predictable in the paths of his thinking. If anything he seemed perversely and dangerously bent on disregarding standard methods. "I think if he had not been so quick people would have treated him as a brilliant quasi-crank, because he did spend a substantial amount of time going down what later turned out to be dead ends," said Sidney Coleman, a theorist who first knew Feynman at Caltech in the fifties.

> There are lots of people who are too original for their own good, and had Feynman not been as smart as he was, I think he would have been too original for his own good.
> There was always an element of showboating in his character. He was like the guy that climbs Mont Blanc barefoot just to show that it can be done. A lot of things he did were to show, you didn't have to do it that way, you can do it this other way. And this other way, in fact, was not as good as the first way, but it showed he was different.

Feynman continued to refuse to read the current literature, and he chided graduate students who would begin their work on a problem in the normal way, by checking what had already been done. That way, he told them, they would give up chances to find something original. Coleman said:

> I suspect that Einstein had some of the same character. I'm sure Dick thought of that as a virtue, as noble.

I don't think it's so. I think it's kidding yourself. Those other guys are not all a collection of yo-yos. Sometimes it would be better to take the recent machinery they have built and not try to rebuild it, like reinventing the wheel.

I know people who are in fact very original and not cranky but have not done as good physics as they could have done because they were more concerned at a certain juncture with being original than with being right. Dick could get away with a lot because he was so goddamn smart. He really *could* climb Mont Blanc barefoot.

Coleman chose not to study with Feynman directly. Watching Feynman work, he said, was like going to the Chinese opera.

When he was doing work he was doing it in a way that was just—absolutely out of the grasp of understanding. You didn't know where it was going, where it had gone so far, where to push it, what was the next step. With Dick the next step would somehow come out of— divine revelation.

So many of his witnesses observed the utter freedom of his flights of thought, yet when Feynman talked about his own methods he emphasized not freedom but constraints. The kind of imagination that takes blank paper, blank staves, or a blank canvas and fills it with something wholly new, wholly free—that, Feynman contended, was not the scientist's imagination. Nor could one measure imagination as certain psychologists try to do, by displaying a picture and asking what will happen next. For Feynman the essence of the scientific imagination was a powerful and almost painful rule. What scientists create must match reality. It must match what is already known. Scientific creativity, he said, is imagination in a straitjacket. "The whole question of imagination in science is often misunderstood by people in other disciplines," he said. "They overlook the fact that whatever we are *allowed* to imagine in science must be *consistent with everything else we know. . . .*" This is a conservative principle, implying that the existing framework of science is fundamentally sound, already a fair mirror of reality. Scientists, like the freer-seeming arts, feel the pressure to innovate, but in science the act of making something new contains the seeds of paradox. Innovation comes not through daring steps into unknown space,

> not just some happy thoughts which we are free to make as we wish, but ideas which must be consistent with all the laws of physics we know. We can't allow ourselves to seriously imagine things which are obviously in contradiction to the known laws of nature. And so our kind of imagination is quite a difficult game.

Creative artists in modern times have labored under the terrible weight of the demand for novelty. Mozart's contemporaries expected him to work within a fixed, shared framework, not to break the bonds of convention. The standard forms of the sonata, symphony, and opera were established before his birth and hardly changed in his lifetime; the rules of harmonic progression made a cage as unyielding as the sonnet did for Shakespeare. As unyielding and as liberating—for later critics found the creators' genius in the counterpoint of structure and freedom, rigor and inventiveness.

For the creative mind of the old school, inventing by pressing against constraints that seem ironclad, subtly bending a rod here or slipping a lock there, science has become the last refuge. The forms and constraints of scientific practice are held in place not just by the grounding in experiment but by the customs of a community more homogeneous and rule-bound than any community of artists. Scientists still speak unashamedly of *reality*, even in the quantum era, of objective truth, of a world independent of human construction, and they sometimes seem the last members of the intellectual universe to do so. Reality hobbles their imaginations. So does the ever more intricate assemblage of theorems, technologies, laboratory results, and mathematical formalisms that make up the body of known science. How, then, can the genius make a revolution? Feynman said, "Our imagination is stretched to the utmost, not, as in fiction, to imagine things which are not really there, but just to comprehend those things which *are* there."

It was the problem he faced in the gloomiest days of 1946, when he was trying to find his way out of the mire that quantum mechanics had become. "We know so very much," he wrote to his friend Welton, "and then subsume it into so very few equations that we can say we know very little (except these equations) . . . Then we think we have *the* physical picture with which to interpret the equations." The freedom he found then was a freedom not from the equations but from the physical picture. He refused to let the form of the mathematics lock him into any one route to visualization: "There are so very few equations that I have found that many physical pictures can give the same equations. So I am spending my time in study—in seeing how many new viewpoints I can take of what is known." By then Welton had mastered the field theory that was becoming standard, and he was surprised to discover that his old friend had not. Feynman seemed to hoard shadow pools of ignorance, seemed to protect himself from the light like a waking man who closes his eyes to preserve a fleeting image left over from a dream.

He said later, "Maybe that's why young people make success. They don't know enough. Because when you know enough it's obvious that every idea that you have is no good." Welton, too, was persuaded that if Feynman had known more, he could not have innovated so well.

"Would I had phrases that are not known, utterances that are strange, in new language that has not been used, free from repetition, not an utterance which has grown stale, which men of old have spoken." An Egyptian scribe fixed those words in stone at the very dawn of recorded utterance—already jaded, a millennium before Homer. Modern critics speak of the burden of the past and the anxiety of influence, and surely the need to innovate is an ancient part of the artist's psyche, but novelty was never as crucial to the artist as it became in the twentieth century. The useful lifetime of a new form or genre was never so short. Artists never before felt so much pressure to violate such young traditions.

Meanwhile, before their eyes, the world has grown too vast and multifarious for the towering genius of the old kind. Artists struggle to keep their heads above the tide. Norman Mailer, publishing yet another novel doomed to fall short of ambitions formed in an earlier time, notices: "There are no large people any more. I've been studying Picasso lately and look at who his contemporaries were: Freud, Einstein." He saw the change in his own lifetime without understanding it. (Few of those looking for genius understood where it had gone.) He appeared on a literary scene so narrow that conventional first novels by writers like James Jones made them appear plausible successors to Faulkner and Hemingway. He slowly sank into a thicket of hundreds of equally talented, original, and hard-driving novelists, each just as likely to be tagged as a budding genius. In a world into which Amis, Beckett, Cheever, Drabble, Ellison, Fuentes, Grass, Heller, Ishiguro, Jones,

Kazantzakis, Lessing, Nabokov, Oates, Pym, Queneau, Roth, Solzhenitsyn, Theroux, Updike, Vargas Llosa, Waugh, Xue, Yates, and Zoshchenko—or any other two dozen fiction writers—had never been born, Mailer and any other potential genius would have had a better chance of towering. In a less crowded field, among shorter yardsticks, a novelist would not just have seemed bigger. He would have been bigger. Like species competing in ecological niches, he would have had a broader, richer space to explore and occupy. Instead the giants force one another into specialized corners of the intellectual landscape. They choose among domestic, suburban, rural, urban, demimondaine, Third World, realist, postrealist, semirealist, antirealist, surrealist, decadent, ultraist, expressionist, impressionist, naturalist, existentialist, metaphysical, romance, romanticist, neoromanticist, Marxist, picaresque, detective, comic, satiric, and countless other fictional modes—as sea squirts, hagfish, jellyfish, sharks, dolphins, whales, oysters, crabs, lobsters, and countless hordes of marine species subdivide the life-supporting possibilities of an ocean that was once, for billions of years, dominated quite happily by blue-green algae.

"Giants have not ceded to mere mortals," the evolutionary theorist Stephen Jay Gould wrote in an iconoclastic 1983 essay. "Rather, the boundaries . . . have been restricted and the edges smoothed." He was not talking about algae, artists, or paleontologists but about baseball players. Where are the .400 hitters? Why have they vanished into the mythic past, when technical skills, physical conditioning, and the population on which organized baseball draws have all improved? His answer: Baseball's giants have dwindled into a more uniform landscape. Standards have risen. The distance between the best and worst batters, and between the best and worst pitchers, has fallen. Gould showed by statistical analysis that the extinction of the .400 hitter was only the more visible side of a general softening of extremes: the .100 hitter has faded as well. The best and worst all come closer to the average. Few fans like to imagine that Ted Williams would recede toward the mean in the modern major leagues, or that the overweight, hard-drinking Babe Ruth would fail to dominate the scientifically engineered physiques of his later competitors, or that dozens of today's nameless young base-stealers could outrun Ty Cobb, but it is inevitably so. Enthusiasts of track and field cannot entertain the baseball fan's nostalgia; their statistics measure athlete against nature instead of athlete against athlete, and the lesson from decade to decade is clear. There is such a thing as progress. Nostalgia conceals it while magnifying the geniuses of the past. A nostalgic music lover will put on a scratchy 78 of Lauritz Melchior and sigh that there are no Wagnerian tenors any more. Yet in reality musical athletes have probably fared no worse than any other kind.

Is it only nostalgia that makes genius seem to belong to the past? Giants did walk the earth—Shakespeare, Newton, Michelangelo, DiMaggio—and in their shadows the poets, scientists, artists, and baseball players of today crouch like pygmies. No one will ever again create a *King Lear* or hit safely in fifty-six consecutive games, it seems. Yet the raw material of genius—whatever combination of native talent and cultural opportunity that might be—can scarcely have disappeared. On a planet of five billion people, parcels of genes with Einsteinian potential must appear from time to time, and presumably more often than ever before. Some of those parcels must be as well nurtured as Einstein's, in a world richer and better educated than ever before. Of course genius is exceptional and statistics-defying. Still, the modern would-be Mozart must contend with certain statistics: that the entire educated population of eighteenth-century Vienna would fit into a large New York apartment block; that in a given year the United States Copyright Office registers close to two hundred thousand "works of the performing arts," from advertising jingles to epic tone poems. Composers and painters now awake into a universe with a nearly infinite range of genres to choose from and rebel against. Mozart did not have to choose an audience or a style. His community was in place. Are the latter-day Mozarts not being born, or are they all around, bumping shoulders with one another, scrabbling for cultural scraps, struggling to be newer than new, their stature inevitably shrinking all the while?

The miler who triumphs in the Olympic Games, who places himself momentarily at the top of the pyramid of all milers, leads a thousand next-best competitors by mere seconds. The gap between best and second-best, or even best and tenth-best, is so slight that a gust of wind or a different running shoe might have accounted for the margin of victory. Where the measuring scale becomes multidimensional and nonlinear, human abilities more readily slide off the scale. The ability to reason, to compute, to manipulate the symbols and rules of logic—this unnatural talent, too, must lie at the very margin, where small differences in raw talent have enormous consequences, where a merely good physicist must stand in awe of Dyson and where Dyson, in turn, stands in awe of Feynman. Merely to divide 158 by 192 presses most human minds to the limit of exertion. To master—as modern particle physicists must—the machinery of group theory and current algebra, of perturbative expansions and non-Abelian gauge theories, of spin statistics and Yang-Mills, is to sustain in one's mind a fantastic house of cards, at once steely and delicate. To manipulate that framework, and to innovate within it, requires a mental power that nature did not demand of scientists in past centuries. More physicists than ever rise to meet this cerebral challenge. Still, some of

them, worrying that the Einsteins and Feynmans are nowhere to be seen, suspect that the geniuses have fled to
microbiology or computer science—forgetting momentarily that the individual microbiologists and computer scientists they meet seem no brainier, on the whole, than
physicists and mathematicians.

Geniuses change history. That is part of their mythology, and it is the final test, presumably more reliable than
the trail of anecdote and peer admiration that brilliant scientists leave behind. Yet the history of science is a history
not of individual discovery but of multiple, overlapping,
coincidental discovery. All researchers know this in their
hearts. It is why they rush to publish any new finding,
aware that competitors cannot be far behind. As the sociologist Robert K. Merton has found, the literature of science is strewn with might-have-been genius derailed or
forestalled—"those countless footnotes ... that announce
with chagrin: 'Since completing this experiment, I find
that Woodworth (or Bell or Minot, as the case may be)
had arrived at this same conclusion last year, and that
Jones did so fully sixty years ago.'" The power of genius
may lie, as Merton suggests, in the ability of one person to
accomplish what otherwise might have taken dozens. Or
perhaps it lies—especially in this exploding, multifarious,
information-rich age—in one person's ability to see his science whole, to assemble, as Newton did, a vast unifying
tapestry of knowledge. Feynman himself, as he entered his
forties, prepared to undertake this very enterprise: a mus-
tering and a reformulating of all that was known about
physics.

Scientists still ask the *what if* questions. What if Edison
had not invented the electric light—how much longer
would it have taken? What if Heisenberg had not invented
the S matrix? What if Fleming had not discovered penicillin? Or (the king of such questions) what if Einstein had

not invented general relativity? "I always find questions like that . . . odd," Feynman wrote to a correspondent who posed one. Science tends to be created as it is needed.

"We are not that much smarter than each other," he said.

10

ELISSA ELY

Dreaming of Disconnecting a Respirator

Boston *Globe*,
July 1, 1989

*The science column is a news format that has been around
for a long time, practiced by writers like Jake Page, Tom Sieg-
fried at the Dallas* Morning Herald, *Dianne Dumanoski of
the Boston* Globe, *David Quammen at* Outside, *contributors
to big-city-newspaper Op Ed pages, editors of science magazines, and many scientists themselves. Today, though, the science column is becoming a more intimate and freewheeling
form than the standard editorial, allowing for and encouraging open discussion of more personal issues that get overlooked in formal science and journalistic venues but affect
deeply the researchers who think about them.*

*Elissa Ely's "Dreaming of Disconnecting a Respirator" draws
from the still hours of the night in a hospital's intensive care
unit, when the only sound is of the bellows whoosh of respirators and, perhaps, a small transistor radio. As an intern, she
says, she realized the extent to which she had become removed
from her own sense of self one night when watching the cardiac monitor of a dying patient. "I watched it slow down, and
start to fibrillate, and I was so absorbed I didn't think until
later that here I had seen a real person die."*

Ely is a gifted writer and now a practicing psychiatrist who chronicled the stages of her medical education in several Boston Globe columns. She comments regularly on science for National Public Radio. Born in 1956, she attended Wesleyan College as an undergraduate. A writer passionate about finding new connections and a place for the individual in the cosmos, she majored in religion. "I feared science terribly," she says. "I still do." She tried her hand as a playwright in Boston and then as a worker in a homeless shelter, where she listened to the poignant stories of alcoholics as she washed their feet. In her writings she tells similarly poignant stories of patients and the bonds that tie them to doctors, to family, and to each other. "I'm looking for that unexpected connection," she says, drawing inspiration from Edith Wharton and Tolstoy. And Arthur Conan Doyle. "Doyle, really, was the ultimate science writer because he created the ultimate scientist, Sherlock Holmes."

L ATE ONE NIGHT IN THE INTENSIVE CARE UNIT, one eye on the cardiac monitor and one on the Sunday paper, I read this story:

An infant lies in a hospital, hooked to life by a respirator. He exists in a "persistent vegetative state" after swallowing a balloon that blocked the oxygen to his brain. This "vegetative state," I've always thought, is a metaphor inaccurately borrowed from nature, since it implies that with only the proper watering and fertilizer, a comatose patient will bloom again.

One day his father comes to visit. He disconnects the respirator and, with a gun in hand, cradles his son until the infant dies. The father is arrested and charged with murder.

In the ICU where I read this, many patients are bound to respirators. I look to my left and see them lined up, like potted plants. Some will eventually be "weaned" back to their own lung power. Others will never draw an independent breath again.

In Bed No. 2, there is a woman who has been on the respirator for almost two months. When she was admitted with a simple pneumonia, there were no clues she would come apart so terribly. On her third day, she had a sudden and enigmatic seizure. She rolled rapidly downhill. Her pneumonia is now gone, but her lungs refuse independence: she can't come off the machine.

I know little about this patient except that she is elderly and European. (It is the peculiar loss of hospital life that patients often exist here with a medical history, but not a personal one.) I sometimes try to picture her as she might have been: busy in a chintz kitchen smelling of pastries. She might have hummed, rolling dough. Now there is a portable radio by the bed, playing Top Ten, while the respirator hisses and clicks 12 times a minute.

The family no longer visits. They have already signed the autopsy request, which is clipped to the front of her thick chart. Yet in their pain, they cannot take the final step and allow us to discontinue her respirator. Instead, they have retired her here, where they hope she is well cared for, and where she exists in a state of perpetual mechanical life.

I have dreamed of disconnecting my patient's respirator. Every day I make her death impossible and her life unbearable. Each decision—the blood draws, the rectal temperatures, the oxygen concentration—is one for or against life. No action in the ICU is neutral. Yet many of these decisions are made with an eye toward legal neutrality—and this has little to do with medical truth. The medical truth is that this patient exists without being alive. The legal neutrality is that existence is all that is required.

Late at night, reading in the ICU, the story of that father—so dangerous and impassioned—puts me to shame. I would never disconnect my patient from her respirator; it is unthinkable. But this is not because I am a doctor. It is because I feel differently toward her than the father toward his son.

I do not love her enough.

11

ROBERT S. CAPERS
AND ERIC LIPTON

Hubble Error: Time, Money and Millionths of an Inch

Hartford *Courant*,
March 31, 1991

The saga of the Hubble telescope has captivated science writers for as long as NASA has been around. The grand dream of seeing the heavens anew echoed the very beginnings of science in Galileo's first observations with his handmade telescope. From the first, though, the Hubble project seemed "snakebit" as one engineer puts it in this first article from a Pulitzer Prize–winning series by Robert S. Capers and Eric Lipton. Originally scheduled to be launched with the space shuttle Challenger *in 1986, for instance, the project was delayed four years by the tragedy of the shuttle explosion. When the telescope did go up, it seemed a stunning setback—and fodder for late-night comics—when the brilliant mirror could not focus on the stars it was meant to see.*

There seemed also a vital, untold lesson in project management to be learned from the initial disaster. America's best planners and technicians had worked hard on the world's most expensive telescope. What had gone wrong? In 1990 two reporters for the Connecticut-based Hartford Courant set out to answer the question.

Their task was almost as formidable as the engineering challenge and just as important in its implication for future big-ticket projects. When they started, Robert S. Capers was a forty-one-year-old, longtime editor who had little experience as a reporter, though he had written a monthly science column and had a background as a biology major. Eric Lipton was twenty-five; he had worked in the Courant's New Britain bureau for a little over a year. They wanted to tell a story of optical physics and big business and government; they knew none of their sources would want to discuss it. They wanted to re-create the unimaginably intense daily pressures on people who had lived through a virtual combat experience—but ten years before the writers visited them. Their approach amounted to a model of sophisticated salesmanship.

Deciding that phone calls would get nowhere, the reporters began knocking on doors. "We knew we had basically one shot to convince them," Lipton says of their ambush interview technique. They gave each person a carefully prepared pitch that, in essence, said: We want to tell your story. They tailored and rehearsed their argument for each individual. They were willing to compromise on conditions—granting anonymity if necessary. They prepared a general list of questions and a specific list for each subject, including questions about the weather, people's clothes, and the noise of the machinery. Only one subject balked; others invited them to interviews that lasted as long as eight or nine hours over successive nights.

The series evolved from a succession of profiles to a dramatic narrative, a style still considered new today in newspapers. Capers and Lipton realized theirs was most of all a story of people forced to scrimp and save and make deadlines while creating the most expensive telescope ever. Weaving together the themes of government and corporate bureaucracy and the day-to-day feelings of brilliant managers, they took the narrative from the realm of esoteric engineering to one of almost Greek tragedy, where a tiny, fatal flaw led to what seemed a national debacle.

That defeat was reversed by an even more stunning shut-
tle mission to give the Hubble, in essence, a new pair of
glasses. It was the subjects' success. Capers gave the engi-
neers the journalist's ultimate compliment: "They were truth
tellers."

ON A CHILLY AUTUMN DAY IN 1978, IN AN UPSTATE New York factory town, Ronald R. Rigby Jr. stared at the glass that would dominate his life for the next three years.

The stocky man ran his thick fingers gently along the smooth face of what looked like a round, transparent waf-fle. The sheer size of it thrilled him. Eight feet in diam-eter, with a 2-foot hole in the center.

No one had ever tried what Rigby's employer, the Perkin-Elmer Corp. of Connecticut, expected him to do.

He was to use a new technology to turn the 1-ton slab from the Corning Glass Works into the finest mirror in the world—the heart of a space telescope.

Rigby would have to make sure his team shaved off just the right amount of glass. Take off too much, and the $1 million blank would be ruined: The correct shape could never be achieved. Polish too little and the tele-scope's images wouldn't be much better than those from any of a dozen good earthbound observatories.

The difference would be measured in millionths of an inch. And in the millions of dollars in this and other gov-ernment contracts.

The enormous expectations for the space telescope, per-haps the most complex scientific instrument ever made, rested largely on Rigby's mirror. It would need a curve so fine, a surface so sublimely smooth, that it could capture and focus light that had traveled billions of years—light that had left the farthest reaches of the universe even be-fore the stars had formed.

Some of the nation's preeminent astronomers had spent decades lobbying for the telescope, and many had planned their careers around its explorations. They believed it would help answer cosmological questions that had intrigued mankind for thousands of years: How big is the universe? How old is it? What is its fate?

The astronomers also hoped that, in the best tradition of scientific inquiry, the telescope's greatest discoveries would be unexpected.

Rigby, a 48-year-old optical engineer, felt up to the challenge. Hadn't he spent 11 years with Perkin-Elmer, proving himself a superior manager time and again in making large mirrors for U.S. spy satellites? Hadn't his work helped the company earn its reputation as one of the finest optical houses in the world?

Rigby and his colleagues didn't know it yet, but this job was not going to be anything like the others.

In quest of perfection and trying to meet all-but-impossible deadlines, the mirror makers would abandon family life and outside interests. Two men would nearly die under the pressure.

In the rush, some of them would ignore repeated evidence of errors. They would brush aside pointed warnings and discourage supervision, making it harder for others to catch their mistakes.

When the $1.5 billion Hubble Space Telescope finally was launched in April 1990 and the terrible truth about its misshapen mirror was revealed, these men would be blamed for a fundamental error.

But the story of their mistake, and how it escaped notice, tells as much about the decline of American space science as it does about their human failings.

The troubled atmosphere was provided by Perkin-Elmer, a company built on basic research and innovation but struggling to adjust to new management techniques and international competition. The unprecedented pressures of time and money came from the National Aeronautics and Space Administration, trying futilely with a dwindling budget to support the kinds of showcase projects that had once defined the nation's greatness.

On that cold day in Canton, N.Y., Rigby wasn't thinking about the external pressures. There was enough to worry about in technology alone.

As long as he could remember, he'd had a special feel for glass. It was his heritage. His grandfather had been an English glass blower who emigrated to the western Pennsylvania town of Jeannette to work in the glass industry.

Walking to school in Jeannette, young Rigby would slow down as he passed two glass factories, fascinated by the craftsmen working the bubbling liquid into crystal bottles. After attending college on a football scholarship—he was a guard, and a mathematics and physics major— Rigby went to work for Pittsburgh Plate Glass. Later he helped develop the technique used for making curved side windows on automobiles.

Rigby joined Perkin-Elmer in 1967 and quickly earned the respect of scientists with his hard-driving competence, his straight talk and honesty. Everyone knew him simply as Bud.

The demands of this new project awed him. The space telescope's mirror would have to be so perfect that if its surface were the size of the Atlantic Ocean, no wave could be higher than 3 inches. On the ground, telescopes couldn't take advantage of such quality because the light that reaches them already is degraded by the earth's atmosphere. So their mirrors always had been made with a good degree of handicraft, shaped roughly by machine, then polished to their final form by opticians whose work fell somewhere between science and art.

To make the space telescope's main mirror, as well as its

12.5-inch secondary mirror, Perkin-Elmer devised a system at its Danbury plant that substantially advanced the science.

Lying on a bed of 134 titanium nails to simulate the gravity-free environment of space, the glass would be polished by a spinning abrasive pad attached to a swiveling arm.

For the first time, computers would control the speed, pressure and direction of the arm. After polishing runs lasting from 6 to 70 hours, the mirror would be trundled on rails to an adjacent room so Rigby's team could determine how much closer they had come to the desired shape.

For that purpose, the company's top scientists had designed an optical measuring system so precise that they used it only in the middle of the night, when there were no vibrations from tractor-trailers rumbling down Route 7 outside the plant. The system, consisting of an instrument called a null corrector and a special camera, was so sensitive the company had to pull out the speed bumps in the parking lot. They even had to shut down the air conditioners when they used it.

The trouble was, NASA designed the schedule and the funding for the program as though space mirrors this smooth were built all the time. The telescope could be finished on time and on budget only if no problems occurred. And even without problems, Rigby knew, his crew would have to put in some long hours to make the mirror's scheduled delivery in early 1980.

Unkind Cuts

At the Corning factory, little things already were going wrong.

The mirror was designed like a sandwich, with two

2-inch-thick plates fused to an interior of glass slats arranged in an egg-crate pattern 10 inches thick.

Inspecting the slats as the mirror was being assembled, another Perkin-Elmer man—David Burch, responsible for quality control—stepped carefully along a wooden board next to the glass. Suddenly the board broke.

An alert Corning worker lunged for Burch's shirt and swung him away, keeping him from crashing down into the middle of the slats. Burch sliced his hand on the glass but didn't damage the mirror.

Then, after the mirror's several parts had been joined in a 3,600-degree furnace, the workers discovered that the round outside band of the glass had fused in several places to the slats inside. This could cause dangerously uneven stresses in the mirror, especially during launch.

For 14 precious weeks, Corning technicians tried to cut out the fused glass without harming the surface.

Instead of fixing the problem, however, they created a new one, leaving straight-edged grooves where they had cut. Rigby sweated; straight edges could cause cracks that could quickly spread.

When the glass finally was trucked in December 1978 to the Perkin-Elmer plant in Wilton for preliminary grinding, Rigby's technicians used acid to eat away at the edges, leaving the glass round. They then used a dental tool to cut the fused places in the glass. The work was successful, but it delayed the start of polishing.

One spring day in 1979, an inspector halted the grinding. He had discovered a tiny cluster of fissures, a flaw that looked like a quarter-inch-wide teacup. Small, but it could ruin the mirror if not removed.

As Burch put it, "Have you ever left your car in the garage with a small crack in the windshield?" You could come back in the morning to find the crack had spread to fill the whole windshield.

It came to be called the Teacup Affair. First, Perkin-Elmer and NASA engineers argued vehemently for two weeks. Some wanted to go in from the side of the mirror, then drill up and under the crack. Rigby, who could out-shout just about everyone, was in this camp. He was anxious about leaving a blemish. "I did not want to cut the face of the mirror," he said.

But drilling from the side would leave glass dust inside the hollow center of the mirror. That wouldn't hurt the mirror, but the dust might escape in space and interfere with the performance of the telescope's instruments.

Drilling in from the top and removing a core of glass, including the crack, was risky as well. But it seemed to be the better choice. So Rigby held his breath as an engineer lowered a drilling tool onto the surface of the mirror and slowly dug a hole in the glass. "It was like brain surgery," he said.

The delicate job was a success; the hole would not go away but it wouldn't affect the mirror's performance. However, the Teacup Affair had cost Rigby another six weeks. A year had been allowed for the rough grinding in Wilton. The mirror had been scheduled for delivery to the Danbury plant for fine polishing in early September 1979; it didn't arrive until late May 1980.

Already Rigby was nine months behind schedule and the hard stuff hadn't even begun.

And Rigby was fully aware what delays in the mirror polishing meant. While Perkin-Elmer and Lockheed Missiles and Space Co. held the major contracts, thousands of people in dozens of companies and laboratories around the world were building parts of the space telescope. NASA wrote a schedule to coordinate all their work. Each bottleneck would have a ripple effect, would cost money. One engineering team might have to sit idle, collecting paychecks, waiting for another team to deliver its job.

A delay in the mirror would delay assembly of the 43-foot-long telescope, delay installation of the scientific instruments, delay Lockheed's work putting together the 12-ton satellite. Ultimately, it would postpone the optimistic launch date of December 1983.

Second thoughts and double-checking were luxuries this program could not afford.

LOWBALLED

From the start, Perkin-Elmer was operating without any flexibility because the company had underbid the telescope contract. With its considerable space experience, Perkin-Elmer desperately wanted the business and the reputation it would gain by building the telescope.

NASA, although confident about the company's technical expertise, admitted to some concerns about Perkin-Elmer's ability to plan and manage such a complex project.

In addition, the company's competitor, Eastman Kodak Co., had proposed two major testing procedures to catch any flaws in the mirror. Kodak proposed to make two main mirrors using different equipment and then to test each mirror with the instruments used to make the other, choosing the better of the two for the telescope. Kodak also proposed testing the telescope's main mirror and its smaller, secondary mirror together before launch.

Perkin-Elmer proposed no such testing. However, Perkin-Elmer said it could do the job for $70 million—$35.5 million less than Kodak.

For public consumption, the company argued, and NASA concurred, that much of the needed technology already was in hand. But many later described the bid as a partnership in deception by NASA and the company's managers.

Perkin-Elmer "had to lie to get the contract. NASA had to lie to get the money," said one key company official. "It was a fable to start with."

Like other government agencies, NASA had winked at underbidding. Richard C. Babish, a former Perkin-Elmer technical director, recalls going to meetings at which U.S. officials would coach corporate officers on winning contracts. The government man would stand up and talk about the game, Babish said, warning that if the company sent a realistic estimate, "Congress will say no."

Once the project was approved, the official would explain, the companies could demand more money for unforeseen technical challenges. Yet by the time work began on the space telescope, Congress no longer was willing to give NASA extra money. In turn, the space agency's top managers became unsympathetic to Perkin-Elmer's pleas, threatening to cancel the project if it didn't stay within budget.

When Donald Fordyce became Perkin-Elmer's telescope project manager in 1982, he found no money budgeted for whole areas of scheduled work. The company wasn't trying to hide the overruns and contract changes that increased its cost, Fordyce felt. Perkin-Elmer had gone to NASA earlier to say that the cost of the contract had quadrupled to $272 million. NASA refused to accept the new figure. The company "just kind of felt snakebit," Fordyce said. "That was the word that was used around the plant. It was like, 'Gee whiz, this program is snakebit, you can't get it done.'"

So corners were cut. "You know the thing to do every time you get in trouble with money is kill the spares, cut that other piece of test equipment, then pare yourself down to the point where you're just hanging on by a thread," Fordyce said.

Sleeping on the Job

In Danbury, Rigby eventually had to put the mirror polishers on back-to-back 10-hour shifts. Rigby tried to be forthright about the time he would need to do the work, but whenever he sent a schedule to management it was cut in half before it even reached NASA.

The crew would polish for days, then move the mirror to the testing room to find out how well they had done. Then they would get a new set of computer instructions and start the next run.

"At the time, it was a matter of everybody working crazy, long, hard hours to pull things back on schedule and save money there," Rigby said.

Under pressure from Perkin-Elmer and NASA, Daniel J. McCarthy, Rigby's boss, said he was "forever bugging him" to move faster.

Rigby protected his mirror and his crew as best he could. "I don't think he ever did anything except the way he thought it should be done, schedule or otherwise," McCarthy said.

While many at Perkin-Elmer saw the space telescope as just another job, although a bigger and more public one, Rigby and others felt it was special.

"It was the trip of a lifetime. I don't think I ever lost sight of the fantasy of it," Burch said. He thought it was wonderful that someone who grew up in an Ohio farm town could end up working on a telescope that would change the understanding of the universe.

The aura of the project added to the pressure. In scheduling the hourly workers, Rigby tried to make sure they did not work too many weekends in a row or too many late nights. But he drove himself hard, coming in at 6:30 A.M. and often not leaving until 10 P.M., sometimes later. He couldn't smoke in the polishing room but managed to go through two packs of Kool menthols a day anyway, largely by smoking in his office. He'd rarely go two hours before chewing one of the antacid tablets he kept in his shirt pocket or taking a swig of Maalox from the bottle in his desk drawer to soothe the ulcer in his esophagus.

When Rigby was a boy, his father worked at a bank during the day and ran his own accounting business at night, and rarely saw his family. Now Rigby was playing the same role for his wife and two college-age children.

"Bud is not what you would call a delegator," said Wilhelm R. Geissler, Rigby's master optician on the project.

Rigby would often call Geissler to his office to talk about the polishing. After a few of these sessions took place at 2 A.M., Geissler figured it would be easier to sleep at the plant than to go home. He brought in a cot and set it up in a trailer in the parking lot.

Geissler had joined Perkin-Elmer in 1956, when he was 19, a few weeks after arriving in America from Germany. Widely regarded as a prodigy, he came from a long and proud German tradition of craftsmanship in glass for lenses and mirrors.

Opticians traditionally did their work with a kind of black magic, even rubbing their thumbs along a lens or mirror to apply the finishing touch. At Perkin-Elmer they told the story of the guy who lost his thumb to a lawnmower and thought his career was over.

But unlike other Old World opticians in the industry, Geissler fully embraced the idea that on this mirror, he would rely on computers to tell him how to polish. "The approach that was used was absolutely fantastic. I happen to be a person who believes in the new approaches," Geissler said.

This reliance on machines—coupled perhaps with fatigue—exacted a price from the mirror.

One morning, Geissler punched the wrong numbers

into the computer, hitting "1.0" instead of "0.1." To every-one's horror, the whirring polishing tool began digging a groove near the inside edge of the mirror.

It could have been much worse. A technician watched the mirror constantly during the hours it was polished, keeping his finger on the kill switch on a long electrical cord that ran to the motor. The job was mind-numbing. But the technician on duty acted instantly when the pol-ishing tool ran amok.

The motor cut off, preventing the arm from leaving a deep scar. The groove was smoothed over somewhat in later polishing runs, but Geissler's mark would never go away completely.

THE FATAL FLAW

What no one knew was that there was a much more se-rious flaw in the project. And it had been there since the beginning of the fine polishing in Danbury.

The flaw was introduced in mid-1980 when technicians assembled that precision piece of optical testing equip-ment, the null corrector.

The cylindrical device, a little taller than a beer keg, consisted of two small mirrors and a small lens. Null cor-rectors had been used before, but Perkin-Elmer's elegantly simple new design could provide unprecedented accuracy, measuring surface smoothness to a fraction of the wave-length of light, a few millionths of an inch.

To test the telescope mirror, light from a laser would be sent through the null corrector and then bounced off the glass. The light then would pass back through the null corrector, creating a pattern of black and white lines. That interference pattern would be photographed; working with a computer, the scientists would analyze the photograph to determine where the mirror needed more polishing.

When the mirror was exactly the correct shape, the

light pattern seen in the photographs would be an evenly spaced series of straight lines.

Perkin-Elmer had to retool the null corrector after making a 5-foot mirror to prove to NASA that the company was up to the job. Company managers were pushing the null corrector technicians to do the adjustments quickly. Rigby's crew needed the null to get going on the fine polishing of the telescope's big mirror.

For one of the technicians, Geoffrey Rogers, the space telescope was the first job out of college. Only later would he realize how rushed and chaotic things had been.

Like the rest of the staff, Rogers understood the importance of his task. "It was so critical that the null corrector be absolutely accurate," he said, "because there was no other check to see if the mirror had the shape it was supposed to have."

The instrument, which worked perfectly on the demonstration mirror, was the responsibility of Rogers' boss, Lucian A. Montagnino, a meticulous, impeccably dressed 42-year-old engineer. Montagnino, a Stamford native and University of Connecticut graduate, had left Eastman Kodak in 1970 to join Perkin-Elmer. He was responsible for seeing that the retooling was done right.

Colleagues respected his intelligence and his sharp tongue, but Montagnino had few close friends in the company. He had little patience for those who didn't share his views or his expertise.

For the telescope mirror, Montagnino's crew spent several weeks making the tiny adjustments in the space between the null corrector's two internal mirrors. They had only a few days left for the final adjustment: the distance between the lower of the mirrors and the lens.

Special rods had been manufactured to measure the spaces. The rods were made of Invar, a material that doesn't expand or contract in heat or cold. They had been measured and cut, then shipped to an independent laboratory that certified their lengths.

But using the rods was not simple. Because an error of even the width of a human hair would make the mirror the wrong shape, a special microscope and a laser were used to make the measurements.

And the harried technicians made a mistake.

To set the distance between the lens and the mirror, the technicians eased a measuring rod into place and looked through the microscope at the end of the rod. They had to bounce the laser beam precisely off the tip, through a hole in a tiny cap on the rod.

The cap was coated with special paint so there would be no reflection unless the laser were aimed at the right spot. But one little spot of paint had worn off. Unknown to the technicians, the laser was set to bounce off that worn spot.

Maybe if they hadn't been so rushed, they would have recognized the problem. Because when they tried to set the null corrector's lens where the laser said to put it, something was wrong. The way the null corrector was built, the lens wouldn't go down far enough without adding something to the bracket that held the lens in place.

Under normal circumstances, this design anomaly might have triggered an engineering inquiry. But the deadline was upon them. There was no time for an inquiry.

There wasn't even time to ask the machine shop to custom-make spacers for the bracket. The technicians grabbed three household washers, the kind you could find in any hardware store for 20 cents. They flattened the washers and put them into the $1 million null corrector.

The technicians moved the lens 1.3 millimeters lower than it was supposed to go. Charles Robbert, the engineer who shimmed the lens with the washers, doesn't remember much discussion about it, just the pressure to finish up the job.

Warning lights should have flashed all around, John D. Rehnberg, who was the company's division head at the time, says now. "Optical design is very precise," he says. "If something isn't working right, you didn't build it the way the designer had it. The guys assumed too much themselves."

The designer himself, Abe Offner, is surprised that he was not consulted. "These things are made so they would not need washers," he says. "I would have expected any questions to be referred to me."

But only the technical crew was in the room. Because there was so much other work going on, company and NASA quality-control inspectors rarely visited the lab where the null adjustments were done.

As the technicians moved the null corrector atop the measuring tower in Danbury, they handled it "like the crown jewels," Rigby remembers. But once it was up there, no one was going to be able to recheck the spacings between its mirrors and lens.

For the next 11 months, Rigby and his crew would rely entirely on the null corrector to tell them whether the mirror was getting closer to the desired shape. It was as if they were cutting and measuring with a 13-inch ruler they thought was a foot long.

During that time, there would be ample evidence of a flaw. It would be staring them all in the face—tacked up on the walls in Rigby's office, distributed among the opticians and engineers, entered in the official logbooks.

Questions were raised, but they were never answered.

There was no time.

Rigby was no expert on null correctors. He relied on Montagnino for that. And Montagnino said to trust him and his device.

DIANE ACKERMAN

Why Leaves Turn Color in the Fall

From A *Natural History of the Senses,*
Random House, 1991

*"We live on the leash of our senses," says Diane Ackerman
of her book* A Natural History of the Senses. *"I wanted to
break that leash." Her writing style, an act of celebration in
words, helps break some of the traditional bounds of prose
with its innovative and imaginative leaps in time and
space.*

*Ackerman began combining science and art in her under-
graduate student days at Boston College and Penn State;
she majored first in psychology and physiology and then in
English. By the time she was pursuing two master's degrees
and a Ph.D. at Cornell University, she was turning that interdisciplinary interest into a first book, a volume of poetry
called* The Planets (1976). *"I've never made the distinction
between science and humanities," she says. "To ignore science is to bankrupt the experience of living."*

*This author of five books of poems calls herself a nature
writer and still feels like a newcomer to prose. "It's taken me
ten years to learn how to write prose," Ackerman says. "I'll
have one thing at the top of the page and one thing at the
bottom and no idea of how to get from one to the other."
Freelance journalism helped her learn how to condense*

without losing the rapture that is the hallmark of her style. Her early projects included contributions to Parade *and* Life *magazines: "I reviewed national monuments that had been sapped of their meaning, like the Grand Canyon, and I learned from the experiences how to pour myself into a subject and let it overtake me."*

Born in Waukegan, Illinois, Ackerman has written four other works of nonfiction: Twilight of the Tenderfoot *(1980),* On Extended Wings *(1985),* The Moon by Whalelight *(1991), and* Natural History of Love *(1994). Now a* New Yorker *staff writer, Ackerman has a unique approach to structure and content. She often keeps her research completely in her head but states: "I wouldn't recommend it."*

"Why Leaves Turn Color in the Fall" was originally a short article for Condé Nast's Traveler. *It picks up on perhaps the most glorious gift to the sense of sight—fall color—and expands to take in subjects as diverse as biblical paradise and our own mortality.*

T HE STEALTH OF AUTUMN CATCHES ONE UNAWARE. Was that a goldfinch perching in the early September woods, or just the first turning leaf? A red-winged blackbird or a sugar maple closing up shop for the winter? Keen-eyed as leopards, we stand still and squint hard, looking for signs of movement. Early-morning frost sits heavily on the grass, and turns barbed wire into a string of stars. On a distant hill, a small square of yellow appears to be a lighted stage. At last the truth dawns on us: Fall is staggering in, right on schedule, with its baggage of chilly nights, macabre holidays, and spectacular, heart-stoppingly beautiful leaves. Soon the leaves will start cringing on the trees, and roll up in clenched fists before they actually fall off. Dry seedpods will rattle like tiny gourds. But first there will be weeks of gushing color so bright, so pastel, so confettilike, that people will travel up and down the East Coast just to stare at it—a whole season of leaves.

Where do the colors come from? Sunlight rules most living things with its golden edicts. When the days begin to shorten, soon after the summer solstice on June 21, a tree reconsiders its leaves. All summer it feeds them so they can process sunlight, but in the dog days of summer the tree begins pulling nutrients back into its trunk and roots, pares down, and gradually chokes off its leaves. A corky layer of cells forms at the leaves' slender petioles, then scars over. Undernourished, the leaves stop producing the pigment chlorophyll, and photosynthesis ceases. Animals can migrate, hibernate, or store food to prepare for winter. But where can a tree go? It survives by dropping its leaves, and by the end of autumn only a few fragile threads of fluid-carrying xylem hold leaves to their stems.

A turning leaf stays partly green at first, then reveals splotches of yellow and red as the chlorophyll gradually breaks down. Dark green seems to stay longest in the veins, outlining and defining them. During the summer, chlorophyll dissolves in the heat and light, but it is also being steadily replaced. In the fall, on the other hand, no new pigment is produced, and so we notice the other colors that were always there, right in the leaf, although chlorophyll's shocking green hid them from view. With their camouflage gone, we see these colors for the first time all year, and marvel, but they were always there, hidden like a vivid secret beneath the hot glowing greens of summer.

The most spectacular range of fall foliage occurs in the northeastern United States and in eastern China, where the leaves are robustly colored thanks in part to a rich climate. European maples don't achieve the same flaming reds as their American relatives, which thrive on cold nights and sunny days. In Europe, the warm, humid weather turns the leaves brown or mildly yellow. Anthocyanin, the pigment that gives apples their red and turns leaves red or red-violet, is produced by sugars that remain in the leaf after the supply of nutrients dwindles. Unlike the carotenods, which color carrots, squash, and corn, and turn leaves orange and yellow, anthocyanin varies from year to year, depending on the temperature and amount of sunlight. The fiercest colors occur in years when the fall sunlight is strongest and the nights are cool and dry (a state of grace scientists find vexing to forecast). This is also why leaves appear dizzyingly bright and clear on a sunny fall day: The anthocyanin flashes like a marquee.

Not all leaves turn the same color. Elms, weeping willows, and the ancient ginkgo all grow radiant yellow, along with hickories, aspens, bottlebrush buckeyes, cottonweeds, and tall, keening poplars. Basswood turns bronze, birches bright gold. Water-loving maples put on a symphonic display of scarlets. Sumacs turn red, too, as do flowering dogwoods, black gums, and sweet gums. Though some oaks yellow, most turn a pinkish brown. The farmlands also change color, as tepees of cornstalks and bales of shredded-wheat-textured hay stand drying in the fields. In some spots, one slope of a hill may be green and the other already in bright color, because the hillside facing south gets more sun and heat than the northern one.

An odd feature of the colors is that they don't seem to have any special purpose. We are predisposed to respond to their beauty, of course. They shimmer with the colors of sunset, spring flowers, the tawny buff of a colt's pretty rump, the shuddering pink of a blush. Animals and flowers color for a reason—adaptation to their environment— but there is no adaptive reason for leaves to color so beautifully in the fall any more than there is for the sky or ocean to be blue. It's just one of the haphazard marvels the planet bestows every year. We find the sizzling colors thrilling, and in a sense they dupe us. Colored like living things, they signal death and disintegration. In time, they will become fragile and, like the body, return to dust. They are as we hope our own fate will be when we die: not to vanish, just to sublime from one beautiful state into another. Though leaves lose their green life, they bloom with urgent colors, as the woods grow mummified day by day, and Nature becomes more carnal, mute, and radiant.

We call the season "fall," from the Old English *feallan*, to fall, which leads back through time to the Indo-European *phol*, which also means to fall. So the word and the idea are both extremely ancient, and haven't really changed since the first of our kind needed a name for fall's leafy abundance. As we say the word, we're reminded of that other Fall, in the Garden of Eden, when fig leaves never withered and scales fell from our eyes. Fall is the time when leaves fall from the trees, just as spring is when flowers spring up, summer is when we simmer, and winter is when we whine from the cold.

Children love to play in piles of leaves, hurling them into the air like confetti, leaping into soft unruly mattresses of them. For children, leaf fall is just one of the odder figments of Nature, like hailstones or snowflakes. Walk down a lane overhung with trees in the never-never land of autumn, and you will forget about time and death, lost in the sheer delicious spill of color. Adam and Eve concealed their nakedness with leaves, remember? Leaves have always hidden our awkward secrets.

But how do the colored leaves fall? As a leaf ages, the growth hormone, auxin, fades, and cells at the base of the petiole divide. Two or three rows of small cells, lying at right angles to the axis of the petiole, react with water, then come apart, leaving the petioles hanging on by only a few threads of xylem. A light breeze, and the leaves are airborne. They glide and swoop, rocking in invisible cradles. They are all wing and may flutter from yard to yard on small whirlwinds or updrafts, swiveling as they go. Firmly tethered to earth, we love to see things rise up and fly—soap bubbles, balloons, birds, fall leaves. They remind us that the end of a season is capricious, as is the end of life. We especially like the way leaves rock, careen, and swoop as they fall. Everyone knows the motion. Pilots sometimes do a maneuver called a "falling leaf," in which the plane loses altitude quickly and on purpose, by slipping first to the right, then to the left. The machine weighs a ton or more, but in one pilot's mind it is a weightless thing, a falling leaf. She has seen the motion before, in the Vermont woods where she played as a child. Below her the trees radiate gold, copper, and red. Leaves are falling, although she can't see them fall, as she falls, swooping down for a closer view.

At last the leaves leave. But first they turn color and thrill us for weeks on end. Then they crunch and crackle underfoot. They *shush*, as children drag their small feet through leaves heaped along the curb. Dark, slimy mats of leaves cling to one's heels after a rain. A damp, stuccolike mortar of semidecayed leaves protects the tender shoots with a roof until spring, and makes a rich humus. An occasional bulge or ripple in the leafy mounds signals a shrew or a field mouse tunneling out of sight. Sometimes one finds in fossil stones the imprint of a leaf, long since disintegrated, whose outlines remind us how detailed, vibrant, and alive are the things of this earth that perish.

13

MIKE TONER

When Bugs Fight Back

Atlanta *Constitution,*
August 23, 25; September 5, 1992

Mike Toner offered two innovations in his 1993 Pulitzer Prize–winning Atlanta Constitution *series, "When Bugs Fight Back." First, like Gleick, Angier, and Brownlee, he gathered dozens of seemingly unrelated, incremental developments in fields from agronomy to medicine, documented in publications as obscure as* Journal of Anti-Microbial Chemotherapy *and* Journal of Hospital Infections. *In these articles he found a frightening and growing world of antibiotic-resistant bacteria, lethal viruses, and pesticide-resistant insects. "We're reaching the stage where we're running out of drugs and pesticides," he says. "It surprised me that no one had written about it before." Much of his material had been previously published, but Toner notes that most science writers concentrate on only the major science journals—like the* Journal of the American Medical Association *or* Science—*and not their more specialized cousins. "There's a treasure trove of story ideas in those other publications," he says.*

His second innovation resulted from the need to sell his four-month odyssey to his editors. To do so, he suggested both major trend pieces, like his article on the antibiotic Cipro, and stories of ordinary people like the Majors, whose

236 / THE NEW SCIENCE JOURNALISTS

sons suffered from today's most common early childhood malady—chronic ear infections. "I asked researchers for the names of people who had been affected by these bugs," Toner says. This attention to victims gives the series a unique impact. "It's important to show how science can be 'news you can use' around here," Toner says. "And I had to do that to make the material come alive."

"When Bugs Fight Back" was published as a twelve-part occasional series between August 23 and October 16, 1992. These three examples show the range of subjects from case studies of a single child's painful rite of passage and a wonder-drug gone awry, to the sweeping examination of ominous trends in hospitals and on farms.

For Toner, born in 1944 and educated at the University of Iowa and Northwestern University's Medill School of Journalism, the key to the series came in a 1990 talk at the annual meeting of the American Association for the Advancement of Science in Chicago. "The researcher discussed the problems of pesticide and antibiotic resistance. I had never connected them before." Toner began keeping a file, which, for a long time, he lacked the ambition to do anything about. Finally, he recalls, "When I switched back from editing to writing at the Atlanta Constitution, I wanted to do something important. So I took out the file and dusted it off."

Toner's clear and direct style is deceptively simple. It comes out of great care in editing. "It's not what you leave in," he says, "but what you leave out that makes a piece."

HOSPITALS AND FARMS UNDER SIEGE

The death certificate attributed the 58-year-old heart patient's demise to "complications" following bypass surgery.

The real reason made even his doctors cringe. Antibiotics didn't work anymore.

For four months, doctors at the University of Michigan Medical Center had struggled to control a bacterial infection that had invaded the man's chest cavity. The germs, however, were resistant to every available drug.

In the end, the bugs triumphed—and doctors at one of the country's premier medical institutions were as powerless to prevent it as doctors were 50 years ago, in the days before penicillin.

"If he hadn't had such a resistant strain, he would have made it," says Dennis Schaberg, professor of medicine at the University of Michigan medical school in Ann Arbor.

"I hate to sound like Chicken Little, but with certain microorganisms, we are back to a point in time where we have no options left. It's tough to explain something like that to the family of the patient. Very tough."

A growing number of patients—and their families—are discovering a grim new reality of medicine in the 1990s. Antibiotics, those too-good-to-be-true compounds that have provided mankind with mastery over infectious disease, don't work like they used to.

The bugs are fighting back. And they are getting very good at it.

On city streets, in remote jungle clinics, on the farm and in back yards, the world's simplest creatures—bacteria, viruses, insects and weeds—are unraveling the chemical security blanket that has nurtured a half-century of progress in both public health and agriculture.

Whether we are conscious of it or not, the ability of these mindless creatures to adapt to the chemical warfare we wage on them has become a significant force in our daily lives. Look closely at any infectious disease for which there is a cure and you'll find bugs with a cure for the cure.

Have a child with an ear infection that won't go away?

Deep in the recesses of your toddler's middle ear, there is probably a resistant bug to blame.

Having trouble getting rid of Fido's fleas or the cockroaches under your sink? Chances are, they're resistant too.

Did your stomach tie itself in knots after your last trip to a restaurant salad bar? If it was food poisoning, chances are one in three that the bug you took home with you was resistant.

Like the villains in a late-night horror show, resistant strains of mankind's oldest enemies are finding ways to sabotage our most sophisticated technology. And even the malevolent microbes of "The Andromeda Strain" or the angry hordes of "Killer Bees" aren't as scary as the real-life "superbugs" that are now emerging throughout the world.

In U.S. hospitals, where most people go to get well, 2 million people a year get sick after they check in—and the Centers for Disease Control (CDC) estimates that 60 percent of those infections are now resistant to at least one antibiotic. Because drug-resistant germs are twice as likely to be fatal, they contribute to 50,000 hospital deaths a year. And because they take twice as long to cure, they add as much as $30 billion a year to the cost of hospital care.

The toll in hospitals, however, is only the most documented facet of an insidious trend. Resistant strains of some of man's oldest enemies—malaria, tuberculosis, gonorrhea, food poisoning, pneumonia, even leprosy—are undermining public health throughout the world.

- Some new strains of tuberculosis, resurgent after 30 years of decline in the United States and Europe, have become resistant to so many drugs that they are virtually as untreatable as they were before the discovery of antibiotics.

- Malaria, which claims at least 1 million lives a year in the tropics, is on the comeback trail too, bolstered by the malaria parasite's growing resistance to drugs, and pesticide resistance of the mosquitoes that carry it.
- Even that familiar nemesis we call pneumonia, which claims more than 3.5 million lives a year world-wide—up to 50,000 of them in the United States—is becoming steadily more resistant to pencillin, which has controlled it for nearly 50 years.

Almost every human infection—from drug-resistant "superclap," which has become a worldwide problem, to stubborn staph infections that linger in nursing homes for years—is now resistant to at least one major class of antibiotics.

Among the insects, things are no better. On Long Island, where the Colorado potato beetle is now resistant to every major class of pesticides, potato farmers use tractor-towed blowtorches to kill the insects—one of at least 17 "superbugs" that are now resistant to all pesticides.

Weeds are getting tougher too. More than 100 species are now resistant to at least one herbicide, and wheat growers in Australia and the United Kingdom are encountering the first multiply-resistant "megaweeds," which scientists say could threaten the world's wheat supply.

Farmers' problems, of course, quickly become consumers' problems.

The clouds of pesticide-resistant sweet-potato whiteflies that devastated last winter's vegetable crops in California, Texas and Florida triggered supermarket sticker shock that gave us $3.50 cantaloupes and $2-a-pound tomatoes.

There is no great mystery about what is happening. The

bugs, whether single-celled microorganisms or the six-legged variety, are doing what comes naturally. They're surviving.

Bacteria have been on the Earth for at least 3 billion years; insects for at least 850 million years. Like all living things, they are constantly mutating, testing new traits that may give them an edge in a hostile environment.

With a new generation of bacteria every 20 minutes, trial and error can be a powerful survival tool. And when one bug finds something that works, it passes it on, sometimes even to other species.

With eons to adapt, bacteria have learned to live in the Earth's most hostile environments—from superheated deep-sea vents to the frozen slopes of Mount Everest. The few thousand antibiotics and pesticides that mankind has thrown at them have been, by comparison, a minor challenge.

The bugs' subversion of man-made chemicals has been unwittingly aided by the industries that market them, by "experts" who overuse them, and by ordinary people who treat them as technological "no-brainers" that promise, for a time, to change the course of evolution.

"The problem is not chemicals; it's the irresponsible way they are used," says University of Illinois entomologist Robert Metcalf. "Our shortsighted and irresponsible use of antibiotics and pesticides is producing strains of monster bugs resistant to nearly everything in our arsenal. The outlook is dismal. And it is getting worse."

The benefits of the 20th century's chemical "miracles" are indisputable. In the decade after the introduction of antibiotics, U.S. death rates from pneumonia, TB and influenza dropped 50 percent. World-wide, penicillin is thought to have added 10 years to life expectancy. And the heavy chemical use that fueled the Green Revolution has helped feed a burgeoning population.

Resistance is not a new phenomenon. The emergence in the 1940s of penicillin-resistant staph infections in hospitals and DDT-resistant houseflies proved that bugs could fight back.

Until recently, however, human ingenuity always pulled some new solution from technology's seemingly inexhaustible bag of tricks. Now, like an audience that has seen the magician's act before, the bugs are getting harder to fool.

In recent years, resistance has become so pervasive that some experts now fear medicine and agriculture are on the verge of regressing into the technological dark ages that preceded the era of antibiotics and pesticides.

For most people, for most illnesses, antibiotics still work. But in a growing number of cases, like the 58-year-old Michigan heart patient who died of mediastinitis caused by a hard-to-treat strain of enterococcal bacteria, the bugs' ability to accumulate resistance swiftly to several drugs at one time conjures up the ultimate nightmare.

"For some infections, we are very close to the end of the road," says Fred C. Tenover, the head of antimicrobics investigations for the CDC. "The worst-case scenario is almost here. We are very, very close to having bacteria resistant to every significant antibiotic ever developed. Only this time, there are no new drugs coming down the pike."

No aspect of the problem has dramatized the predicament more than the resurgence of tuberculosis—a disease that was once thought to have been vanquished by antibiotics. Although the numbers are relatively low—26,283 cases in the United States last year, 909 in Georgia—the upward trend and the growing prevalence of resistant TB worry many experts. A 50 percent increase in cases in Atlanta last year left the city with the highest TB rate in the country.

"TB is out of control," says Dixie Snider, who heads the

CDC's tuberculosis control division. "These outbreaks we have seen in the last year may be just the beginning."

But while tuberculosis gets the headlines, resistant strains of other diseases have been spreading almost unnoticed. Salmonella infections, which cause up to 4 million cases of food poisoning a year in the United States, have been rising steadily for 15 years—and antibiotic-resistant strains now make up one-third of all cases.

Health officials say the spread of resistant food-borne germs, which often acquire resistance genes from exposure to antibiotics used to treat farm animals, will mean larger outbreaks of food poisoning in the future—like a 1985 case of contaminated milk that sickened 180,000 in the Midwest.

New strains of resistant bugs are spreading globally. In Georgia, soaring rates of penicillin- and tetracycline-resistant gonorrhea—once unknown outside of Southeast Asia—have rendered obsolete drugs that controlled the disease for three decades. In five years, drug-resistant gonorrhea has increased tenfold in Georgia, enough to give the state the highest rate in the country.

Several antibiotics are still effective against gonorrhea, but pockets of resistance to these "last resort" drugs are already emerging in other countries.

"There is a global movement of these gonococcal strains, so it is probably only a matter of time before we have them in the United States," says Joan Knapp, an epidemiologist with the CDC's division of sexually transmitted diseases. "We are standing at the edge of a crisis. Every new antibiotic we have thrown at this bug has ended up making it more resistant."

Old enemies aren't the only ones learning new tricks. The AIDS virus is already resistant to the first three drugs approved to treat it.

Development of two other AIDS drugs were curtailed

this year after researchers discovered that the virus had developed resistance after only 12 weeks of treatment.

Insects are proving every bit as adept at chemical countermeasures as the microscopic "bugs" that cause human disease.

When Rachel Carson warned in 1962—two decades after the introduction of DDT—that repeated pesticide use would create a crisis in which "only the strong and fit remain to defy our efforts to control them," 137 insects were resistant to at least one pesticide.

Today, resistance has been documented in 504 species of insects and mites, 273 weeds, 150 fungi and other plant pathogens, and five kinds of rats. And, there are at least 17 insects that are resistant to all major classes of pesticides.

When pesticides fail, the consequences can assume almost biblical proportions, as they did during last year's invasion of sweetpotato whiteflies in California, Texas and Florida.

"We had fields that were completely devastated," says Nick Toscano, an entomologist at the University of California at Riverside. "It was like the plagues of locusts and grasshoppers that they have in the Middle East and Africa. At times, the clouds of whiteflies were so thick, it looked like a dust storm. If you drove through one of the clouds, you had to stop and scrape off your blackened windshield so you could see."

The U.S. Department of Agriculture has launched a five-year research program to seek new solutions to the problem.

But "Invasion of the Sweetpotato Whitefly II," the sequel, may be only months away. Experts say the insects, which thrive on cotton and peanuts, could soon become a major headache in Georgia, Mississippi and New Mexico, too.

"Control may not be impossible, but it's going to be

very expensive," says Gary Herzog, research entomologist at the University of Georgia's Coastal Plain Experiment Station in Tifton. "I had to tell a farmer the other day to expect a couple of years of serious hardship before we come up with a solution."

The rising tide of resistance is by no means an unbroken trend. The boll weevil, which almost instantly became resistant to DDT, is as susceptible to parathion as the day in 1949 when it was first sprayed on Southern cotton fields. Penicillin is still as effective against syphilis as it was when GIs were treated with it during World War II.

At other times, compounds that took years to develop have sometimes been rendered ineffective within months of their introduction.

Sometimes the bugs leapfrog ahead of technology. Farmers, using a class of chemicals called pyrethroids for the first time, have discovered insects that were already resistant. The same gene the bugs used to beat DDT also works against pyrethroids—and the trait has persisted even though DDT hasn't been used in the United States for 20 years.

Man-made chemicals of all kinds apply the same kind of "selective pressure" that Charles Darwin first described more than a century ago.

But the unrelenting use of antibiotics and pesticides has, in effect, thrown the evolution of resistance into fast forward.

In 50 years, bacteria have evolved more than 100 resistance factors to survive the onslaught of antibiotics. The same 50 years have seen the evolution of at least 1,640 combinations of insect-insecticide resistance.

From the bugs' point of view, the pressure to succeed is enormous.

Americans use 700 million pounds of pesticides and herbicides and 30 million pounds of antibiotics each year to treat everything from acne and gum disease to farmed catfish and feedlot cattle. Worldwide use of antibiotics and pesticides is three to five times that of the United States.

In the long run, the effects of this chemical blitz are not all for the better. Even though U.S. farmers use 33 times more pesticides than they did in the 1940s, pests now destroy 37 percent of the annual harvest, about what they did in medieval Europe, where farmers lost "one of every three grains grown."

The record on antibiotics is no more encouraging. Doctors write 220 million prescriptions for oral antibiotics a year, one for nearly every person in the country. But surveys show that about half are unnecessary or incorrectly prescribed. In addition to wasting billions of dollars a year, the misuse encourages the spread of resistant infections.

"The widespread, often inappropriate use of antibiotics ensures their phased obsolescence as new resistant organisms emerge," says Calvin Kunin, professor of medicine at Ohio State University, who has studied doctors' prescribing practices for more than a decade.

"Too many people think antibiotics are harmless," says Thomas F. O'Brien, a specialist in infectious diseases at Brigham and Women's Hospital in Boston. "We need to start persuading them that resistant bacteria can be just as dangerous as high blood pressure or cholesterol. You don't want it—and the way to avoid it is not to take antibiotics unnecessarily."

Although experts in infectious disease and agriculture seldom discuss their problems with each other, they think remarkably alike on one point. As bugs of all shapes and sizes grow more resistant, urgent efforts are needed to preserve the weapons that still work. That means abandoning the quick-fix mentality that has shaped the use of these chemicals for 50 years, and adding an ingredient that often has been missing—common sense.

246/ THE NEW SCIENCE JOURNALISTS

Some farmers are discovering that simple biological control—insects eating insects—works better than chemicals. Others believe advanced technology will ride to the rescue. Scientists, for instance, are already engineering insecticidal traits and herbicide resistance into hundreds of crops—a generation of plants that could reduce the need for chemical pesticides.

Some insects, however, have already developed resistance to these biological pesticides, and some experts worry that widespread use of such plants could actually promote resistance.

"History is repeating itself," says Marvin K. Harris, an entomologist at Texas A&M University. "Every time we come up with a new class of chemicals, we think we are finally home free. In every instance we have been wrong. There's no reason to think we won't be wrong again."

Advances in genetic engineering also promise a new generation of anti-infective drugs and vaccines, as well as speedier diagnosis of resistant microbes. But if hope springs eternal, it no longer flows with the optimism that greeted the introduction of penicillin a half-century ago.

"This is a race between man and bugs," says Colin Marchant, associate professor of pediatrics at the Tufts University School of Medicine. "The bugs have been very clever about finding ways to evade the drugs we make. So far we have been very clever about devising new ones, but I don't know how much longer we will be able to."

A Child's Painful Rite of Passage

Not yet 2, Manny Major has taken virtually every antibiotic doctors have for infections of the middle ear. With growing frustration, his parents have watched as each new prescription has failed to correct his problem.

"Every four to six weeks we would go back to the doctor

and he would switch antibiotics," says Donata Major, whose older son, 4-year-old Zane, also has suffered a half-dozen middle-ear infections.

"But the antibiotics always seemed to stop working after a week or so. I got tired of giving it to them. They got tired of taking it."

Manny's ordeal has become almost a national rite of passage for young children. The same kind of ear infections that last year sent the Majors, residents of DeKalb County, to the doctor nine times also prompted 30 million office visits nationwide.

Middle ear infections range in severity from the kind that require a 10-day course of amoxicillin ($5) to those that demand Pediazole ($22), Augmentin ($43), Suprax ($51) or, if all else fails, an operation to install tiny tubes in the child's ears ($2,000 and up).

Nationwide, middle-ear infections account for 20 million antibiotic prescriptions and more than $1 billion in medical expenses a year.

America's epidemic of middle-ear infections, however, is a sign of something more ominous than earaches. Made increasingly resistant by repeated exposure to antibiotics, the bugs that cause these infections are fighting back. In some cases, there are simply no antibiotics that work anymore.

Not all persistent ear infections are because of antibiotic failures. Some result from underdeveloped eustachian tubes, the passages between the nose and the middle ear, which can become blocked when a child has a cold.

"Kids are also in contact with more children at an earlier age these days, so there is more opportunity for the spread of infections," says Benjamin White, a pediatric otolaryngologist who inserted tubes in the Major children's ears at Atlanta's Scottish Rite Children's Medical Center.

But researchers say resistant germs play a large and growing role in this now nearly universal affliction of childhood.

A Centers for Disease Control study of children undergoing tube-placement surgery at Scottish Rite showed high-level resistance—up to 100 percent—among the three dominant bacterial causes of middle-ear infections.

"In kids with chronic ear infections, we found strains that could not be effectively treated with antibiotics," says CDC epidemiologist Ben Schwartz.

Resistance complicates an already difficult dilemma. When parents see their child in pain or discover pus oozing from an infant's ear, they want action. Neglected, such infections can lead to hearing loss, even life-threatening meningitis or encephalitis.

In more than half of all cases, however, the inflammation of the middle ear subsides on its own, making antibiotics unnecessary. Even the doctors can't be certain of the outcome.

"Most physicians rely only on a physical exam of the ear," says Robert Breiman, chief of epidemiology in the CDC's respiratory disease branch. "Antibiotics may not be warranted for inflammation due to an allergic reaction, a virus or structural problems, but when a mother wants something, it's difficult for a doctor not to prescribe an antibiotic."

Even when antibiotics are needed, the choice poses a second dilemma. Susceptibility of the microbes can be determined only by piercing the child's eardrum to sample the fluid—a painful process—so treatment usually involves an element of trial and error.

"On the first visit, a doctor usually puts the child on a 10- to 14-day course of amoxicillin," explains Dr. White. "But you don't know an antibiotic is working unless the child gets better. If it doesn't clear up after four to six weeks, you try a different antibiotic. You may switch two or three times before resorting to surgery."

Even if an infection subsides, doctors often prescribe low doses of antibiotics to keep it from returning. In the process, they may unwittingly encourage the remaining germs to become resistant.

That strategy is most likely to backfire in what doctors call the "culture clubs"—day-care centers, where children swap germs like Tinkertoys.

"Children who have recently received antibiotics—even for something other than an ear infection—are far more likely to have resistant organisms," says Dr. Schwartz. "The risk is highest in day-care centers, where children may acquire resistant organisms from other children who are taking antibiotics."

In a study at a Cleveland, Ohio, day-care center, the CDC found 52 youngsters with an identical strain of Streptococcus pneumoniae that was resistant to nearly all of the commonly used antibiotics. Children with the resistant germs were four times as likely to have received preventive doses of antibiotics.

"For the individual child, the benefits outweigh the harm, but low-dose antibiotics increase the chances of selecting resistant organisms that can be passed to others."

In time, vaccines, which marshal the body's natural defenses against germs, may replace antibiotics for the treatment of ear infections. A vaccine against Haemophilus influenzae, one of the major causes, already is available, and researchers are testing a potential vaccine against Streptococcus pneumoniae.

In the meantime, parents confronting the difficult choices that chronic ear infections pose can't expect much in the way of clear guidance.

Many doctors won't prescribe costly broad-spectrum antibiotics until they have tried first-line drugs. But studies by the Otitis Media Research Center of the Children's Hospital of Pittsburgh suggest that amoxicillin, the first choice of many doctors today, is so ineffective for serious ear infections that there no longer is much point in prescribing it.

Preventive, or prophylactic, antibiotic use is even more controversial. The American Academy of Pediatrics recommends it for children who have had three or more ear infections in the past six months. Amid rising concern over resistance, however, those guidelines are under review.

"The judicious use of prophylactic antibiotics is still probably the right thing to do," says Dr. Breiman. "But as resistance becomes more common, we may have to consider being more conservative with such uses of antibiotics."

"BEST OF DRUGS, WORST OF DRUGS"

The promotional banners, baseball hats and ballpoint pens all said, "Cipro Power." The free samples of white tablets and caplets that inundated doctors' offices throughout the country said, "Try me."

They did. In droves. In Cipro's first year on the market, doctors wrote 5 million prescriptions for the powerful new antibiotic that had taken German chemists nearly a decade to develop.

It took the bugs three months to find the first crack in its armor.

The pharmaceutical division of Miles Inc. launched sales of the new antibiotic in October 1987. By January 1988, staph infections resistant to it had emerged in several New York City hospitals. By late 1988, 31 hospitals and 28 nursing homes were reporting resistant germs, including one institution where the new strain was blamed for one-quarter of all staph-related deaths.

Bacterial resistance has been a problem since the dawn of the antibiotic age. But the rapid spread of resistance to ciprofloxacin in the past five years—a period in which Cipro has become one of the world's hottest-selling antibiotics—provides a chilling demonstration of how swiftly germs can subvert medicine's most advanced weapons.

The problem also provides a glimpse of how aggressive marketing of a new drug—and doctors' overuse of it—hastened the development of resistance and may have mortgaged the future of the entire class of infection-fighting drugs to which it belongs, the quinolones.

"Resistance has basically destroyed Cipro's usefulness for a number of infections," says Robert Gaynes, who heads the Centers for Disease Control's National Nosocomial Infections Surveillance System, which tracks national trends in hospital infections. "And when you get resistance to one quinolone, you pretty much lose the others. In just a few years, it has almost ruined a whole class of antibiotics."

To researchers at the Bayer AG laboratories in Leverkusen, Germany, where ciprofloxacin was developed, it looked like the perfect antibiotic. It worked against dozens of nasty germs—the causes of respiratory and urinary tract infections, gonorrhea, infectious diarrhea, typhoid fever and tuberculosis.

Best of all, Cipro could be given orally, with few side effects. It was far cheaper ($2.50 per tablet, $50 for a 10-day course) than the intravenous antibiotics it replaced. And because it blocked the replication of bacterial DNA, researchers dared to hope that it might be free of the resistance problems that had plagued other antibiotics.

With such obvious benefits, Cipro might have sold itself. But even in an industry that spends $1 billion more a year on promotion than it does on research, the selling of Cipro—hailed by Miles officials as "a major advance in the treatment of infections"—was something special.

"Cipro was—and probably still is—the most heavily promoted antibiotic on the market," says Calvin Kunin, professor of internal medicine at Ohio State University College of Medicine and a frequent critic of drug company efforts to influence doctors' prescribing practices. "There were free samples everywhere, and if doctors have free samples, they're going to use them on their patients."

Doctors, eager for an oral antibiotic that would work against almost anything, voted with their prescription pads. Within a year, Cipro was on the shelves of a record 78 percent of the nation's hospitals and sales had topped the $100 million mark, another record.

Last year, in fact, Americans spent $470 million on Cipro, more than $1.2 million a day. Virtually unknown five years ago, Cipro and similar quinolone antibiotics developed by other manufacturers now account for $1 in every $5 spent on antibiotics in the United States.

But as sales soared, trouble was brewing among the bugs. Even before the drug went on sale in the United States, reports of resistance were trickling in from Europe, where Cipro was first approved—and embraced—by doctors.

"Cipro was classic Dickens—the best of drugs and the worst of drugs," says Fred C. Tenover, head of the CDC's antimicrobics investigations division. "The dramatic rise in resistance occurred, in part, because physicians used these drugs to treat so many infections, even when less expensive drugs could be used. In some hospitals, they became almost universal antibiotics."

As the use of Cipro and other quinolones has soared, resistance has been reported in scores of U.S. hospitals as well as in France, Spain, Japan and the Philippines.

The Veterans Affairs Medical Center in Atlanta discovered just how swiftly Staphylococcus aureus, especially a strain called MRSA, which was already resistant to methicillin, could rise to the challenge.

The VA added Cipro to its pharmacy in May 1988. By August, the 500-bed hospital had its first cases of Cipro-resistant staph. Within a year, 79 percent of MRSA infections were resistant to Cipro, too.

"I don't think we've ever seen anything develop so quickly," says David Rimland, chief of infectious diseases for the Atlanta VA. "It surprised us."

Staph is a major concern in hospitals because it causes severe wound infections, meningitis, pneumonia and life-threatening blood infections.

But because Cipro is widely used outside hospitals, many patients now have resistant infections even before they are admitted.

Miles officials say nationwide surveys by a private laboratory, the Institutes for Microbiology in Franklin, Tenn., show that most hospital infections still respond well to Cipro.

But the laboratory's director, Clyde Thornsberry, says his surveys also show that 76 percent of the methicillin-resistant staph infections in his sample of U.S. hospitals are resistant to Cipro.

"Cipro is no longer a drug that should be considered for treatment of these staph infections," he says. Dr. Thornsberry also says there are "significant" levels of resistance in pseudomonas bacteria, which thrive in IV tubes and catheters, as well as in some of the germs that cause pneumonia and intestinal infections.

"What we saw with Cipro could have happened with any of the new quinolones if they had been abused with equal enthusiasm," says Christine Sanders, a medical microbiologist at the Creighton University School of Medicine, who did some of the early tests on ciprofloxacin. "Other drugs that have been greeted with over-exuberant enthusiasm have been met by a similar increase in resistance."

"This is the way physicians have grown up in the antibiotic era," Dr. Sanders says. "But our overuse of antibiotics has cost us billions of dollars we don't need to be spending—and billions more to find new drugs to replace ones that don't work anymore."

With advertising, samples, seminars and generous research "grants" to interested doctors, drug manufacturers do little to discourage such habits.

"Pharmaceutical companies don't worry about resistance," says Dr. Kunin. "It's like planned obsolescence in automobiles. The industry is interested in selling its products tomorrow. It's not interested in 10 years down the line."

In spite of the early emergence of resistance to Cipro, Miles officials say the antibiotic's benefits—millions of people cured and released from hospitals sooner than they might have been—outweigh any problems it has created. But the company is sponsoring an international effort to learn more about the problems and to try to minimize them.

"Resistance is still very specific, but Cipro and the other quinolones are clearly not going to be the magic bullet that people thought," says Roger Echols, director of anti-infectives research for Miles Inc.

Some researchers, however, say the bugs' ability to dodge this bullet should have come as no surprise. Today's quinolones are modified versions of nalidixic acid, a drug first used during the 1960s to treat urinary tract infections, but prescribed infrequently because of resistance.

"When Cipro was first identified, our scientists were well aware that one of the problems with nalidixic acid had been the development of resistance," says Dr. Echols. "Based on the laboratory experience, they concluded that resistance was much less likely."

With little evidence of resistance in early tests on humans, European countries began approving the new drug in mid-1987. In October 1987, the Food and Drug Administration approved Cipro for more than 40 kinds of infections, including staph and pseudomonas. It was the broadest-spectrum oral antibiotic ever marketed.

But independent researchers were already reporting—in communications with Miles scientists and in nationally circulated medical journals—that some bacteria, particularly staph and pseudomonas, were prone to develop resistance.

"We predicted that Cipro and other quinolones would quickly result in resistance in staph and some other organisms," says Dr. Sanders. "Miles knew that when they marketed the drug. The FDA probably knew it too."

The potential for resistance, however, receives little attention from federal regulators when they decide the fate of a new antibiotic.

"Our primary function is to ensure an antibiotic's safety and efficacy," says Albert T. Sheldon, supervisory microbiologist for the FDA's division of anti-infective drug products. "It would not be realistic to require 100 percent of the organisms to be susceptible. The FDA has never, that I know of, refused to label a drug because it might induce resistance."

To prevent the kind of overuse that encourages resistance, many hospitals now keep their most effective drugs under lock and key. At Grady Memorial Hospital in Atlanta, for instance, doctors aren't allowed to prescribe Cipro for their patients without a supervisor's approval.

But 75 percent of all prescriptions for Cipro are written by private practitioners, and a 1990 survey by Thomas R. Frieden, an infectious disease specialist at Yale University School of Medicine, found "widespread, inappropriate use" for infections that could have been treated as effectively with older, cheaper drugs. Dr. Frieden says there has been no slackening in misuse; sales of Cipro have soared since then. "Many physicians take the attitude, 'Why treat strep throat with penicillin when you have something bigger and better?' " says Dr. Tenover. "No matter what happens, it gets you out of trouble."

Although medical journals regularly carry detailed information about new antibiotics and FDA-approved uses are spelled out in the fine print of inserts in every package, doctors are too busy to read everything that crosses their desks. Many get their information from advertising or direct contact with sales representatives.

"The average clinician is frustrated," says Ronald Jones, director of the Anti-infectives Research Center at the University of Iowa College of Medicine. "With 80 different antibiotics, they have to sort out claims from counter-claims and blatant attacks on one company's product by another. They want one drug that works."

Miles officials say the company's claims about Cipro — whether in person or in print — are always within FDA and industry guidelines.

"Our salesmen emphasize what the appropriate uses are," says Dr. Echols. "We're concerned about the development of resistance too."

But skeptics say whether company representatives are dispensing free samples, promotional "freebies" such as notepads and pens, company-sponsored research or consulting fees, their principal aim is sales.

"The pharmaceutical industry doesn't control how a physician uses drugs," says Dr. Tenover. "But the industry has been very effective in showing the best side of their drugs to physicians."

Some doctors say advertising in medical journals, another major source of information for busy doctors, often makes misleading claims.

Even as hospitals in Europe grappled with outbreaks of

Cipro-resistant staph, Miles' ads in medical journals were touting the antibiotic as "highly active" in laboratory tests against staph. A two-line footnote in fine print cautioned that such claims did not "imply a correlation" with clinical use.

A recent study for the inspector general's office of the U.S. Department of Health and Human Services concluded that 70 percent of the advertising for antibiotics—including a Cipro advertisement in the journal *Family Practice*—was misleading or unbalanced. The rate of questionable claims was surpassed only in ads for birth control pills.

In the wake of the findings, FDA Commissioner David Kessler called on the pharmaceutical industry to clean up its ads and eliminate "the enormous potential" the practice has for enticing doctors to misuse drugs of all kinds.

But profit-minded manufacturers and busy doctors are not the only reason that antibiotics are misused.

"It's not all industry's fault; it's everybody's fault," says Dr. Sanders. "It's the mind-set that sees antibiotics as miracle drugs.

"Many doctors—and many patients—think we can just pick something off the shelf and it will make them well. If it doesn't work, get a different one. If one is good for you, two must be better."

14

DENNIS OVERBYE

The Endless Good-bye

From *Lonely Hearts of the Cosmos,*
HarperCollins, 1991

*If many science writers see James Watson or Tracy Kidder as
models, Dennis Overbye looked to Tom Wolfe's* The Right
Stuff *as inspiration for his book on cosmology,* Lonely
Hearts of the Cosmos. *Focusing primarily on Allan
Sandage, the brilliant scientist who ran Mount Palomar
Observatory, the book follows the grand quest for the origin
of the universe through numerous conferences and long-
range friendships and rivalries. Like Wolfe, Overbye captures the haphazard social collegiality of science, the way
scientists talk to each other, their thoughts and repartee,
and sometimes the poignant stories of their lives.*

*The story of Overbye's life seemed to put him on an end-
less good-bye from science. Born in 1944 in Seattle and
raised on nearby Mercer Island, as a boy he devoured the
science fiction of Robert Heinlein, Isaac Asimov, and Arthur C. Clarke. But his love for science was crushed, he
says, after four years as a physics major at MIT. After a
stint working on a novel in the style of Thomas Pynchon, he
started as a typesetter at* Sky & Telescope *in 1976 and was
soon writing articles. In 1980 his profile of Stephen Hawking for the third issue of* Omni *magazine won an American*

Institute of Physics writing award, leading him to Science '80 *and then* Discover *magazine.* "I was constantly writing for magazines that hadn't begun publishing yet," *he says.*

At Discover *he fell into the creative upheaval of a new publication with all its talents and rivalries. There Natalie Angier became his closest confidante and muse for* Lonely Hearts of the Cosmos. *Where other writers look back in fondness on the* Discover *years, Overbye recalls it as an "intimidating time you would not willingly go through again. There's a certain masthead roulette in a magazine start-up. Plus, in the Time-Life Building, I was surrounded by guys in three-piece suits who acted as if they had invented journalism."*

This book rose out of several articles and a lifelong love for the passionate arcana of cosmology. To write the book, Overbye pursued Allan Sandage — notorious for his isolation and egoism — for a year before getting him to talk. Many more years of following him around the world at conferences left Overbye a silent observer, like "part of the furniture," he says. His access makes for a science book that reads like a novel of very bright friends growing older — arguing, marrying, divorcing, learning.

On the global issues facing science writing today, Overbye agrees there is a ferment in the field and says his dream has always been to write like an art critic for science. But he disagrees with the attack-dog style of science journalism. "Like using Freedom of Information Act requests to get at a guy's raw data. I wouldn't do that."

"The Endless Good-bye" tells the story of a major challenge to Allan Sandage's theory of a closed universe, coming from an outspoken astrophysicist named Beatrice Tinsley. Tinsley spent ten years in a bitter feud with the far more powerful researcher. The cast here includes Gustave Tammann, a debonair Swiss physicist and Sandage disciple, and the three scientists who allied with Tinsley as grad-

uate students, at great risk to their careers but with full commitment to their interpretation of the data.

THE FATE OF THE UNIVERSE WAS THE $64,000 question in cosmology. "The fate of the universe"—by what possible audacity could a person even say those words? What did they mean? Which was more absurd: the notion that the universe went on forever, or the notion that it didn't? The idea that one might be able to predict the future condition of everything that existed—yea, or existence itself—might seem preposterous and a little foolhardy. As preposterous, perhaps, as the idea that the universe could have had a beginning, and yet the skies were ringing with testimony of its fiery birth. The cosmological question, as Sandage called it, had riveted the attention of astronomers and their public ever since Hubble had begun cosmology by discovering that the universe was expanding. Would it continue to expand forever, the galaxies departing each other for good? Or would it slow down gradually and eventually recontract, the galaxies swarming back together in a final cataclysm that was a backward replay of the explosion that brought it into existence? Would existence wink out into a black hole at the end of time? If it did, would the universe rebound Phoenix-like from its own crushed ashes? For twenty years, every astronomical discovery, every new paper or newspaper Sunday supplement article, came with those questions tagging along— what did this mean about the fate of the universe?

Sandage had hoped that the answer would come from the Hubble diagram, on which the redshift velocities of nearly identical galaxies at vastly different distances—so-called standard candles—were compared to see if the cosmic expansion was slowing down and by how much. The

Hubble diagram seemed to indicate that the universe was closed, that it would one day, some 60 billion years from now, collapse. In his heart Sandage wanted to believe that result, that he was getting The Answer, but his faith was buffeted as the hideous complications of the Hubble diagram were pointed out.

On the other hand, preliminary data from his and Tammann's project to measure the Hubble constant showed the universe expanding evenly and uniformly in all directions, both toward and away from imposing concentrations of galaxies, which implied that there was not enough gravity in the universe to affect the expansion. The galaxies would sail on, lonely and free. Which was it? The answer seemed buried in shadows and ghostly errors.

It was long dry work, this systematic combing of the cosmos. Sandage had lost his enthusiasm long before the end was in sight. In the early seventies the end was drawing near. But while he fiddled with his Hubble diagrams and continued his long march with Tammann through the cosmos, a new generation of cosmologists had grown up, less inclined to wait decades for someone else to get the answer.

In 1967 Sandage took a trip to the University of Texas to give a talk about cosmology. Before he could speak, a young woman, a graduate student, stood up and told the audience that everything they were about to hear was wrong. Sandage was stunned and outraged—an outrage he never was to forget. "It was typical of him to recall with exaggeration," said Tammann. "She was a graduate student. Allan was already Allan."

The woman who had announced herself into Sandage's life so unforgettably was Beatrice Tinsley. She was short with dark, curly hair and resembled the Peanuts character Lucy, in temperament as well as looks. Tinsley was only the loudest of many astronomers who argued that Sandage's standard candles—giant elliptical galaxies—were not standard enough to reveal the fate of the universe. On one level the argument between Sandage and Tinsley was a technical dispute about which kind of stars generated the most light in elliptical galaxies—red giants or normal hydrogen-burning stars. On another level it was about the fate of the universe. She and Sandage were to spend the next ten years dueling.

Tinsley had taken a circuitous but determined route to cosmology, and once there she was not to be denied. She had been born Beatrice Hill, the daughter of an Anglican clergyman, in Cambridge, England, during the Blitz, and had been raised in New Zealand, where her father gradually became involved in politics. Writing about her later, her father described her as a genius in Newton's sense, of being able to take infinite pains.

Her two loves were music and mathematics. At the University of Canterbury in Christchurch, she played in a chamber music group four nights a week and fell under the spell of physics, which, she felt, combined the seductive elegance of pure math with a certain amount of practicality. She learned, she said, "to question everything." She emerged in 1962 with a master's degree and married Brian Tinsley, an atmospheric and auroral physicist. When he got a job at the Southwest Center for Advanced Studies in Dallas, she followed him to the United States.

She brought with her a scholarship from New Zealand. Having decided to go into astrophysics, she used it to wheedle a position with the mathematics group of the Dallas center. She arrived just in time for the first Texas Symposium and the parade of Wheeler, Schmidt, Greenstein, Gold, and Hoyle wrestling with the issues of quasars and singularities.

In a short while she found life in Dallas scientifically and culturally stagnant. Although she loved to travel around the country and took delight in its rambling possibilities, she was appalled at the civil rights situation in the South. A feminist slightly ahead of her time, Tinsley also did not fit into the life of a scientist's wife in Dallas and caused a minor scandal by refusing to host a tea when it was her turn. She preferred to hang out with the other scientists, the men, but even that soon palled; relativity was still a mathematical game to the center theorists.

When she and Brian failed to conceive a baby, she enrolled in graduate school at the University of Texas, 200 miles away in Austin. The astronomy department there was being built up by the energetic Harlan Smith, who had hired a French cosmologist Gérard de Vaucouleurs, among others. Tinsley commuted twice a week from Dallas and commenced a thesis. As her speciality she picked the evolution of galaxies. It was here that she crossed swords with Sandage.

The bone of contention between them was the Hubble diagram. Sandage had concluded that the Hubble diagram indicated that the universe was closed. That conclusion, however, depended on how much the diagram had to be corrected for the supposed tendency of elliptical galaxies to redden and dim as they got older and the brightest and bluest of their stars burned out. How much did these galaxies change? Not enough, Sandage decided, based on observations and his knowledge of the H-R diagram, to change the overall conclusion.

Tinsley was not impressed by Sandage's result; she was not alone in feeling that it had been based on lazy thinking. In her thesis she tackled the problem theoretically, asking how various collections of stars would evolve and how their collective properties would change as they aged. The answer was quite a bit, enough to change the verdict of the Hubble diagram from a closed universe to an open one.

Tinsley's thesis was published in 1968, after a long struggle with an "anonymous referee," with the cosmology section greatly curtailed. Sandage rejected her conclusion, say Tinsley's friends. He simply treated it as if it didn't exist. Tinsley was wounded by Sandage's reaction but she was a combative person. It made her work all the harder, and she launched into the problem of galaxy evolution.

She and Brian had adopted children, and she spent the years after her thesis at home in Dallas taking care of them and doing cosmology on the side. She got involved as well in antiwar activities and joined Zero Population Growth. She kept her hand in enough to plague Sandage, who once told a colleague that he opened each new Tinsley paper with trembling.

Then, in 1972, to add insult to injury, Tinsley came to Caltech and Palomar–Mount Wilson.

The person who brought her there was a Caltech professor named Jim Gunn, who would become the second member of what would soon become a young cosmological gang of four. "Sandage didn't like Beatrice from the very beginning," he recalled one afternoon in the large corner office he now inhabits at Princeton. "She was right and she knew it. She was assertive."

Gunn, a wiry figure, now baldish with long brown curls cascading down the back of his neck, a bushy beard, and squarish wire-frame spectacles, had come to Caltech as a graduate student in 1961, after studying physics at Rice. He met Sandage when he was working on his Ph.D. thesis about the background light in the universe and whether its grainy pattern could be used to discriminate between the cosmological world models. Gunn found Sandage fascinating—"He's a religious man, a peculiarity among our breed"—but their relationship was distant. "Sandage was well known not to be interested in students," he said in an Oxbridge accent that belied his rural Texas roots. "I never thought about working for him. Mount Wilson never took students, anyway."

After two years in the army, which he spent assigned to Caltech's Jet Propulsion Laboratory (JPL) building spacecraft instruments, Gunn went to Princeton. By 1970 he was back at Caltech teaching Robertson's old course. While at JPL he had built a small electronic spectroscope for studying planets that turned out to be perfect for looking at dim galaxies as well. With that he was pitched into the front line of observational cosmology, a discipline in which progress was driven largely by improvements in instrumentation. The giant 200-inch telescope had sparked one revolution; electronic light detectors that were more sensitive and versatile than photographic plates would spark the next. Gunn, who was enamored of high technology, could design and build state-of-the-art instruments, observe with them, and do theoretical calculations when it rained. He became one of the few astronomers, in an age of ferocious specialization, who could do everything.

Once, when asked who was the best astronomer in the world, Sandage had replied, "Well, young Jim Gunn is doing pretty well. If he keeps it up, he could be number two."

In 1970 Gunn had served notice that nothing was sacrosanct anymore, neither in cosmology nor in Pasadena. He and Beverly Oke, another Caltech astronomer, decided to take up the elusive Hubble diagram. They applied for time on the 200-inch telescope to perform modern observations of the bright elliptical cluster galaxies. "Sandage wasn't doing anything in that regard," said Gunn. "We didn't consider it a direct assault."

Sandage, of course, did, just as he had when Greenstein rushed into quasars. When he objected to Gunn's getting

200-inch time to pursue what was in essence Mount Wilson and Sandage's project, he was overruled. After all, it was in the best traditions of science that everybody's work is checked by someone.

But, of course, it was not in the Gentleman's Code to do it at the same observatory.

The rival project went ahead. Gunn had been following Tinsley's work and, knowing they needed a theorist to unravel the effects of galactic evolution on their measurements, arranged for her to spend several months in Pasadena in 1972, giving her a new lease on life after her domestic confinement. They became close friends as well as professional allies.

There were now two groups doing cosmology in Pasadena, trooping to Palomar, that did not speak to each other except in the angry language of referees' reports and peer reviews. Sandage eventually published an eight-part series of papers on the Hubble diagram. He and Tinsley made contradictory statements about the evolutionary correction in the Hale Observatories annual report.

The next member of the rebel cosmological team was recruited in Cambridge, England, in the summer of 1972 when Gunn, who was visiting Hoyle's institute for the summer, spent some time hiking and talking with David Schramm, another summer visitor. Schramm, a hulking outgoing redhead and the Caltech wrestling coach, was a graduate student of Fowler's. He was an expert on nucleosynthesis and interested in the big bang.

Peebles had pointed out, recall, that the amount of deuterium (a heavy isotope of hydrogen) produced in the big bang was extremely sensitive to the density of nuclear matter in the early universe. The definitive calculations had been done by Hoyle, Fowler, and Robert Wagoner in the late sixties. Only recently, however, had space techniques made it possible to measure the abundance of interstellar deuterium, which in turn made it possible to estimate that density: the mass density of the universe when it was a few minutes old. The results strongly suggested that the universe only had about a tenth of the mass needed to generate enough gravity to ever recollapse itself. The implication was that the universe would expand forever. Schramm was enthusiastic about using the nucleosynthesis data to resolve the cosmological question.

Gunn was impressed. Work he had been doing with a Caltech postdoc named J. Richard Gott on the dynamics of galaxies and clusters pointed to a similar conclusion: that the galaxies *in toto* were neither massive nor numerous enough to arrest the expansion of the universe.

In the fall both Schramm and Tinsley were at the University of Texas, talking about doing a paper, when Gott came to town for a colloquium. The four of them decided to combine forces and write one paper, reviewing the growing preponderance of evidence that the universe was open, that Wheeler's big crunch, the collapse and snuffing of the laws of physics, was not in the cosmic cards after all. Most of these data were not new, and much of them were not even the young scientists' own work, but it was the first time anyone had assembled all the evidence together and dared to stand behind it. "We were sort of young Turks wanting to upset the establishment," said Schramm, chuckling. "One of the motivations was to show the best way to solve cosmology was not the Hubble diagram."

It was a formidable quartet. Gott, a moon-faced Kentuckian who speaks in a slow drawl, was the youngest and also perhaps the deepest. A pure theorist and expert on relativity and the life of Einstein, he specialized in concocting strange universes. In one celebrated example, he theorized that at the moment of the big bang the universe had split into three parts: a universe of ordinary matter going forward in time; a universe of antimatter going backward in time; and a universe of tachyons—hypothetical particles that go faster than the speed of light. None of these universes could ever connect with one another.

Schramm was the physicist, the representative of a new breed who regarded the universe as a physics problem, and the most aggressive. Gunn, the closest of the four to being a classic "Sandagean" astronomer, was the most versatile. As for Tinsley, "Beatrice," sighed Gunn fondly with a faraway look in his eyes, "Beatrice was the glue."

She did most of the writing. The paper was called "An Unbound Universe?" If Sandage's prose tended to sound like cosmic groans reeking of dry authority, Tinsley's tone had the snap of youthful impertinence. It began with a quote from the Greek philosopher Lucretius:

> Desist from thrusting out reasoning from your mind because of its disconcerting novelty. Weigh it, rather, with a discerning judgment, then, if it seems to you true, give in. If it is false, gird yourself to oppose it. For the mind wants to discover by reasoning what exists in the infinity of space that lies out there, beyond the ramparts of this world. . . . Here, then, is my first point. In all dimensions alike, on this side or that, upward or downward through the universe, there is no end.

Tinsley and her comrades made the case for a new way of doing cosmology. Instead of asking, How is space-time curved?—a task involving dauntingly long-distance astronomy with all its mystical uncertainties and Hubble diagram perplexities—they asked, Is the universe heavy or dense enough to drag itself back down to oblivion?

According to the Friedmann equations of the expanding universe there was a critical density of mass and energy—equivalent to about one hydrogen atom per cubic meter. If the universe were denser than that, it would eventually stop expanding and collapse; if it were less dense the galaxies would fly out forever. In equations, the ratio of the actual density of the universe to this critical density was denoted by a capital omega, the last letter of the Greek alphabet, symbol of kingdom come. Written it looks like a horseshoe: Ω. Mathematically, omega is just twice q_0. An omega of exactly 1.0, the critical density, corresponded to the universe with q_0 equal to 0.5: flat space, a universe balanced on the edge that would stop expanding after an infinite amount of time, the galaxies flying apart like rocks thrown just at escape velocity. If omega were less than 1.0, the universe would expand forever. If it were greater than 1.0, gravity would slow the expansion to a halt one day far in the future. Then the universe would recollapse and eventually swallow itself in the big crunch. In effect their paper enshrined omega as the new Holy Grail of cosmology, replacing the quaint and tiresome q_0.

To measure omega an astronomer need only stake out a suitably representative volume of space—the larger the better, but there was no need to survey all the way to the quasars—and somehow add up all the mass inside. Gott, Gunn, Schramm, and Tinsley (listing themselves alphabetically) showed that however you added up the mass in the universe, omega came out to be pitifully small— much, much less than 1.0—and therefore, way too small to close the universe.

One way to measure omega was to add up all the light from the galaxies; the mass of all the stars needed to produce that much light only amounted to 0.01 of the critical mass. A more powerful way to estimate the masses of galaxies was by analyzing their motions and the way they tugged on each other in pairs and clusters. That method included the gravitational contributions of black holes, dim stars, and any other dark stuff in galaxies; it increased the imputed masses of galaxies tenfold (apparently, most of the material in galaxies didn't shine), but still left omega at only 0.1, the four reported, far short of the density needed to close the universe.

The final way to estimate omega was by measuring deuterium. Schramm's line of thought was the centerpiece of their argument. The beauty of deuterium was that it made no difference to the calculations what form the matter was in *today*—whether it was in a black hole, dust, or a blazing star—as long as it had passed through the thermonuclear cauldron of the big bang. Just by determining the relative abundance of deuterium in some representative sample of the cosmos, astronomers could calculate directly what the density of matter—ordinary matter, that is, neutrons and protons—had been when the universe was a few minutes old. The deuterium abundance gave the same answer as the galaxies: that omega was only 0.1

"The verdict is not yet in [on the fate of the universe]," they concluded, "but perhaps the mood of the jury is becoming perceptible."

It took them longer to get the paper published than it did to write it. They sent it first in 1973 to *Nature*, where it was rejected as "inappropriate." It was finally published in the *Astrophysical Journal* in December 1974.

If Tinsley and her friends were right and the universe was open, then Sandage had been beaten to the greatest prize in cosmology, the end of Hubble's road. But he hadn't been beaten by much. The race was in fact virtually a dead heat. Sandage's route to the answer was pure astronomy in the classic Hubble vein. In 1961, he had invented an alternative to the slippery uncertainties of the Hubble diagram; he called it the time-scale test. It was a way of comparing two independent "clocks" to see how much the expansion of the universe had slowed down. Globular clusters were the first clock. Globular clusters were made of the oldest stars in the galaxy, maybe the universe, and figuring out how to date them had been his first big accomplishment. Suppose, he said, that you knew the ages of the oldest stars. Because the universe couldn't be younger than its inhabitants, he would then know that the universe had to be at least that many billion years old.

The second clock was the expansion of the universe. If he knew how fast the universe was expanding he could calculate how long it would have taken the galaxies to spread out to their current distances from each other at the present expansion rate. That would give him a second estimate of the age of the universe. The universe, like a person, had surely grown faster when it was young than it is growing now. Therefore the second clock, based on today's expansion rate, should always give a greater age than the globular cluster clock. By comparing the readings of these two "clocks," Sandage could determine how much gravity had slowed the expansion. For example, suppose the globular clusters proved to be 5 billion years old, while the so-called Hubble time was 10 billion years. Then Sandage would know that expansion must have been slowed down by at least half since the birth of the universe; at that rate it would soon coast to a complete stop and then reverse. Knowing those two "ages," he could solve the equations for q_0.

In effect, having launched the Hubble constant project in quest of one of the sacred numbers of cosmology, at the end Sandage would harvest them both.

Sandage and Tammann, based on their study of the spiral galaxies, finally concluded that the Hubble constant was 57 kilometers per second per megaparsec, plus or minus 15 percent.[1] Shortly thereafter an adjustment to stellar theory

1. The same amount of uncertainty that Hubble had allowed for a constant ten times larger.

nudged the Hyades star cluster farther out, which made everything else in the universe farther and bigger and brighter. The Hubble constant became an even 50.

The latter value made the so-called Hubble time 20 billion years, which was how old the universe would be if it had expanded at the same speed, without slowing down, ever since creation. If that was the oldest the universe could be, what was the youngest it could be? Surely not younger than the stars. According to Sandage's most recent calculations, the oldest globular cluster stars were 14 billion years. He added a billion years or so for the galaxy to form and figured out that those two ages were pretty close. The universe had hardly slowed down at all. And it wasn't going to slow down. Ever.

In March 1975, these words, written by Sandage, appeared in the *Astrophysical Journal*.

> From this analysis we conclude that if H_o has the value given . . . and if the age of globular clusters is about 14 billion years, then q_o cannot be as large as 1. It may be as small as 0.03, in which case (a) most of the mass is in galaxies, (b) the Universe has happened only once, and (c) the expansion will never stop.

In the Tinsley and Gunn camp, despite all their bravado, there was quiet relief that the old man had come up with the same answer as they had. "It's a terrible surprise," Sandage told *Time* magazine.

What about the contradictory evidence from the Hubble diagram that the universe was closed? In the eyes of most astronomers, Tinsley had won that argument. The Hubble diagram based on giant elliptical galaxies had fallen. The crux of the argument came down to a technical disagreement about what kind of stars produced most of the light in elliptical galaxies. The answer would determine whether the galaxies got radically dimmer with age, as Tinsley claimed, necessitating a drastic correction to the Hubble diagram and its message of a closed universe. Sandage said they were normal hydrogen-burning stars; Tinsley said they were red giants—one of the stages of evolution that stars pass through after they exhaust their hydrogen fuel and leave the so-called main sequence.

In 1974 the astronomer Jay Frogel, now at Ohio State, made infrared observations of elliptical galaxies and found in their light the unmistakable signature of red giant stars. Tinsley had been right.

Tammann got a preprint of Frogel's paper in the mail. "I was about to give a talk," explained Tammann. "I called up Allan and asked, 'Can I say the universe is open?'

" 'Of course.' He wasn't angry or even sad. It just shows how flexible he is when he is presented with the data. Up to then, q-nought was always 0.5 or more. It changed overnight."

Sandage, in fact, had fulfilled his quest nobly. His disappointment was tempered by the realization that the final result was a great vindication of the cosmological framework in which first Hubble and then he had toiled for decades. The Friedmann equations worked. The time scales matched—that was a miracle. The answer didn't mean as much to him as the fact that there *was* an answer. So what if it wasn't the answer that the theorists thought was the prettiest? We lived in a Friedmann universe. The simplest model worked. But it didn't feel like God.

"So the universe will continue to expand forever," Sandage said, "and galaxies will get farther and farther apart, and things will just die. That's the way it is. It doesn't really matter whether I feel lonely about it or not."

The open universe gave a new meaning to loneliness. It

opened vast, unbelievable realms of time and space to informed speculation—gulfs that made all of cosmic history
to date an indistinguishable splinter. If the closed, oscillat-
ing universe punctuated physical existence with a big
crunch like a pair of clashing cymbals, the open universe
was like the piano chord struck at the end of the Beatles
song "A Day in the Life"—a single brief jangly burst of
light and sound, quavering and ringing as it slowly fades
out into the blackness.

In this scenario, apocalypse (such as it is) will happen
in stages. The first thing that will happen is that the stars
will burn out and the galaxies will fade. The sun will run
out of hydrogen in a mere 5 billion years and swell up
into a red giant, turning the earth into a black cinder. In
100 billion years the Milky Way will be a cemetery full
of stellar corpses: black holes, neutron stars, and white
dwarfs. Within a billion billion (10^{18}) years, these will all
be conglomerated into a single giant black hole at the
center of the former galaxy. In 10^{27} years, all the galaxies
in a cluster will have merged into one supergalactic black
hole; the universe will consist of black holes rushing away
from each other through dead cold space. In 10^{100} years
these black holes, billions of times as massive as the sun,
will evaporate. Nothing will remain but feeble, dilute
pools of particles and radiation separated by trillions of
light-years.

What else might happen depended on how seriously
you took the more exotic theories of physics. For example,
some speculative theories of particle physics predicted that
protons, the fundamental building blocks of atoms and
thus of all ordinary matter, were unstable and would fizz
away radioactively after about 10^{30} (a million trillion trillion) years or so. There would be nothing but lightweight
junk particles left in the universe. Some scientists envisioned the formation in the far far future of pseudo-atoms

composed of these junk particles—electrons and positrons circling each other at a distance equal to the radius of today's universe. No matter how huge and empty the universe got, they pointed out, it could never be completely empty. By virtue of the uncertainty principle there would always be vacuum fluctuations; space would at least be microscopically alive even if there was no one to look at it.

What were the prospects for life in such a universe? The imaginative Freeman Dyson suggested that civilizations could sustain themselves almost indefinitely by tapping the energy that could be extracted from a rotating black hole. Of course, it would prove futile if the protons in their bones meanwhile decayed. Still, there was nothing in principle, he concluded, to keep life from going on forever if it could adapt itself to the infinitely slow rhythms of the far future.

Wheeler, the eternal prophet, found this prospect of eternal decay, a one-way universe that was born and never died, distasteful aesthetically and emotionally, as well as intellectually. It was unsymmetrical. It was like being trapped in a football stadium with the home team hopelessly behind in a fourth quarter that would never end. A universe that could never die could never be reborn. There was no second chance for creation. Where was the frame that gave meaning to existence? Wheeler insisted that the extra mass that would raise omega and close the universe would be found somewhere some time.

He was not alone. The preponderance of evidence in favor of an open universe was impressive, and yet . . . One night during a 1974 Texas Symposium, *New York Times* reporter Walter Sullivan took a group of astrophysicists to dinner and asked them to vote on whether they thought the universe was open or closed. The vote, he reported, was unanimous for a closed universe. After 1974, looking for the other 90 percent of the universe was to become one of the major themes of cosmology.

Tinsley was one of the few astronomers who *liked* having an open universe. "It may be 'bad science' to like the universe being open because it feels better, but there is in me a strong delight in that possibility," she wrote her father. "I think I am tied to the idea of expanding forever—like life in a sense—more than spatial infinity."

On another occasion she wrote, "I don't think it is weakness to be motivated by emotions. What else is the driving force, or the inspiration to think of useful theories? Only if emotional attachment to one's own theory makes one blind to alternatives is it bad."

Another who did not join in the quest for the missing mass was Sandage. "For some reason I would like to have it closed," he admitted haltingly. "Yes, but to think the universe happened only once—that makes it even more mysterious, in a sense. It's outside the realm of science, what happened before the first microsecond. Why it got itself into that, how it got itself into that state?

"But it's no more mysterious than noting the tremendous complexity of the chemical balance of the human body. You cut yourself—and why is it the white corpuscles know exactly where to go to close the wound? That's a miracle. And I don't believe that's due to progressive selection of the fittest. It's just too fine a mechanism. I don't know what I'm saying now, I don't know what the next sentence is.

"I don't mean that points to the existence of God, whatever that means. Newton's laws are God, in a sense. But I find it all so rational and so amazingly beautiful and so mysterious."

That same line of thought often ran through Sandage's conversations, that the world was too magical to be an accident, although in his milder moments he admitted that he didn't know enough about evolution to be shooting his mouth off. In 1975 he was eating lunch with Graham Berry, the director of the Caltech news service, when he got on the subject of religion in his usual enthusiastic manner. The couple at the next table started following the conversation. Finally the man got up, introduced himself as a minister, and asked if he could join them. He thought Sandage was a minister, too. Sandage was thrilled.

"I don't know what I would call myself," he said in 1977, describing the strange nexus between science and religion into which his pursuit of the stars had stuck him.

"If you believe anything of the hard science of cosmology, there was an event that happened that can be age-dated back in the past. And just the very fact that science can say that statement, that cosmology can understand the universe at a much earlier state and it did emerge from a state that was fundamentally different. Now that's an act of creation. Within the realm of science one cannot say any more detail about that creation than the First Book of Genesis.

"Well, I think that the whole rationality of the universe is a mystery. The fact that Newton's and Einstein's equations work is one of the world's great mysteries. And in that sense I'm very religious."

Reaching the end of a quarter-century trail gave Sandage no relief. To Tammann, Sandage was at his worst when he finished something. The frenzy of completion would fend off the larger pressure for a while, but then, as soon as it was gone, what Tammann called the "debt of nature" would come crashing back in on Sandage. He would start pestering Tammann for work that was due on the next paper.

Sandage plunged into new projects. He had to finish

measuring redshifts of the 1300 brightest galaxies in the sky, which had been compiled in a catalog by the astronomers Harlow Shapley and Adelaide Ames at Harvard in 1932. In collaboration with a pair of younger astronomers, Jim Westphal and Jerome Kristian, he set out to redo the Hubble diagram, remeasuring the magnitudes of elliptical galaxies with a sensitive new television system—one of his few ventures into high technology.

The pressure and pace invariably left his collaborators by the wayside. Tuton remembered Sandage badgering Kristian during their attempts to extend the cursed Hubble diagram. There was never enough time for Sandage at the telescope; every second counted. Kristian was too slow. He would be up in the cage trying to make some measurement and Sandage would be prowling restlessly down in the control room calling up over the intercom. "What's taking so long, Jerry? Are you done yet? What's going on? C'mon, talk to us, Jerry."

Only Tammann seemed to be able to endure Sandage's blasts year in and year out. Once, even he rebelled against the accelerating workload, and curiously it was a comfort to Sandage. He had always worried about drowning Tammann, but now he knew that Tammann would fight back.

Deadlines were a particular burden to the two of them. Writing, Sandage moaned, was "turning blood into ink." Every calculation was hell. Sandage often copped out on appearing at conferences, but to Tammann's chagrin, never on delivering a paper once the deadline was agreed to. "It makes life hard and, therefore, has to be done," said Tammann. The debt of nature could never be repaid.

"Allan is so talented, so powerful," Tammann said, marveling, "and so unhappy because he can never accomplish what he sees as his duty, what people expect of him." He recalled Sandage complaining once, why hadn't it been given to him to discover a great law of nature, as it had been to Hubble? "Allan Sandage wanted to be Hubble. Hubble wanted to be Einstein. And Einstein wanted to be a peacemaker," he sighed. "The great ones pay."

The competition from astronomers outside Pasadena was increasing. The Mount Wilson monopoly had ended. In 1974 a 158-inch telescope began operation at the Kitt Peak National Observatory outside Tucson, run by a consortium called Associated Universities for Research in Astronomy (AURA) and funded by the National Science Foundation. A couple of years later AURA and NSF built a twin telescope in Chile to open up the southern skies. The Europeans followed suit. Putting a large telescope in Chile had actually been Mount Wilson's idea; Hale had dreamed of a 200-inch in the Southern Hemisphere. Carnegie, Mount Wilson's owner, had lost a tug of war over Ford Foundation funding for the telescope when the head of the Ford Foundation moved over to become the director of the National Science Foundation, AURA's patron. Carnegie finally built a 100-inch telescope at Las Campanas in Chile. The new telescopes were being equipped with electronic detectors like the charge-coupled device (CCD), a silicon wafer on which light was collected as electric charge and then read out by a computer. A good photographic emulsion might capture 5 percent of the light falling on it to blacken grains; a CCD gobbled 50 to 80 percent of the available light. One of these transformed an ordinary telescope into a giant. Now anybody could reach the edge of the universe, the depths of redshift and the time where even the quasars fell off, the era before which there might not have been galaxies.

Even with all this new equipment, observatories could not keep up with the rising demand for telescope time. In the wake of the space program, quasars, black holes, and the big bang, astrophysics had become a glamour field.

New astronomy departments were starting every year, staffed by freshly minted Ph.D.s and by physicists flooding across interdisciplinary lines to join the Great Work. In the face of this population pressure Sandage was somehow able actually to increase his observing time. In 1977 he spent 105 nights on various mountains. He particularly liked the Las Campanas telescope, which could photograph more than two square degrees of sky in one shot, 41 times more than the 200-inch could image.

Sandage didn't make it easy for the younger astronomers and the physicists to get to know him. His door at Santa Barbara Street was usually closed, and he virtually stopped going to meetings and conferences. In his office he sat with the heritage of Hubble and Baade and Humason stacked around him. Asked a question he was liable to wave at the locked file cabinets and plate boxes and answer aloofly, "The answer's in there."

There were two Sandages, really. According to legend a young acolyte might first meet Uncle Allan, the charismatic teller of tales with a dry wit and religious intensity about the creation event, a puller of legs and nudger of elbows in the Lyndon Johnson style, kidder of the young ladies, drinker of Manhattans, speller of bromides and Bondi theorems. Sooner or later there would be the clash of scientific opinion, and the disillusion and disappointment would set in; the acolyte had failed him. The jollity would slide off like an old snakeskin. Out came That Son-of-a-Bitch Sandage with a dry-ice voice, slumped shoulders, cold half-lidded blue-gray eyes, and all the warmth and empathy of some patch of sky next to Virgo, lowering the boom, writing devastating referee's reports on one's paper or proposal, telling one not to publish, delivering edicts. We at Mount Wilson . . .

It was rumored in astronomical circles that it was Sandage who had driven Gunn out of Pasadena to Princeton, where he became a full professor and MacArthur "genius grant" fellow. Gunn denied it. The principal reason he left, he said, was to get out of building instruments all the time (he was drafted to help build one of the cameras for the space telescope) and to do more theoretical work.

"Allan does not like competition. He established the discipline of observational cosmology and he thinks it should be his. I think he feels, and I can sympathize," Gunn said frowning, "that many sloppy and shoddy papers are rushed to print. He is seldom nasty in person."

Tinsley's star also soared in the wake of the unbound universe, but according to Schramm her personality changed shortly thereafter. An uncle had been on the DC-10 that crashed taking off in Paris in 1976, killing all aboard. Before, said Schramm, she seemed happy. Afterward she was more driven, more determined to do what she did best.

Eventually Dallas became too small. Yale and Chicago were pursuing her with professorships, while the head of the University of Texas, Dallas—which is what the old Southwest Center had become—failed to answer her letters asking for a promotion. Feeling her children were old enough to do without her, she divorced Brian and went to Yale, where she moved in with Richard Larson, a mild-mannered astronomer she had known in Pasadena.

At Yale she became a role model and champion for the tiny but growing band of women in astronomy. Tinsley never lost her combative edge and had difficulty accepting the fact that people respected her and took her seriously. "She never lost the feeling of fighting the world," said Larson.

Tinsley continued to wage war against the Hubble diagram, railing against its usefulness as a cosmological tool in several papers. The last straw for the credibility of the

Hubble diagram came when the Princeton theorists suggested that everybody had been on the wrong track: Giant elliptical galaxies, they said, did not get dimmer with age—as everyone had thought—but might actually get brighter by swallowing smaller galaxies that wandered too close. Subsequently, photographs of giant elliptical galaxies with two or more bright central spots in them— presumably the half-digested nuclei of victim galaxies— gave credence to the notion of galactic cannibalism.

In 1977 Tinsley organized a major symposium at Yale on the evolution of stars and galaxies. Sandage was invited but didn't show up. That same year a lump showed up on her thigh that turned out to be a melanoma. Tinsley's years at Yale were shadowed by a fight that she finally couldn't win. By 1980, despite surgery to remove the original tumor, the disease had spread through her body, and she spent the last year of her life checking in and out of the Yale infirmary undergoing radiation and chemotherapy while holding seminars in her room. Toward the end, in 1981, she wrote a poem:

> Let me be like Bach, creating fugues,
> Till suddenly the pen will move no more
> Let all my themes within—of ancient light,
> Of origins, and change and human worth—
> Let all their melodies still intertwine,
> Evolve and merge with growing unity,
> > Ever without fading,
> > Ever without a final chord . . .
> Till suddenly my mind can bear no more.

15

CHARLES BOWDEN

Bats

From *Blue Desert*,
University of Arizona Press, 1989

*"I have zero background in science," Charles Bowden likes
to explain. "It's been a help. I have no concern about peers,
and my curiosity has not been destroyed."*

*For Bowden, writing about science, about anything, re-
quires mainly an insatiable curiosity. Some scientists escape
the stultifying effect of their academic training and keep the
childlike fascination that got them into science in the first
place. "Read the biography of Feynman," he suggests, referring to James Gleick's work, a chapter of which appears in
this anthology. "He was unusual, not just in his physics,
but in the broadness of his interests. The ecologist Eugene
Odum also had an incredibly curious mind. That's the
main prerequisite."*

*Born in 1941, Charles Bowden grew up near Chicago.
His brash style can be traced to an upbringing that combined Midwestern farm wisdom and the more elliptical intelligence of the desert. While still a child, he moved from
the Midwest to Tucson, where he now lives. He has an undergraduate degree from the University of Arizona and a
master's from the University of Wisconsin in American intellectual history. He therefore likes science but does not con-*

sider himself a science writer, just a reporter. "In a decent world there wouldn't be science writing, just good writing," he states.

In addition to Blue Desert (1989), in which "Bats" was reprinted, Bowden has written articles and books on the wildlife of the Sonoran Desert in Arizona and Mexico (Frog Mountain Blues [1987]; The Secret Forest [1993]) and a book-length profile of Charles Keating, convicted of fraud in Arizona's share of the savings and loan scandal in the 1980s. "I sold the Keating book by saying I'd write about him like I'd write about a panther," he says.

Bowden was working for the Tuscon Citizen when he wrote this story on bats. He has lived and traveled in the Southwestern deserts for the last few decades. He reads widely and eccentrically, including Dostoyevsky's novels, nature writer David Quammen's essays, and "anybody who can take me where I can't go." The bat story here takes us somewhere we can't, or most of us wouldn't want to, go. Ostensibly a profile of bat researcher Ronnie Sidner, it's a tour de force of description—just the kind of story Bowden himself would want to read.

THE AIR SCREAMS, RUSTLING MOVEMENTS FEATHER against the skin, squeaks and screeches bounce off the stone walls, and a sweet acrid stench rolls across the room. My mouth chews the darkness like a thick paste.

We stand in feces, hills of feces, and the grey powder slops over our running shoes and buries our ankles. Behind us the light glows through the cave entrance, a slit sixty-five feet high and twenty-four feet wide. Above us the screams continue, the rustling frolic of life. The rock walls feel like cloth to the touch; a wilderness of fungus thrives in the warm room.

We climb. The hills of feces roll like trackless dunes. Our feet sink deeply into the grey powder as we move up toward the ceiling. Here and there a feather: a primary off a turkey vulture; a secondary off a black hawk. There is no explanation for their presence. The odor seems to ebb as our senses adjust to the stench. The dunes toss like waves and in between the dark mounds writhe masses of beetle larvae. Here we find the bones—skulls, femurs, rib cages, and the like.

This is the forbidden place, the dark zone claimed by nightmares. The air can be rich with rabies, and people and animals have died from visiting such places. Up high, up near the ceiling, the rustling grows louder and louder. They are disturbed as we march into their world. The eye sees blackness but the skin feels the rustling, the swoosh of something near our brows, our throats, our mouths. We are enveloped in a swirling mass of energy and we keep walking toward the center of this biological bomb.

Something is crawling up our bare legs, across our bellies, down our arms, past our necks and onward into the curious contours of our faces. Mites move up from the dunes of feces and explore us like a new country. When we pause and look up, our eyes peer into a mist, a steady drizzle of urine and feces cascading from the ceiling.

I have no desire to leave. The feces and urine continue to shower down, the mites tickle the surface of my body, the atmosphere tastes like a bad meal and always the air drifting like a thick fog promises the whisper of rabies.

We have come to the charnel house, a bastion of a world in the twilight of its life. The crackling energy swirling in the air around us is dying. And we and our kind are the killers.

This is the bat cave and 25,000 *Tadarida brasiliensis mexicana* wrap us with their anxiety. Night is falling outside the cave. Soon our world will become theirs.

Then they will exit and plunder the canyons, the mesas, the hillsides, the towns, the fields. They will bring back deadly reports of our world, details buried deep in their bones and body chemistry.

The sound tightens now, a shrill spike of screeches and squeaks. The mites scramble across the skin. The larvae writhe like shiny stones at our feet.

We stand inside a brief island of life, a hiding place of our blood kin.

We have known each other a good long while. We would pluck the eye of a live bat, stick it in a wax figure of a dog, put the effigy at a crossroads and hope a lover would come to our bed. We would make an ointment of frankincense, the blood of a lizard, the blood of a bat and treat trachoma. We would carve the image of a bat on the tip of a rhinoceros horn to ward off demons. We would cut the head off a live bat and place it on someone's left arm to cause insomnia. We would crucify live bats, heads downward, always downward, and place the result over our doors to fight evil, to protect our sheep, to insure our wakefulness.

We have hated bats. We still hate bats. They own the night and mock our helplessness. Their faces to our eyes look cruel, fierce, ugly.

For thousands of years, they rode through our dreams, they drank our blood, they stood as symbols of a world we were reluctant to enter but a place we lusted for—the black nights, the witches' sabbaths, the magic chants, the scream under a full moon.

This time we have come for them wearing the mask of science. Ronnie Sidner is in her thirties now and she was raised in a tract house along a wooded draw outside Phil-adelphia. She wanted to become a veterinarian and found her path blocked by a male-dominated profession. She is a small, light-boned woman with red hair but she looks large and angry when she recalls this part of her life.

She decided to go West and wound up a schoolteacher in Parker, Arizona, a small town in the hard ground along the Colorado River where the Mojave and Sonoran des-erts rub against each other. She stayed six years and then the emptiness of the American classroom burned her out and left her barren of ambitions. She took a summer course at Northern Arizona University in Flagstaff and the class focused on bats.

Something quickened in her, perhaps the memory of walks along the wooded draw behind her childhood home, the drive to be a veterinarian, or some simple, an-imal need. She enrolled in the University of Arizona at Tucson and rode to a master's degree in biology. And she rode bats.

I first met her in the Chiricahua Mountains. She was wearing a t-shirt that proclaimed: I LOVE BATS. By then she was deep into her doctorate, a sprawling, undefined inves-tigation held together solely by bats, thousands and thou-sands of bats. We talked and then there seemed nothing to do but go to the dark stone room.

I keep thinking it is something about the newspaper business, something about the killings and the people with defeat on their faces, that has kindled a bat appetite within me for gore, for ruin and bankruptcy, for bulldoz-ers knocking down giant cactuses so that shopping centers may flourish. But I constantly reject this sense of myself and am angered when others force this black cloak on my shoulders. I like to remember being a boy on that Illinois farm and I am holding a cane pole down by the creek and the fish are jumping. The sun skips off the quiet pools of water and the air comes fresh from Eden. Up by the house the old man and his cronies are drinking beer from quart bottles and marching toward a Saturday afternoon drunk. Below the barn, the Holsteins graze and cool spring water skims across the limestone floor of the milk house. And I am in the sun, and this is what I want and who I am.

I sit at my desk at the paper and stare at the blank wall and when the call comes, and it always comes, I volunteer for the bad deaths, the slaughters called meaningless in our silicon chip society. The ones that do not compute. Because for me, on some level I cannot say, they do compute. I am the one basking in the hot blaze of the Sunbelt who always senses these periodic eclipses when the land goes suddenly dark.

The assistant city editor is standing before my desk with a crooked smile. I can see him just past my boots propped up on my idle typewriter. He wears an Izod shirt. He tosses a police report down and says, "You'll like this one, Captain Death." And I go, I always go, and my entire being picks up and rises. I can sense this eclipse and I want to write it down. The Sunbelt has so much energy, so many slabs being poured, so much land being slain, so much action, and I know amidst this frenzy there are these eclipses when the sun goes black and the temperature drops, these little deaths of the blazing white light. And I do not want these moments to go unnoticed. I am certain of this lunatic mission when I flip on the evening news and see the smiling faces or when I read the front page and the headlines chatter about growth, new jobs, booms, and dreams of freeways.

So when I hear of this hole in the earth where bats linger, I must go. Right now, not a moment's delay. There is a huge eclipse of the sun taking place and attention must be paid. I know my job.

The cave is near Clifton and Morenci, two eastern Arizona mining towns at the foot of a wilderness country stretching northward toward Blue River. In the early 1960s, millions of bats lived in the colony. E. Lendell Cockrum, a University of Arizona professor in the Department of Ecology and Evolutionary Biology, tried to tally them once. He made sample counts, multiplied and came out with 50,000,000 bats. Trying to be conservative, he published a figure of 25,000,000.

The big colony once devoured 80,000 pounds of Arizona insects a night. By the late 1960s, there were 25,000 bats and they ate about ninety-eight pounds of insects a night. The devastation of the bat colony came quickly and that fact is what has brought us to the cave. A holocaust has taken place here and I want to visit the place of the great death. Few have noticed this event; fewer cared.

The walk in means miles of wading a stream guarded by light brown canyon walls. As we hike, a zone-tailed hawk explodes from a tree and slashes across the canopy of cottonwoods and sycamores. A red hepatic tanager and his mate watch from a mesquite, the blaze of a vermilion flycatcher spins and twirls off a bare limb. Half-wild steers charge through the brush before us. The water feels warm, the stone bottom slippery under our shoes. Fish dart from our footsteps. Stretches of the stream form still ponds reflecting the high canyon walls and the blue sky.

This is a throwaway canyon in Arizona, a place that in much of the United States would qualify as a national monument, but here in the careless riches of the West's wild land is regarded as simply another slit through the high country, a name on a map that few visit.

The smell hits us like a slap in the face. We look up and there is the huge vaulting door to the cave. We have found the core of the dying.

We pitch our packs under cottonwoods on the canyon's

far side and wade back across the stream. Ronnie leads the way and her excitement quickens our steps.

Like us, they are mammals. Their blood is warm and they nurse their young. One out of every five species of mammals is a bat. Forty-five million years before the first beast that looked like a human being walked this earth, bats took to the sky. The early bat jumped from tree to tree after insects and over time the arm became the wing and the air became a new floor for life.

Eight hundred fifty species now swirl across the planet's skin and twenty-four can be found in Arizona. *Tadarida brasiliensis mexicana*, the Mexican freetail, roams from Texas westward and winters deep in Mexico. This small bat rides on a wingspan of about a foot. The hair runs from dark brown to dark gray. They favor caves—thirteen in Texas, five in Oklahoma and one each in New Mexico, Arizona and Nevada.

These hunters search the desert and sometimes feed as high as 9,200 feet. They can live in colonies of millions, huge masses of bats squeaking, chattering, and crawling across each other. When big colonies once exited from their caves, the sound, according to early observers, thundered like the roar of white water and the dark cloud could be seen for miles. They fly into the night at about thirty-five miles per hour, then accelerate to around sixty. At dawn, they make power dives back into the cave, sometimes brushing eighty miles per hour.

They feed on small moths, ripping the abdomens from them in flight, and may travel forty miles in any direction seeking prey. The young, one per female per year, immediately crawl up the mother hunting the breast. At first, the mother returns several times during the night to nurse and then less frequently. No one is certain if the females find their own young in the huge colonies or nurse the first young bat they encounter. They can live perhaps fifteen years—no one is sure.

Bats remain a mystery in many ways. Science has come to them late in the day. They have been banded and migrations of 1,000 miles recorded. They have been kidnapped and released to test their homing instincts and a return of 328 miles has been observed.

And they have been dying. Oklahoma had 7 million Mexican freetails and is now down to fewer than 1 million. Carlsbad Caverns had around 9 million and is down to 250,000. And the cave on the creek in the canyon near Clifton and Morenci had its 25 million or perhaps even 50 million and is down to 25,000 or fewer.

There have always been ways for bats to die. In the 1960s, man offered them a new way.

White bones lace across the dark guano like thin wires. The remnants outline a wing that fell from the ceiling. Small skulls peek through the feces, the tiny craniums empty of brains. Ronnie and I keep moving further into the cave. The room stretches 288 feet across, 65 feet high. Up at the peak runs a deep crevice where the bats now live. We have forgotten about the outside world and joined the darkness.

Ronnie picks up a skull and runs her fingers over the white smoothness.

"Oh, skulls," she says, "look at the baby skulls. It's a graveyard."

Bats circle over our heads. They are warming up for the evening flight. At 6:32, they suddenly swoosh out of the cave and stream from the top of the vault. A funnel forms in the center of the canyon and vanishes as the cloud of bats goes north. The flight is over in moments. It is merely the preliminary to the main evening takeoff.

We look back down at the bones, the lacework of bones

on the dark guano in the hot cave squeaking with the life of the dwindling colony.

Around the turn of the century, they packed guano out on burros and then loaded it onto trains for fertilizer needs of the West Coast. The haul reportedly earned a profit of $30,000. Later owners of the cave would mine it every five years or so with the last excavation occurring in 1958.

Scientists heard of the cave in the fifties and Cockrum came in 1958. He had been banding bats since the early forties and published books on the mammals of Kansas, Arizona, and the Southwest.

He tried various schemes to catch the bats for banding and finally found a trap that worked. Bats present special problems. Rabies shots are often necessary because the caves form a perfect medium for the virus. Caged animals placed beneath the colonies have died from the disease although no bat could possibly have reached through the mesh containers to bite them.

Banding offered its own woes. The bats chew off bands within six weeks and less than one tenth of one percent of the banded bats were ever recovered.

Cockrum reveled in the bat colony at its height—one estimate made in June 1964 pegged the population at 50 to 100 million bats. By June 1969 the census estimate was 30,000.

Cockrum remembers the cave in the good times when the first evening flight required thirty minutes and the main event began at dusk and roared on until midnight.

"At dawn," he laughs, "we'd be sitting there banding these goddamn bats and you could hear the flutter of the bats as they came in on a power dive."

Inside the cave, the ceiling and walls were covered, the crevice could not even be seen under the mass of bats, and the animals hung far down the sides. Cockrum could just reach up and pluck them.

Cockrum is a hearty man now in his sixties. He sits in his university office and drifts easily back to the bat cave of the sixties.

"It was a constant, loud, intensive noise," he says, "a constant stream of bats flying. A constant rain of mites as well as urine and guano. After you'd been in there ten minutes, you could feel things crawling on your skin and you'd go out and see these dots crawling up your arms."

But what he remembers best is the seething mass of beetle larvae on the cave floor.

"This was fresh guano," he says. "This surface was almost a sea of larvae and any bat that died or baby that fell to the floor was immediately devoured. Within thirty minutes you'd have a clean skeleton."

Outside green blazes off the trees and the stream slides like a brown skin over the rocks. Light ebbs from the canyon. We climb down from the dunes of guano, slip off the rock shelves to the cave opening. The night begins to come down.

Ronnie holds a feather and the delicate finger bone of a bat. And then it begins.

"Oh, my God," she says. "Oh, look at them all. This is great!"

Urine and feces rain down on us. We look up and we cannot look away. Bats storm across the top of the vault, a torrent of wings and squeaks. They streak to the canyon center and swirl and then funnel off. This is the major flight. The freetails give a faint echo of the thunder of twenty years ago when perhaps 100 million tiny mammals squealed from the room in the rock wall and took to the night sky, an army of hearts, lung, and fangs ranging out twenty, thirty, forty miles, beasts ripping the soft abdomens from moths, feasting in the dark hours.

A crescent moon hangs and the bats become fine lines etching the glowing face. In four minutes it is over. A flight that once took hours is now 240 seconds. The cave falls silent.

They are gone.

When Cockrum finished his banding, 88,176 bats had been tagged. From this he plotted the colony's migration route from Arizona to Sonora and Sinaloa in Mexico. This helped him understand the dying.

When the bodies were examined back in the laboratory, the scientists found dieldrin, toxaphene, and DDT. The colony kept shrinking and Cockrum began to understand why. He had already noticed that bats had deserted Tucson. Once they had roosted in the old buildings of the university campus and were a common sight under the streetlights. Then with the massive use of household pesticides they vanished.

He began tracking DDT sales in Arizona. Five hundred and forty thousand pounds were sold in 1965, and by 1966 the quantity had reached 1.07 million pounds. In 1967, 2.52 million pounds were poured onto the land. The agricultural district of the Gila Valley lies within easy reach of the bat cave and they fed heavily there.

That might be part of the answer.

When the United States ended the use of DDT in the late sixties, the colony did not repopulate. Below the border, the use of DDT continued, as it does to this day.

The bats acted as sensors for a world man created but ignored. They roamed the global skin where the insects fly and swallowed the parts per million and per billion that human beings measured and monitored. These chemicals were concentrated in the mother's milk and the young suckled lustily.

Cockrum thinks the tradeoff was reasonable. He likes bats and hates the idea of man causing the extinction of any creature. But, he hastens to add, he has worked in the Third World.

He puts it this way: would you rather die of a tropical disease in your twenties or perish in your sixties because of toxic chemicals? But of course, no one polls the bats on their views.

They simply die, humans live, the crops grow. It is part of this time in this century.

The dying goes like this. The young drink the milk laced with pesticides, the pesticides attack their central nervous systems. The small animals start to shake, then motor skills decline. Eventually the feet clinging to the mother or to the ceiling let go. They fall. The mass of beetle larvae move in. In thirty minutes the bones are clean, a fine wire of calcium across the dark guano in the warm cave.

The scream sounds faraway at first, then nearer. We walk out the mouth of the cave. The howling continues, a screech, a long winding yowl as the cry of a big cat shreds the night stillness. We pan with the flashlight.

Twenty feet away two green eyes glow. We move toward the eyes, move instinctively and without hesitation. The cat bounds into the brush and is gone. We crash down the hillside through the thicket of mesquite and hackberry. The stream cools our legs. Bats skim the water sipping drinks. Now outside the warmth of the cave, the mites flee our bodies.

We eat dinner, have a drink of whiskey, and throw our bags down on the ground. Rocks fall from the nearby cliffs as bighorn sheep hop from ledge to ledge.

We are very excited by the memory of the bats brushing

against our faces, by the roar of the evening flight, by the green glow of the mountain lion's eyes. Around midnight, the screaming returns. The cat moves around our camp howling. Scientists speculate that this behavior is territoriality, that the lion is staking out its share of the earth. We listen to the screams in the warm night and we do not wonder at what they mean. They say this is my ground, my place.

The sound pierces our half-sleep and then after fifteen or twenty minutes drifts down the canyon. Quiet returns and the screams persist only in our dreams.

Bats squeak overhead as they begin to hunt the poisoned skies and fields. They have few friends in the world of man. They are the demons of our dreams and their slow chemical death is not a matter of concern for many.

We lie under a roof of stars, wings rustling above our faces.

The lion does not return.

1 6

ELISABETH ROSENTHAL

The Forgotten Female

Discover,
December 1991

*Elisabeth Rosenthal has been a contributing editor at Dis-
cover since 1986. She is one of the new science writers who
practices the craft, working both as an emergency room physician and medical writer for the New York Times. Her specialty is the inside wisdom of the physician, the shoptalk or
gossip that has brought her to such different subjects as doctors who supply drug addicts, the overuse and overproduc-
tion of expensive magnetic resonance imaging machines,
and the slick marketing of drugs to doctors by huge pharmaceutical companies.*

*In "The Forgotten Female" she profiles the University of
Michigan primatologist Barbara Smuts, who has carved a
controversial role for herself as a kind of feminist Jane
Goodall. " 'It's a task I've been struggling with for twenty
years,' " Rosenthal quotes Smuts as observing. Among the
advantages of being a woman in the field, Rosenthal reports, is that the animals are apparently less disturbed and
more natural when approached by a woman. And Smuts
was careful to leave time at the end of each day for a kind
of Zen observation, with no notebooks or plan. In a sense
she was willing to sit at the side of the monkeys and let*

them come to her. It was a practice from which many of her key theories sprang.

Smuts was inspired to pursue primatology when she was thirteen years old and saw a National Geographic *article on Jane Goodall. One of the key functions of science writing overlooked by many of its new practitioners, according to scientists, is to inspire young people to take up the arduous and often draining pursuit of science.*

If anything, many of the new science writers who are women are more aware of the need to highlight female role models in a male-dominated discipline—a mission echoed by writers like Ellen Ruppel Shell, director of the Boston University science writing program. For her work Elisabeth Rosenthal has received the 1991 Front Page Award from the Newswomen's Club of New York and a 1990 Prize in Writing from the New York State Society of Anesthesiologists.

BARBARA SMUTS'S FAVORITE PHOTO SHOWS HER sitting under a scrawny acacia thorn tree in the Kenya plains, surrounded by ten wild olive baboons, some almost equal to her in size. "Venus, Alexander, Pan, Cressida"— she recognizes the seemingly indistinguishable creatures instantly and fondly recites their names. In the picture Smuts is smiling broadly. The baboons, in contrast, seem indifferent to her presence: they groom, sleep, pick at leaves or tree bark. And that makes Smuts swell with pride.

"I can never get over the incredible privilege of being accepted into their society," she says, sitting in her office at the University of Michigan, where she is an associate professor of anthropology and psychology. "To be right inside a society of wild animals, to be able to see the nuances of their behavior at close range, is a miracle."

Now 41, Smuts has spent two decades studying wild baboons, chimpanzees, and, lately, bottle-nosed dolphins to figure out what makes these animals tick and how their complex societies function. But she is not interested in just any large-brained mammals: she focuses on females. Feminism has been an undercurrent in her work since college. But at the outset, she recalls, she had no idea just how radical an approach that would turn out to be. "I was too young and naive to realize that evolutionary biology and feminism were not natural bedfellows," she says, "and I began to put these two perspectives together as best I could. It's a task I've been struggling with for the past twenty years."

Traditional evolutionary theory has tended to focus on males and their aggressive competition as a major force behind evolution: the more successful a male was at winning fights with his rivals and acquiring mates to bear his offspring, the more likely he was to pass on his genes and shape future generations. Females, on the other hand, were simply assumed to be passive players, with no choice but to submit to the generally larger, beefier males. It didn't seem to occur to nineteenth-century biologists that females, who not only contributed their genes to their offspring but nurtured them as well, might also invest in the welfare of future generations by picking suitable mates.

"There's been a lot more research done on males than females," says Smuts, and then she sighs. She's spent most of her career filling in the missing half of the picture.

The findings from her tireless field studies fly in the face of many of these traditional assumptions. Her observations of baboons have revealed that, far from simply awaiting male overtures, female baboons usually have an active say in selecting their mates. She recalls, for instance, watching Delphi, a young female, rebuff 42 sexual advances within three hours from a male named Vulcan.

When he attempted to mount her, she would disdainfully walk away or simply sit down, the baboon equivalent of just saying no. Later that day Delphi copulated willingly and repeatedly with another male clearly more to her liking.

That incident, and many others like it, prompted Smuts to ask the questions that have influenced much of the baboon research that would make her famous. Why do females choose some males over others? From a female's point of view, what makes a good mate? Or, to turn the question around, what does a male have to do to win her consent? One way or another, Smuts has been pondering the themes of cooperation and conflict between the sexes ever since. Many of the ideas she touches on seem to resonate with the concerns of society in the late twentieth century. She is currently studying male aggression toward females, including forced sex in primates, which may shed light on such human problems as wife-battering and rape.

It's hard to imagine Smuts as a field scientist on the African savanna, crouching alone from dawn to dusk among a group of wild baboons. She is small—about five feet— and very outgoing, not a loner by nature. On the door to her ramshackle office at the University of Michigan is a sampling of Gary Larson cartoons, many of which depict intelligent—and sarcastic—primates. Inside, pride of place goes to the portraits of three particular primates who have touched her life, the "three Ds," as she calls them: Charles Darwin, Bob Dylan, and Digit, Dian Fossey's favorite gorilla, who was decapitated by poachers in the late 1970s.

Smuts was 13 when she decided to become a primatologist, after seeing Jane Goodall's first article about chimpanzees in *National Geographic*. She had always loved animals, and she'd been somewhat fanatic about science, precociously dissecting sheeps' eyes provided by a local butcher when she was in fifth grade. But Goodall's example cemented her interest. "I was thrilled that you could have a job watching animals and knew right then I wanted to work with her." After graduating from Harvard in 1972 and beginning her graduate studies in biology at Stanford, she flew to Goodall's Gombe Stream Research Center in Tanzania to study foraging patterns and social relationships in female chimps.

Her first few years of research were plagued by false starts, caused less by the science than by Africa's complex politics. Two months after her arrival at Gombe, Smuts and three other students were kidnapped from their huts by Marxist rebels from neighboring Zaire. The four were taken by boat across Lake Tanganyika and held hostage in exchange for a ransom and the release of political prisoners held in Tanzania. Although all four were released unharmed, Gombe was temporarily declared off-limits to Western researchers with the exception of Goodall herself.

Discouraged but determined, Smuts went with a fallback plan. Although she had originally wanted to study chimps, she decided to settle for olive baboons instead. Even then, her first baboon project fell through because of another flare-up of local trouble in Masai Mara, Kenya. Finally, in 1977, she arranged to study a troop residing in the Eburru Cliff area in central Kenya.

"Olive baboons turned out to be the perfect species, since I am interested in social relationships and they are so social," says Smuts. Males, females, and offspring live together in large gregarious groups, feeding, grooming, and sleeping together. Yet their groups are also highly structured, with a pecking order for both males and females based on a complex web of kinship, friendship, alliances, and power plays. "By comparison, female chimps are pretty solitary," comments Smuts. "I would have spent my time watching lone animals eat."

Armed with a backpack and data sheets, Smuts followed the nomadic baboon troop on and off for six years in their wanderings through the dry grasslands around Eburru's rocky cliffs. In the field there were no days off and no quitting early; she would trail the baboons to the cliffside spot they chose as a bedroom each night so she'd know where to intercept them early the next morning. If on occasion she lost the troop in their 30-square-mile home turf, she had to search their favorite cliff outcroppings for several days to find them. After dark she would retire to a sprawling turn-of-the-century farmhouse with a sweeping veranda from which she could watch herds of zebra and gazelle amble by. "It was the nicest place I'll ever live," she says wistfully.

Smuts's goal when she was observing the Eburru baboons was to be a "neutral presence," not frightening but not frightened either. "The key is to be boring, so that you don't disrupt their normal behavior," she says. "That can be hard, especially when the little ones bound up laughing," she adds, imitating the breathy sound that baboons make during play. For her own safety, she learned to turn away. In the rough and tumble of play, she explains, "an infant could get hurt and squeal, and then an adult male would blame me." Adult male baboons can weigh 70 pounds, and they have canines longer and sharper than a lion's.

But Smuts also learned to hold her ground. Baboons, being hierarchical animals, will try to dominate humans they sense are scared, she says. "But I came to understand their body language, and when they charged I knew they were bluffing. If I just stood there, they stopped." Only once did she blow her professional cool, and that was with an adolescent chimp named Goblin, in the very early days at Gombe.

Goblin was the most status conscious, driven male ever observed at Gombe, a sort of Donald Trump of the chimp world. He rose to be alpha male of his troop at the very early age of 16. When he first encountered Smuts, though, he was still zealously working his way to the top, intimidating small females, even human ones, with his brawn. "He would stalk me, bursting from the bushes, knock me over, and roll me down hills," Smuts recalls. One day he started grabbing relentlessly for her raincoat, and enraged, she instinctively swung it and smacked Goblin in the nose. "In retrospect it was risky, and I shouldn't have done it," she says, "but it worked." Goblin never bothered her again.

At Eburru, though, being small and female worked to her advantage. She suspects that the troop felt less threatened by the presence of a five-foot human female than a large human male. "Everyone says that baboons habituate to women more readily," she says. "I could walk through the troop and not a single baboon would look up." Yet when she brought along a male companion, the baboons nervously moved away. Many researchers now believe that women, who have come to dominate primatology in the past 20 years, may be better suited to the fieldwork than men. "They feel women tend to be more patient, better able to sit still for hours in solitude," Smuts says.

Smuts herself takes pride in her keen powers of concentration and rigorous data gathering. Her approach is to follow one animal at a time, systematically entering its activities and social interactions on a gridlike check sheet. At Eburru she would concentrate on a single female for half-hour periods; every five minutes she would record which other animals were within one yard, 2 yards, 5 yards, and 15 yards of her subject. (Close, comfortable proximity is a yardstick of trust and friendship.) Every minute on the minute, she'd note the female baboon's activity—say, nursing or grooming—and note the location of the female's infant. If the baboon associated with others in her troop, she would note that too, describing the gestures and noises—whether challenging, submissive, or friendly—that the female made as a new animal approached.

"Recording everything in the check-sheet system helps to translate their behavioral language into statistical patterns I can understand," Smuts says. In isolation each observation seems a trivial detail. But when Smuts puts together these tiny bits of data, like a high-tech pointillist painter, she creates a picture of the individual and of what it means to be a female in baboon society. In the process, she transforms the impressionistic world of observations into a hard science: quantitative, reproducible, and testable.

Such meticulous fieldwork is what enabled Smuts to make her astute observations about friendships between the sexes in her baboon troop. Her charts revealed that certain males and females often showed up in close proximity—the males took the females under their protective wing, and they frequently rested and groomed together. Remarkably, these affectionate bonds usually developed between animals that were not sexual partners at the time. Even more surprisingly, the protective males helped females care for their children, even if they hadn't fathered the infants.

For example, in her book, *Sex and Friendship in Baboons*, Smuts describes a scene in which a female baboon, Daphne, and her male friend Handel were resting in the grass while Daphne's infant by another male played on a rock nearby. Although Handel was not the baby's father, when the baby fell and made a squeaky distress sound, it was he who came running over, drew the infant into his arms, and comforted it. "The two adults had a long-term bond, and the male was quick to help his friend and her infant," Smuts recalls.

Observations like these seemed completely at odds with the old assumptions that males consort with females only when mating and invest only in infants that carry their genes. What did the solicitous males hope to gain? Smuts had a hunch that the answer had something to do with female choosiness. By befriending females and nurturing their infants, males got into the females' good graces and increased their chances of mating with them in the future. Six years of careful note-taking among the Eburru baboons has shown that Smuts's hunch was right.

Still, every day, half an hour before calling it quits, Smuts would put away her notebooks and just watch in "a sort of Zen state of mind." On the cliffs at Eburru, the baboons are at their most social near sundown: amicably grunting, grooming, having sex. It was at these times, she says, that she often gained new insights into baboon society—perhaps noticed a new call or gesture—that would direct her future study. "I let them tell me what to look for."

During one such evening meditation, for example, she "first had the idea that some males were kind of cool, while others seemed very tense." Pursuing this observation in 1978, she did one of her few field studies on males: she observed how different animals reacted when other males came within two yards, and she discovered that while some became agitated, others were indifferent to the intrusions. Moreover, "coolness" turned out to be the best predictor of a male's popularity with females. "I think acting cool was a good measure of the male's social savvy," says Smuts, "and those same qualities made it easier for the male to form friendships and get sexual cooperation from females."

Smuts has gone against the scientific grain in her willingness to use seemingly anthropomorphic terms in reference to her animals. She is convinced, for example, that baboons get depressed. When infants are abandoned, they show the classic signs of grief that psychiatrists find in humans: loss of appetite, sleep disturbance, lowered heart rate, emaciation. "If I took you to look at such an animal," says Smuts, "you'd say right away she's depressed."

Her experience at Eburru also convinced Smuts that each animal had its own personality. "The one hundred twenty baboons in the troop I studied are as individual to me as the one hundred twenty people I know best," she says. "When you follow them day in, day out, the stereotypes fall apart and you come to know them as sentient beings." She defends her approach by adding, "If you want to understand their social world, I think it's valid to learn each face and personality because that's how they relate to each other." She remembers a nervous animal named Olympia who was not very popular in the troop. "You could see why," Smuts says. "She was so jittery even I got tense when I followed her." At the other end of the spectrum was Lysistrata, an outgoing animal with a mischievous streak. Smuts describes watching Lysistrata playfully bat an infant that was being carried on its mother's back. When the mother craned her head back to see what was happening, Smuts recalls, "Lysistrata just sat there, nonchalantly grooming her foot."

In the late 1980s Smuts turned her attention from African baboons to Australian bottle-nosed dolphins. The shift seems odd at first, but as she explains the evolution of the project, the links become apparent. From 1985 to 1987 Smuts took a break from her field studies to concentrate on academic commitments at the University of Michigan. While there she learned about a graduate student, Richard Connor, who was studying wild dolphins in a remote area of Western Australia called Shark Bay. Connor and another young researcher, Rachel Smolker (now one of Smuts's graduate students), were observing this society of dolphins from small outboard skiffs and had attracted the attention of several prominent anthropologists. "They kept saying, 'You've got to go. You've got to see this,'" Smuts recalls. "Finally I said okay and went."

From the first day on the water of Shark Bay, Smuts found herself thinking of primate societies. "Superficially the dolphins were as different as they could be," says Smuts. "Yet as I watched them swim, so many things reminded me of higher primates. It was clear that these aquatic mammals had distinct personalities and very complicated social interactions." Males, females, and infants frequently engaged in petting—sliding across another animal's body while stroking it with a fin—an activity that seemed to play a role akin to primate grooming. And they engaged in exuberant displays of social solidarity, such as synchronous surfacing and leaping. The degree of synchrony seems to be a good indicator of the strength of the bond between the animals. "It's a clear message: We're in this together," Smuts says.

Smuts has brought to Shark Bay her rigorous method of focusing attention on one animal at a time, cataloging its every gesture and social interaction. The researchers now recognize, and have christened, about 300 resident dolphins. What quickly became apparent was that individuals of both sexes have friends with whom they prefer to spend time and that males in particular form enduring coalitions, usually consisting of pairs or triplets. Forming purposeful alliances is what makes large-brained mammals like dolphins, apes, and humans unusual, Smuts notes. It means that the survival of the fittest "no longer depends on individual fighting ability, but on the strength of the team."

On one occasion she and Connor witnessed a dramatic illustration of that principle. Three dolphin males, Trips, Bite, and Cetus, were attempting to steal a choice female from a competing trio that had captured her. Swimming toward the hoarding threesome, the rival males suddenly hesitated, then retreated—only to return a short time later with two more friends to reinforce their challenge. They won.

"At the moment we're just scratching the surface of dolphin society," Smuts says. "Remember, Goodall started in the early sixties and it wasn't until the late seventies that a clear picture of chimp society emerged." Among the intriguing questions she would like to answer is how dolphins raise their young. What strikes you immediately about these highly social animals, says Smuts, is that the urge to socialize starts so early—long before they are weaned, in fact. Small six-month-old dolphins stray from their mothers' side to hang out with other infants and favorite adolescent females referred to as aunts.

Another question Smuts's team would like to answer is whether females stick together to fend off coercive males. Anecdotal evidence suggests that they might. In one episode a trio of males was sighted trying to herd and mount an uncooperative female, when a group of females moved in to protectively surround their sister. As with the baboons, Smuts's dolphin work continues to explore the tangled web of cooperation and conflict between the sexes.

Lately, though, it is the darker side of male-female relationships that has absorbed Smut's attention. To her dismay, male aggression toward females is quite widespread among primates and other mammals. Even among baboons, where males and females form affectionate friendships, males also resort to outright violence against the opposite sex. At Eburru she recalls seeing a female mercilessly pummeled and bitten; after escaping from her male attacker, the animal ran screaming into a thicket where she sat shaking uncontrollably.

To date, no primatologist has studied male aggression toward females in a systematic way. Smuts thinks the oversight is partly due to queasiness about broaching a subject that touches a raw nerve in humans. Perhaps that explains the skeptical reaction that her new work has received from some of her colleagues. They have maintained, she says, that aggression is "just a part of courtship, and not harmful," a position Smuts rejects.

"To me," she replies, "that's like saying, 'She wants it.' When males deliberately attack females, leaving them screaming and sometimes seriously injured, it's hard to deny their aggression is dangerous." Next year she hopes to travel to Africa with colleague John Mitani to begin studying relations between the sexes in chimps, pygmy chimps, and mountain gorillas. By simultaneously observing male and female individuals, they hope to learn what situations predispose the animals to violence.

On the basis of the small amount of previously published literature, Smuts theorizes that the cultures most prone to violence against females are those in which males bond in groups. She remarks that there are only five mammalian species in which males are known to deliberately gang up against the opposite sex: chimps, spider monkeys, lions, dolphins—and humans. "In this case I think the animal data speak to us," she adds, pointing out that fraternities and sports teams have recently been implicated in a number of rapes and acts of harassment.

It does not particularly surprise Smuts that the issues she grapples with as a primatologist can sound so human. "Obviously my passionate interest in cooperation and conflict between the sexes is a reflection of what's going on in our society," Smuts replies. "But we shouldn't lose sight of the fact that cooperation and conflict are also important themes in animal societies—and that we are animals, too."

This is not to say, of course, that friendship between two baboons is the same as friendship between two humans. As an outward observer, however astute, Smuts can only guess at what the psychic rewards, if any, might be for baboons. But what's abundantly clear to her is that cooperative bonds and alliances are critical to survival and reproduction in both their species and ours.

"I like to approach our species as a primate among primates and see how far the comparison can take us with any given problem," she says. And obviously there are some comparisons that are more apt than others. "If you're interested in art, animals aren't very relevant. But if we're asking about mother-infant bonding, there are incredible similarities."

As a scientist, Smuts must of course be cautious in taking the analogies between human and nonhuman primates too far. But, honestly, doesn't she sometimes see all-too-telling resemblances? "Oh, all the time," she admits. "Not with my behavior, of course, but if I'm at a party where I don't know a lot of people, I'll catch myself watching the action and thinking about baboons." She also admits that she and her students sometimes refer to senior colleagues as silverbacks, the dominant males who lead gorilla groups.

"Certainly my work affects the way I see people," Smuts says. "It helps you to distance yourself from tiny human dramas when you realize that we're going through the same stuff as baboons."

17

JOHN CREWDSON

Fraud in Breast Cancer Study

Chicago *Tribune*,
March 13, 1994

If there is one writer who represents the most controversial edge of investigative science writing, it would be the Chicago Tribune's *John Crewdson. Born in 1946 and raised in Berkeley, California, Crewdson resembles a bear in person. He has no formal science background. But what he lacks in training he more than makes up for in persistence and intellect, earning a reputation as the best reporter in any field in America. Describing him in a 1991 profile, his former editor at the* New York Times, *David Jones, said: "You could say to him: 'John, see that brick wall over there? I want you on the other side' . . . and he'd get there."*

Crewdson began his career as a young reporter covering Watergate for the New York Times. *He won a Pulitzer Prize in 1981 for a series of forty articles tracing the flow of illegal aliens from Mexico, Cuba, and Haiti and corruption at the Immigration and Naturalization Service. By the time the* Tribune *wooed him in 1982, Crewdson could virtually tell the paper where he wanted to live, what stories he wanted to work on, and how much time and money he would need.*

When it came to science writing and the AIDS story, though, he was at first reluctant to take on the task. Only after he began experiencing the same reactions he had had with Watergate—late-night clandestine meetings for revelations off the record—did he warm to the story of fraud in the research of Dr. Robert Gallo. By the time he was finished, Congressional, National Institutes of Health, and criminal investigations were under way. Nothing like it had ever happened before to a scientist of Robert Gallo's reputation.

Many journalists and scientists criticized Crewdson, who fell victim to a public relations campaign that painted him as obsessive and misguided. In the end, however, Crewdson's version of events largely prevailed. On July 11, 1994, the Department of Health and Human Services formally acknowledged that, in developing the American version of the AIDS blood test, Gallo had used an AIDS virus originally discovered at the Pasteur Institute of Paris, and not in his lab as he claimed. That "milestone" acknowledgment gave the French an additional $700,000 a year in patent royalties. The decade-long controversy revealed science at its worst—the collusion between French and American laboratories, the campaign against a reporter, the arrogance of researchers who receive millions of dollars in government money. Little of it would have been publicized without Crewdon's investigative zeal.

But it seemed an aberration in the annals of science journalism. Then came breast cancer fraud. This story began with one paragraph in the June 1993 Federal Register. Nobody spotted its significance until a whistleblower contacted Crewdson, who admits he would have otherwise missed the story. Eight months later, when the following article appeared, a kind of hysteria broke out. Officials from the University of Pittsburgh, Montreal's St. Luc Hospital, and Washington's National Cancer Institute scrambled to cover their backs. A senior medical researcher was forced to resign, a seminal study was suspended, and again Congress an-

nounced immediate hearings. More important, thousands of women called their doctors, newspapers, and each other, trying to understand the effect of the fraudulent data on their treatment and lives.

"The hysteria could have been avoided," said Crewdson from the center of the maelstrom. "It was the Watergate paradigm all over again—arrogance, reluctance, cowardice, and a cover-up that may have been worse than the original offense."

The remarkable thing was not that it was an aberration, but that it followed on the heels of several other science fraud cases—more than one at the University of Pittsburgh alone—leading the New York Times's science writer, Lawrence K. Altman, to ask why new examples of misconduct kept cropping up. The case reads like a whodunit, casting into doubt "some of the most frequently cited [articles] in the modern medical literature," according to Crewdson. A method of breast cancer treatment widely used since 1985 was based in part on findings from a doctor who lied for ten years.

Most news coverage focused on the clinical relevance of the fraud, claiming it would not contravene the study's overall conclusion: Lumpectomy, the least invasive of breast cancer surgeries, could be as effective as mastectomy in certain cases. True, perhaps, but the reassurances were premature because no other precisely comparable studies existed. Few other reporters picked up or commented on the essential, frightening two-year chain of dishonesty on the part of the study's directors in covering up the fraud.

Crewdson regretted the outcome. "The forced resignation of [study director] Bernie Fisher was a cover-up again. The sad thing is, if they had come forward in the beginning, then all this would have been avoided." The fact that these researchers did not come forward when they uncovered their own flawed data, and that perhaps many others do not do *so, is perhaps John Crewdson's main legacy in science writing. "It certainly keeps me busy," he laughs.*

FEDERAL INVESTIGATORS HAVE DOCUMENTED more than a decade of fraud in some of the most important breast cancer research ever conducted, including a landmark 1985 study that established the relative safety of the operation known as lumpectomy and made it a common surgical procedure.

The organizers of the study privately assured investigators nearly two years ago that the fraud had not affected the "direction" of their findings about lumpectomy, or any of the other major conclusions that since have been drawn from a complex of related breast cancer studies.

But Dr. Bernard Fisher, the Pittsburgh surgeon who heads the giant research consortium that changed the course of breast cancer treatment in this country, has yet to publish a promised reanalysis of his data or to make any other public acknowledgment of the fraud.

Asked how soon, and in which journal, the reanalysis would be published, Fisher replied last week that "We don't know yet."

Responsibility for the fraud has been assumed by one of Fisher's principal collaborators, Dr. Roger Poisson, a professor of surgery at the University of Montreal. He served for more than a decade as a major contributor to the U.S.-Canadian research group known as the National Surgical Adjuvant Breast and Bowel Project (NSABP).

Beginning in 1977, astonished investigators found, Poisson enrolled at least 100 of his cancer patients at the university's St. Luc Hospital in breast cancer studies conducted by Fisher even though they were ineligible on medical, technical or consensual grounds.

Poisson and his assistants then falsified or fabricated the medical records they forwarded to NSABP headquarters at the University of Pittsburgh to make the patients appear to have been eligible.

Investigators said Poisson apparently was not trying to influence the outcome of the studies but simply to enroll as many patients as possible. One investigator described Poisson's motive as an "ego trip" that gained him co-authorship on several of Fisher's most prominent scientific articles and more than $1 million in research funding from the U.S. National Cancer Institute (NCI).

The federal Office of Research Integrity (ORI), which investigates science fraud, subsequently barred Poisson from performing any U.S.-funded research for eight years. Officials said it was the stiffest sanction ever imposed in a scientific misconduct case.

In all, investigators documented 111 separate instances of data falsification or outright fabrication involving 99 patients enrolled in 14 NSABP breast cancer studies between 1977 and 1990. There were cases in which women who previously had cancer were reported as cancer-free, cases of breast cancer that were deliberately downgraded or misclassified, dates of treatment that were falsified, and cases in which proper informed consent was never obtained.

Last month, asserting the data compiled by Poisson from more than 1,500 patients over 12 years no longer could be deemed reliable, the NCI began efforts to recover the money it has paid Poisson and St. Luc's since 1980, both directly and through the NSABP. Sources said the total involved was well over $1 million.

St. Luc's executive director, Jean Leblanc, said in a written statement that the hospital did not accept the conclusion "that 12 years of research had been invalidated" by the fraud. Leblanc said the hospital continued, at its own expense, to treat more than 1,000 of Poisson's patients and report data on them to the NSABP, which was still supplying the hospital with cancer drugs.

In addition to the validity of the research data, the Poisson case has raised questions about the administration of the 35-year-old NSABP, which many physicians regard as the nation's premier breast cancer research effort.

Officials at ORI and NCI particularly have questioned how systematic fraud of the sort that occurred in Montreal could have gone undetected by the NSABP for more than a dozen years. They also asked why, once Fisher and his staff learned of data discrepancies, they failed to inform the cancer institute for more than eight months.

"They should have reported this immediately to the National Cancer Institute," said the ORI's Dr. Dorothy Macfarlane, the government's chief investigator in the case.

In addition to its sheer scope and potential significance, investigators said the Montreal case may well be the only instance of fraud in which several members of the same research unit are known to have conspired.

For years, investigators said, Poisson's staff kept duplicate sets of reports, some actually labeled "true" and "false" in French, and forged the signatures of other physicians at St. Luc's on documents they sent to Pittsburgh.

The staff members, none of whom have been charged in the case, told investigators Poisson had assured them the falsifications were being done "for the good of the patient" and would not affect the study's results.

Jerome Kassirer, the editor of the *New England Journal of Medicine*, where several of Fisher's most influential articles have appeared, said last week he never was told about the fraud or the possibility that it might affect the conclusions of research studies published by the journal. Kassirer said he would "try to find out what's going on."

The articles include some of the most frequently cited

papers in the modern medical literature, among them the seminal 1985 article showing that many women with early breast cancers have essentially the same chance of disease-free survival following a partial mastectomy, or lumpectomy, as with a more disfiguring total mastectomy.

That study, to which Poisson contributed about 16 percent of the patients, is generally credited with having promoted a far greater willingness to perform lumpectomies among American breast cancer surgeons, many of whom previously had presented total mastectomy to their patients as a far safer option.

Although the NSABP has been supported mostly with U.S. government funds, many of the patients in the lumpectomy study came from Canadian hospitals. The reason, a former cancer institute official said, was the greater willingness of Canadian surgeons to essentially roll the dice by assigning patients at random to undergo a then-unproven lumpectomy.

Poisson was also a major contributor to a 1989 NSABP study, which triggered a "clinical alert" from the cancer institute, showing that many women whose cancers had not spread significantly beyond the breast could benefit from post-operative treatment with various anti-cancer drugs, including the controversial drug tamoxifen.

Because Fisher and the NSABP have yet to publish a statistical reanalysis, the precise effect of the Montreal fraud on these and related studies remains unclear.

For more than a year, ORI and NCI officials have urged Fisher to publish a "corrected analysis" of those articles whose conclusions rely on data submitted by Poisson, a step one investigator said was necessary "to restore public confidence in the studies and to allow scientists to re-evaluate the conclusions."

Even if the conclusions are not affected, the final ORI report on the Poisson case points out, and independent statisticians confirm, the predictive power of some of the NSABP findings is automatically diminished when the data provided by Poisson is discarded.

Carol Redmond, the NSABP's chief statistician, said that nothing would be made public until the other members of the NSABP had been told about the problems at St. Luc's, and that that would not happen before June.

"We have to follow certain processes in terms of reporting to our group," she said, adding that the reanalysis "had to be put in the priority scheme with a lot of other publications.

"Obviously, if there was any major impact on our trial, the priority associated with that would be very, very high," Redmond said. "The bottom line was that analyzing our data with the data from St. Luc's entirely removed did not affect any major conclusion of any of our trials."

Redmond said that while she was "in no way interested in justifying what Dr. Poisson did," the falsifications for which he was responsible "had to do with the characteristics of people, but not the fact that they were cancer patients."

The initial clue in the case emerged more than three years ago when a member of Fisher's staff discovered that the Poisson group, apparently having fallen victim to its own double recordkeeping, had submitted two reports of a breast cancer operation for the same patient.

The records were identical, with one glaring exception: One contained a date for the woman's surgery that made her eligible for the study, while the date on the other record made her ineligible.

Further examination revealed other discrepancies, including an alteration of the date on the "informed consent," a document in which the patient acknowledged having been advised of the risks of post-operative treatment with tamoxifen.

Although tamoxifen, which blocks the hormone estrogen, appears to be effective in reducing the recurrence of breast cancer in some women, recent data from the NSABP and other studies have fueled concern that women who use the drug may have an increased risk of uterine cancer.

When other patient records from Montreal were examined by Fisher's staff, more alterations were found, along with documents that appeared to show that Poisson had enrolled at least two patients in the tamoxifen study after they explicitly had refused to participate.

Rather than notifying the cancer institute or demanding an explanation from Poisson, NSABP officials decided to wait for the results of the next scheduled audit of the Montreal program, then three months away.

That audit, in September 1990, unearthed further problems, including numerous other changes in hospital records and more than a dozen instances in which treatment apparently was begun before informed consent documents were signed.

"It makes you wonder how informed these people really were," the ORI's Macfarlane said.

Although the NCI should have been provided with the results of the audit within six weeks of its completion, it was told nothing for another five months. Even after Fisher's assistants advised him that the alterations represented a "serious violation of acceptable standards," his response was to admonish Poisson that "such practices must not continue."

It was not until February 1991, more than eight months after the first discrepancies were discovered, that Fisher finally suspended Poisson's authority to enroll new patients in the NSABP studies. A few days later he notified the NCI that unspecified "irregularities" had been discovered in the data from Montreal.

The NCI quickly informed the ORI, whose fraud investigators immediately began their own inquiry. Over the next four months, teams of investigators flew to Montreal, where they compared each of the 1,511 files on patients enrolled by Poisson with the data Poisson had sent to Pittsburg.

What they found, according to the ORI's report, was nearly 100 cases in which Poisson, or someone acting on his instructions, had altered medical data—or simply made it up—to render patients eligible for one of the NSABP's many protocols.

Some of the falsifications were relatively minor, such as changing the date of a surgical operation by a few weeks. Many were more serious, including numerous cases in which the nature of a patient's breast tumor was deliberately misrepresented to make her eligible for a particular study.

One woman with advanced breast cancer was falsely reported as having a less-advanced condition—and, as a result, enrolled in a NSABP study in which she was given a less-than-optimal therapy.

Another woman with a history of congestive heart failure was reported as free of heart disease, then enrolled in a study testing a cancer drug that was known to pose a specific danger to heart patients.

In a third case, a woman whose cancer had spread from one breast to the other was classified as having cancer in only one, with the result that she did not receive post-operative radiation therapy in both breasts.

When one of its patients died, the Montreal group not only failed to inform Pittsburgh of the death but continued to report "followup" contacts with the woman for the next two years.

Non-government cancer experts called in to assess the evidence suggested that the investigators might have found only the "clumsy," or most obvious, falsifications in the Montreal data, and that the 99 documented cases of fraud merely represented "the tip of the iceberg."

As a result, the ORI's report says, the experts "questioned whether any data from the St. Luc Hospital patients could be considered reliable in light of the audit findings."

Within days of the experts' warning, new data fabrications began to turn up, including some pointed out by a contrite Roger Poisson, who then volunteered to investigators that he had falsified laboratory data in an unknown number of other cases.

Concluding it was "likely that additional data changes in other cases were not recognized during the audit," the ORI warned the cancer institute that "little confidence" could be placed in any of the data Poisson had amassed from the 1,500 patients he had enrolled in the NSABP.

The exasperated investigators pointedly noted that eight months had elapsed before the fraud was reported by Fisher, more than enough time to afford Poisson and his staff "the opportunity to destroy or alter evidence" if that had been their inclination.

Poisson pleaded to be allowed to continue his participation in the NSABP studies, telling investigators in a letter he had "learned my lesson the hard way" and suggesting that "a simple warning" would be sufficient punishment for what he termed "silly little mistakes."

Poisson's plea was in vain. Last April, he was barred from receiving federal research grants for eight years and prohibited for life by the Food and Drug Administration from access to experimental drugs. A St. Luc's spokeswoman, Monique Paquet, said that while Poisson remained on the hospital's staff and continued to do research there, he was no longer chief of its oncology center.

As the investigation was winding down, the investigators asked Fisher's group to reanalyze its massive breast-cancer database. "We were concerned that we might have a public health crisis," the ORI's Macfarlane said, "women making decisions about how their breast cancer should be treated on information that was not valid."

Macfarlane said the Fisher group later showed her and the other investigators a "preliminary reanalysis" of their published conclusions but not the actual data, without which the investigators were unable to perform their own reanalysis or to confirm the NSABP's conclusions.

Although Fisher's staff agreed to publish a corrected analysis of its most important studies within a few weeks of the misconduct finding against Poisson, nearly a year later the reanalysis still has not appeared in print.

Macfarlane said she remained puzzled by the NSABP's failure to publish a reanalysis. She said she was told more than a year ago "that everyone was behind the strategy of trying to get out a publication as quickly as possible."

18

EDWARD O. WILSON

Is Humanity Suicidal?

New York Times Magazine,
May 30, 1993

One of the most prominent scientist authors today, winner
of two Pulitzer Prizes, biologist Edward O. Wilson might
well be our generation's Charles Darwin. Like Darwin, Wil-
son combines the rigors of close observation with a deeply
humanistic sense of the world. Both scientists drew from ex-
tensive studies a new understanding of human identity—
with controversial repercussions in society and politics. Both
wrote for a popular public. Both men tackled enormously
complex issues and subjects.

Wilson's books include The Insect Societies *(1971),* Sociobiology *(1975),* On Human Nature *(1978),* Genes, Mind and
Culture *(1981), and, most recently,* The Diversity of Life—*a*
New York Times *Notable Book of the Year in 1992. Begin-*
ning as an evolutionary biologist and then evolving into a
kind of pundit for the planet, Wilson has managed to enrage
Marxists, liberals, and Stephen Jay Gould in studies that
looked at island evolution, the social life of insects, and a
field he called sociobiology—the application of evolutionary
theory to behavior in human and animal societies. Combin-
ing acute observational, mathematical, and analytical skills
with a Southerner's storytelling ability, Wilson writes like no

other scientist or essayist. He frequently uses novelistic technique—plot, drama, a cast of characters facing an impending crisis—to convey his scientific conclusions, and he draws upon numerous disciplines and a deeply religious sense of the world. In early works he saw religion as an evolutionary development that enabled humans to cultivate key virtues to survive despite our violent self-destructiveness.

The perspective in "Is Humanity Suicidal?"—that of an alien being looking down at Earth—is one of Wilson's favorite devices, echoing the opening to his explosive final chapter to Sociobiology. *In that chapter he argued that human flaws like deception and hypocrisy, and strengths like entrepreneurship and competitiveness, were natural traits well evolved to "conduct the complex business of everyday life." The chapter analyzed the effect of genes on human behavior, an idea even more relevant today with science's ambitious Human Genome Project to map every human gene. But back in 1975 Wilson's work made him a pariah among leftist student groups, colleagues, and friends. "There were several prominent professors here at Harvard, and substantial numbers of students and outsiders and so on, who were declaring me a very dangerous person and not fit to be on the faculty," Wilson said once in an interview. "You can get a feeling of isolation and exclusion."*

In The Diversity of Life *Wilson examines the costs of losing millions of yet uncatalogued animal species. That work led to this article. "When the* New York Times *called," Wilson reports, "I seized the opportunity to evangelize." In a meticulous argument, he counters the notion that science can somehow reconstruct biosystems for future generations, like a natural Disneyland. "That is simply not in our grasp, nor in our dreams, nor should it be."*

I MAGINE THAT ON AN ICY MOON OF JUPITER — SAY, Ganymede — the space station of an alien civilization is concealed. For millions of years its scientists have closely watched the earth. Because their law prevents settlement on a living planet, they have tracked the surface by means of satellites equipped with sophisticated sensors, mapping the spread of large assemblages of organisms, from forests, grasslands and tundras to coral reefs and the vast plank-tonic meadows of the sea. They have recorded millennial cycles in the climate, interrupted by the advance and re-treat of glaciers and scattershot volcanic eruptions.

The watchers have been waiting for what might be called the Moment. When it comes, occupying only a few centuries and thus a mere tick in geological time, the for-ests shrink back to less than half their original cover. At-mospheric carbon dioxide rises to the highest level in 100,000 years. The ozone layer of the stratosphere thins, and holes open at the poles. Plumes of nitrous oxide and other toxins rise from fires in South America and Africa, settle in the upper troposphere and drift eastward across the oceans. At night the land surface brightens with mil-lions of pinpoints of light, which coalesce into blazing swaths across Europe, Japan and eastern North America. A semicircle of fire spreads from gas flares around the Per-sian Gulf.

It was all but inevitable, the watchers might tell us if we met them, that from the great diversity of large animals, one species or another would eventually gain intelligent control of Earth. That role has fallen to Homo sapiens, a primate risen in Africa from a lineage that split away from the chimpanzee line five to eight million years ago. Un-like any creature that lived before, we have become a ge-ophysical force, swiftly changing the atmosphere and climate as well as the composition of the world's fauna and flora. Now in the midst of a population explosion, the human species has doubled to 5.5 billion during the past 50 years. It is scheduled to double again in the next 50 years. No other single species in evolutionary history has even remotely approached the sheer mass in protoplasm generated by humanity.

Darwin's dice have rolled badly for Earth. It was a misfortune for the living world in particular, many scientists believe, that a carnivorous primate and not some more benign form of animal made the breakthrough. Our species retains hereditary traits that add greatly to our destructive impact. We are tribal and aggressively territorial, intent on private space beyond minimal requirements and oriented by selfish sexual and reproductive drives. Cooperation beyond the family and tribal levels comes hard.

Worse, our liking for meat causes us to use the sun's energy at low efficiency. It is a general rule of ecology that (very roughly) only about 10 percent of the sun's energy captured by photosynthesis to produce plant tissue is converted into energy in the tissue of herbivores, the animals that eat the plants. Of that amount, 10 percent reaches the tissue of the carnivores feeding on the herbivores. Similarly, only 10 percent is transferred to carnivores that eat carnivores. And so on for another step or two. In a wetlands chain that runs from marsh grass to grasshopper to warbler to hawk, the energy captured during green production shrinks a thousandfold.

In other words, it takes a great deal of grass to support a hawk. Human beings, like hawks, are top carnivores, at the end of the food chain whenever they eat meat, two or more links removed from the plants; if chicken, for example, two links, and if tuna, four links. Even with most societies confined today to a mostly vegetarian diet, humanity is gobbling up a large part of the rest of the living world. We appropriate between 20 and 40 percent of the sun's energy that would otherwise be fixed into the tissue of natural vegetation, principally by our consumption of crops and timber, construction of buildings and roadways and the creation of wastelands. In the relentless search for more food, we have reduced animal life in lakes, rivers and now, increasingly, the open ocean. And everywhere we pollute the air and water, lower water tables and extinguish species.

The human species is, in a word, an environmental abnormality. It is possible that intelligence in the wrong kind of species was foreordained to be a fatal combination for the biosphere. Perhaps a law of evolution is that intelligence usually extinguishes itself.

This admittedly dour scenario is based on what can be termed the juggernaut theory of human nature, which holds that people are programmed by their genetic heritage to be so selfish that a sense of global responsibility will come too late. Individuals place themselves first, family second, tribe third and the rest of the world a distant fourth. Their genes also predispose them to plan ahead for one or two generations at most. They fret over the petty problems and conflicts of their daily lives and respond swiftly and often ferociously to slight challenges to their status and tribal security. But oddly, as psychologists have discovered, people also tend to underestimate both the likelihood and impact of such natural disasters as major earthquakes and great storms.

The reason for this myopic fog, evolutionary biologists contend, is that it was actually advantageous during all but the last few millennia of the two million years of existence of the genus Homo. The brain evolved into its present form during this long stretch of evolutionary time, during which people existed in small, preliterate hunter-gatherer bands. Life was precarious and short. A premium was placed on close attention to the near future and early reproduction, and little else. Disasters of a magnitude that occur only once every few centuries were forgotten or transmuted into myth. So today the mind still works comfortably backward and forward for only a few years, spanning a period not exceeding one or two generations. Those in past ages whose genes inclined them to short-term thinking lived longer and had more children than those who did not. Prophets never enjoyed a Darwinian edge.

The rules have recently changed, however. Global crises are rising within the life span of the generation now coming of age, a foreshortening that may explain why young people express more concern about the environment than do their elders. The time scale has contracted because of the exponential growth in both the human population and technologies impacting the environment. Exponential growth is basically the same as the increase of wealth by compound interest. The larger the population, the faster the growth; the faster the growth, the sooner the population becomes still larger. In Nigeria, to cite one of our more fecund nations, the population is expected to double from its 1988 level to 216 million by the year 2010. If the same rate of growth were to continue to 2110, its population would exceed that of the entire present population of the world.

With people everywhere seeking a better quality of life, the search for resources is expanding even faster than the population. The demand is being met by an increase in scientific knowledge, which doubles every 10 to 15 years. It is accelerated further by a parallel rise in environment-devouring technology. Because Earth is finite in many resources that determine the quality of life—including arable soil, nutrients, fresh water and space for natural ecosystems—doubling of consumption at constant time intervals can bring disaster with shocking suddenness. Even when a nonrenewable resource has been only half used, it is still only one interval away from the end. Ecologists like to make this point with the French riddle of the lily pond. At first there is only one lily pad in the pond, but the next day it doubles, and thereafter each of its descendants doubles. The pond completely fills with lily pads in 30 days. When is the pond exactly half full? Answer: on the 29th day.

Yet, mathematical exercises aside, who can safely measure the human capacity to overcome the perceived limits of Earth? The question of central interest is this: Are we racing to the brink of an abyss, or are we just gathering speed for a takeoff to a wonderful future? The crystal ball is clouded; the human condition baffles all the more because it is both unprecedented and bizarre, almost beyond understanding.

In the midst of uncertainty, opinions on the human prospect have tended to fall loosely into two schools. The first, exemptionalism, holds that since humankind is transcendent in intelligence and spirit, so must our species have been released from the iron laws of ecology that bind all other species. No matter how serious the problem, civilized human beings, by ingenuity, force of will and—who knows—divine dispensation, will find a solution.

Population growth? Good for the economy, claim some of the exemptionalists, and in any case a basic human right, so let it run. Land shortages? Try fusion energy to power the desalting of sea water, then reclaim the world's deserts. (The process might be assisted by towing icebergs to coastal pipelines.) Species going extinct? Not to worry. That is nature's way. Think of humankind as only the latest in a long line of exterminating agents in geological time. In any case, because our species has pulled free of old-style, mindless Nature, we have begun a different order of life. Evolution should now be allowed to proceed along this new trajectory. Finally, resources? The planet has more than enough resources to last indefinitely, if human genius is allowed to address each new problem in turn, without alarmist and unreasonable restrictions imposed on economic development. So hold the course, and touch the brakes lightly.

The opposing idea of reality is environmentalism, which sees humanity as a biological species tightly dependent on the natural world. As formidable as our intellect may be and as fierce our spirit, the argument goes, those qualities are not enough to free us from the constraints of the natural environment in which our human ancestors evolved. We cannot draw confidence from successful solutions to the smaller problems of the past. Many of Earth's vital resources are about to be exhausted, its atmospheric chemistry is deteriorating and human populations have already grown dangerously large. Natural ecosystems, the wellsprings of a healthful environment, are being irreversibly degraded.

At the heart of the environmentalist world view is the conviction that human physical and spiritual health depends on sustaining the planet in a relatively unaltered state. Earth is our home in the full, genetic sense, where humanity and its ancestors existed for all the millions of years of their evolution. Natural ecosystems—forests, coral reefs, marine blue waters—maintain the world exactly as we would wish it to be maintained. When we debase the global environment and extinguish the variety of life, we are dismantling a support system that is too complex to understand, let alone replace, in the foreseeable future. Space scientists theorize the existence of a virtually unlimited array of other planetary environments, almost all of which are uncongenial to human life. Our own Mother Earth, lately called Gaia, is a specialized conglomerate of organisms and the physical environment they create on a day-to-day basis, which can be destabilized and turned lethal by careless activity. We run the risk, conclude the environmentalists, of beaching ourselves upon alien shores like a great confused pod of pilot whales.

If I have not done so enough already by tone of voice, I will now place myself solidly in the environmentalist school, but not so radical as to wish a turning back of the clock, not given to driving spikes into Douglas firs to prevent logging and distinctly uneasy with such hybrid movements as ecofeminism, which holds that Mother Earth is a nurturing home for all life and should be revered and loved as in premodern (paleolithic and archaic) societies and that ecosystematic abuse is rooted in androcentric—that is to say, male-dominated—concepts, values and institutions.

Still, however soaked in androcentric culture, I am radical enough to take seriously the question heard with increasing frequency: Is humanity suicidal? Is the drive to environmental conquest and self-propagation embedded so deeply in our genes as to be unstoppable?

My short answer—opinion if you wish—is that humanity is not suicidal, at least not in the sense just stated. We are smart enough and have time enough to avoid an environmental catastrophe of civilization-threatening dimensions. But the technical problems are sufficiently formidable to require a redirection of much of science and technology, and the ethical issues are so basic as to force a reconsideration of our self-image as a species.

There are reasons for optimism, reasons to believe that we have entered what might someday be generously called the Century of the Environment. The United Nations Conference on Environment and Development, held in Rio de Janeiro in June 1992, attracted more than 120 heads of government, the largest number ever assembled, and helped move environmental issues closer to the political center stage; on Nov. 18, 1992, more than 1,500 senior scientists from 69 countries issued a "Warning to Humanity," stating that overpopulation and environmental deterioration put the very future of life at risk. The greening of religion has become a global trend, with theologians and religious leaders addressing environmental problems as a moral issue. In May 1992, leaders of most of the major American denominations met with scientists as guests of members of the United States Senate to formulate a "Joint Appeal by Religion and Science for the Environment." Conservation of biodiversity is increasingly seen by both national governments and major landowners as important to their country's future. Indonesia, home to a large part of the native Asian plant and animal species, has begun to shift to land-management practices that conserve and sustainably develop the remaining rain forests. Costa Rica has created a National Institute of Biodiversity. A pan-African institute for biodiversity research and management has been founded, with headquarters in Zimbabwe.

Finally, there are favorable demographic signs. The rate of population increase is declining on all continents, although it is still well above zero almost everywhere and remains especially high in sub-Saharan Africa. Despite entrenched traditions and religious beliefs, the desire to use contraceptives in family planning is spreading. Demographers estimate that if the demand were fully met, this action alone would reduce the eventual stabilized population by more than two billion.

In summary, the will is there. Yet the awful truth remains that a large part of humanity will suffer no matter what is done. The number of people living in absolute poverty has risen during the past 20 years to nearly one billion and is expected to increase another 100 million by the end of the decade. Whatever progress has been made in the developing countries, and that includes an overall improvement in the average standard of living, is threatened by a continuance of rapid population growth and the deterioration of forests and arable soil.

Our hopes must be chastened further still, and this is in my opinion the central issue, by a key and seldom-recognized distinction between the nonliving and the living environments. Science and the political process can be adapted to manage the nonliving, physical environment. The human hand is now upon the physical homeostat. The ozone layer can be mostly restored to the upper atmosphere by elimination of CFC's, with these substances peaking at six times the present level and then subsiding during the next half century. Also, with procedures that will prove far more difficult and initially expensive, carbon dioxide and other greenhouse gases can be pulled back to concentrations that slow global warming.

The human hand, however, is not upon the biological homeostat. There is no way in sight to micromanage the natural ecosystems and the millions of species they contain. That feat might be accomplished by generations to come, but then it will be too late for the ecosystems—and perhaps for us. Despite the seemingly bottomless nature of creation, humankind has been chipping away at its diversity, and Earth is destined to become an impoverished planet within a century if present trends continue. Mass extinctions are being reported with increasing frequency in every part of the world. They include half the freshwater fishes of peninsular Malaysia, 10 birds native to Cebu in the Philippines, half of the 41 tree snails of Oahu, 44 of the 68 shallow-water mussels of the Tennessee River shoals, as many as 90 plant species growing on the Centinela Ridge in Ecuador, and in the United States as a whole, about 200 plant species, with another 680 species and races now classified as in danger of extinction. The main cause is the destruction of natural habitats, especially tropical forests. Close behind, especially on the Hawaiian archipelago and other islands, is the introduction of rats, pigs, beard grass, lantana and other exotic organisms that outbreed and extirpate native species.

The few thousand biologists worldwide who specialize in diversity are aware that they can witness and report no more than a very small percentage of the extinctions actually occurring. The reason is that they have facilities to keep track of only a tiny fraction of the millions of species and a sliver of the planet's surface on a yearly basis. They have devised a rule of thumb to characterize the situation: that whenever careful studies are made of habitats before and after disturbance, extinctions almost always come to light. The corollary: the great majority of extinctions are never observed. Vast numbers of species are apparently vanishing before they can be discovered and named.

There is a way, nonetheless, to estimate the rate of loss indirectly. Independent studies around the world and in fresh and marine waters have revealed a robust connection between the size of a habitat and the amount of biodiversity it contains. Even a small loss in area reduces the number of species. The relation is such that when the area of the habitat is cut to a tenth of its original cover, the number of species eventually drops by roughly one-half. Tropical rain forests, thought to harbor a majority of Earth's species (the reason conservationists get so excited about rain forests), are being reduced by nearly that magnitude. At the present time they occupy about the same area as that of the 48 conterminous United States, representing a little less than half their original, prehistoric cover; and they are shrinking each year by about 2 percent, an amount equal to the state of Florida. If the typical value (that is, 90 percent area loss causes 50 percent eventual extinction) is applied, the projected loss of species due to rain forest destruction worldwide is half a percent across the board for all kinds of plants, animals and microorganisms.

When area reduction and all the other extinction agents are considered together, it is reasonable to project a reduction by 20 percent or more of the rain forest species by the year 2020, climbing to 50 percent or more by midcentury, if nothing is done to change current practice. Comparable erosion is likely in other environments now under assault, including many coral reefs and Mediterranean-type heathlands of Western Australia, South Africa and California.

The ongoing loss will not be replaced by evolution in any period of time that has meaning for humanity. Extinction is now proceeding thousands of times faster than the production of new species. The average life span of a species and its descendants in past geological eras varied according to group (like mollusks or echinoderms or flowering plants) from about 1 to 10 million years. During the past 500 million years, there have been five great extinction spasms comparable to the one now being inaugurated by human expansion. The latest, evidently caused by the strike of an asteroid, ended the Age of Reptiles 66 million years ago. In each case it took more than 10 million years for evolution to completely replenish the biodiversity lost. And that was in an otherwise undisturbed natural environment. Humanity is now destroying most of the habitats where evolution can occur.

The surviving biosphere remains the great unknown of Earth in many respects. On the practical side, it is hard even to imagine what other species have to offer in the way of new pharmaceuticals, crops, fibers, petroleum substitutes and other products. We have only a poor grasp of the ecosystem services by which other organisms cleanse the water, turn soil into a fertile living cover and manufacture the very air we breathe. We sense but do not fully understand what the highly diverse natural world means to our esthetic pleasure and mental well-being.

Scientists are unprepared to manage a declining biosphere. To illustrate, consider the following mission they might be given. The last remnant of a rain forest is about to be cut over. Environmentalists are stymied. The contracts have been signed, and local landowners and politicians are intransigent. In a final desperate move, a team of biologists is scrambled in an attempt to preserve the biodiversity by extraordinary means. Their assignment is the following: collect samples of all the species of organisms quickly, before the cutting starts; maintain the species in zoos, gardens and laboratory cultures or else deep-freeze samples of the tissues in liquid nitrogen, and finally, establish the procedure by which the entire community can be reassembled on empty ground at a later date, when social and economic conditions have improved.

The biologists cannot accomplish this task, not if thousands of them came with a billion-dollar budget. They cannot even imagine how to do it. In the forest patch live legions of species: perhaps 300 birds, 500 butterflies, 200 ants, 50,000 beetles, 1,000 trees, 5,000 fungi, tens of thousands of bacteria and so on down a long roster of major groups. Each species occupies a precise niche, demanding a certain place, an exact microclimate, particular nutrients and temperature and humidity cycles with specified timing to trigger phases of the life cycle. Many, perhaps most, of the species are locked in symbioses with other species; they cannot survive and reproduce unless arrayed with their partners in the correct idiosyncratic configurations.

Even if the biologists pulled off the taxonomic equivalent of the Manhattan Project, sorting and preserving cultures of all the species, they could not then put the community back together again. It would be like unscrambling an egg with a pair of spoons. The biology of the microorganisms needed to reanimate the soil would be mostly unknown. The pollinators of most of the flowers and the correct timing of their appearance could only be guessed. The "assembly rules," the sequence in which species must be allowed to colonize in order to coexist indefinitely, would remain in the realm of theory.

In its neglect of the rest of life, exemptionalism fails definitively. To move ahead as though scientific and entrepreneurial genius will solve each crisis that arises implies that the declining biosphere can be similarly manipulated. But the world is too complicated to be turned into a garden. There is no biological homeostat that can be worked by humanity; to believe otherwise is to risk reducing a large part of Earth to a wasteland.

The environmentalist vision, prudential and less exuberant than exemptionalism, is closer to reality. It sees humanity entering a bottleneck unique in history, constricted by population and economic pressures. In order to pass through to the other side, within perhaps 50 to 100 years, more science and entrepreneurship will have to be devoted to stabilizing the global environment. That can be accomplished, according to expert consensus, only by halting population growth and devising a wiser use of resources than has been accomplished to date. And wise use for the living world in particular means preserving the surviving ecosystems, micromanaging them only enough to save the biodiversity they contain, until such time as they can be understood and employed in the fullest sense for human benefit.

ABOUT THE EDITORS

TED ANTON has written for *The Sciences, Publishers Weekly, Lingua Franca,* the Chicago *Tribune, Chicago, The Latino Studies Journal, Teaching, Learning,* and many other magazines. A winner of the National Teachers As Writers Award (1989), he has received grants from the Arts Councils of Illinois and New Jersey and the Fund for Investigative Journalism. In 1993 his work was nominated for a National Magazine Award in Reporting. In 1994 he was named a Fulbright Research Fellow in Eastern Europe. He teaches nonfiction writing in the English Department at DePaul University in Chicago.

RICK MCCOURT is both a scientist and science writer. Starting with an American Association for the Advancement of Science Mass Media Fellowship, he has contributed over one hundred stories to National Public Radio on biology, astronomy, anthropology, and medicine. In 1985 he won the AAAS–Westinghouse Science Journalism Award for a radio series on aquaculture. He has written for *Discover, Science '86, International Wildlife,* and *Outside,* and for numerous technical journals and books on ecology. In 1994 he received a grant from the National Science Foundation for the study of algae. He teaches biology at DePaul University in Chicago.